Esther Higgins

SIERRA SOUTH

100 Back-country trips in California's Sierra

Thomas Winnett, Jason Winnett and Kathy Morey

Wilderness Press
BERKELEY

FIRST EDITION May 1968
Second printing January 1969
Third printing March 1970
Fourth printing January 1971
Fifth printing June 1971
Sixth printing March 1973
Seventh printing April 1974
SECOND EDITION March 1975
Second printing July 1977
Third printing April 1978
THIRD EDITION May 1980
Second printing Sept. 1981
Third printing July 1983
Fourth printing April 1984
FOURTH EDITION April 1986
Second printing August 1988
FIFTH EDITION June 1990
Second printing August 1991

Photos by the authors except as noted
Front-cover photo by Jason Winnett
Back-cover photo by Howard Weamer
Design by Thomas Winnett
Map by Jeff Schaffer

Library of Congress Card Number 90-12325
ISBN 0-89997-115-6
Manufactured in the United States of America
Published by   Wilderness Press
                  2440 Bancroft Way
                  Berkeley, CA 94704
                  (415) 843-8080
                  Write for free catalog

Library of Congress Cataloging-in-Publication Data
Winnett, Thomas.
     Sierra South : 100 back-country trips in
California's Sierra. -- 5th ed. / by Thomas Winnett
and Kathy Morey.
        p.   cm.
     ISBN 0-89997-115-6
1. Backpacking--Sierra Nevada Mountains (Calif. and
Nev.)--Guide-books. 2. Hiking--Sierra Nevada Mountains (Calif. and Nev.)--Guide-books. 3. Backpack-
ing--California--Guide-books. 4. Hiking
--California-- Guide-books. 5. Sierra Nevada Mountains (Calif. and Nev.)--Guide-books. 6. Califor-
nia--Description and travel--1981--Guide-books. I.
Morey, Kathy. II. Title.
GV199.42.S55W564 1990
917.94'4--dc20
                                         90-12325
                                         CIP

ACKNOWLEDGEMENTS

In preparing this fifth edition, I had input from a number of Sierra lovers who checked out some places where I hadn't been for several years. I deeply appreciate the help of Lyn and Ralph Haber, Ruby and Bill Jenkins, Peter Browning, Don Deck, Jeff Schaffer and Andy Selters. Cecelia Hurwich has, over the 22 years of this book's life, been a continual source of encouragement and information. My wife Lu walked wilderness trails with me, reminding me to take more pictures, and then cooking delicious dinners while I reviewed the results of the day's trail-scouting.

T. W.

I am grateful to all who have helped me, both directly and indirectly, with this fifth edition. I wish there were room to list them all here. I would like to give special thanks to Melanie Findling, who helped me stay on the path both in and out of the backcountry.

J.W.

I shall always be indebted to those who encouraged me, shuttled me around the Sierra, and generally put up with me. In particular, alphabetically: Barbara Dallavo, Christina O'Keefe, Ed Schwartz, and Thomas Winnett.

K.M.

Preface to the Fifth Edition

As guidebook writers we strive to provide the most up-to-date information possible. *Sierra South* is actually an ongoing process—it is never finished. This fifth edition—the latest and the most complete—is a report on the progress so far. Because mountains change—both physically and politically—we have in this edition emphasized process over form. In our discussions of natural history, especially geology, we have tried to give you a feel for change in the wilderness by describing events that occurred on a time scale that you can relate to, such as a human lifetime. Discovering how the environment changes will help you become more aware of the relationships in your environment. If the human race is to survive, then more and more people must come to respect our dependence on this life-giving earth. It is in the wilderness where we can best understand the statement of Chief Seattle, "Man did not weave the web of life; he is merely a strand in it."

Contents

Introduction

The backcountry traveler knows the exhilaration of the out-of-doors in a rich, personal way that is beyond the ken of the ordinary car camper. Far from the crowds that infest the roadside campgrounds, he comes to realize the value of solitude, and he learns the calmness of spirit that derives from a fundamental relationship with the mountains. He comes to know the simple satisfactions of deep breaths, hardened muscles and a sound sleep under brilliant stars. But, above all, in renewing his bond with the wilderness he rekindles that cherished spark of childlike innocence that is so easily extinguished by the pressures of city life. It is these pressures that account for the dramatic increase in the demand for wilderness experiences. The Sierra, offering some of the finest and most spectacular wilderness in the United States, has drawn more than its share of the demand, and its backcountry sees thousands of new faces each year.

Together with the companion volume *Sierra North,* this book is a discriminating effort to meet the demands of both the newcomer and the "old hand." Taking up where *Sierra North* left off, this book describes backcountry trails between Mono Creek and the southern end of Sequoia National Park. Here are trips ranging in length from overnighters to two-week expeditions; trips that will sate the appetite of the most avid angler, naturalist or camera bug.

These trips were chosen after considerable screening that entailed interviews with rangers, packers and mountaineers, and substantial research. Finally, they were all walked. The final selections were made on the basis of (1) scenic attraction, (2) wilderness character (remoteness, primitive condition), and (3) recreational potential (fishing, swimming, etc.). After walking the trip, the authors decided how long it should take if done at a leisurely pace, how long at a moderate pace, and how long at a strenuous pace. In deciding, they considered not only distance but also elevation change, heat, exposure, terrain, availability of water, appropriate campsites and finally, their subjective feeling about the trip. For each trip, then, we suggest how many days you should take to do it at the pace ("Leisurely," "Moderate" or "Strenuous") you prefer. Some trips simply don't lend themselves to a leisurely pace—maybe not even a moderate pace. Such trips have a blank in the number-of-days spot for the corresponding pace at the beginning of the trip. Some are not strenuous unless you do the whole thing in one day. Such trips have the word "Day" after "Strenuous."

The last decision about pace was the decision of which pace to use in describing the trip, day by day. Since this book is written for the average backpacker, we chose to describe most trips on either a leisurely or moderate basis, depending on where the best overnight camping places were along the route. The exceptions were the trips that involve an initial climb of more than 3000 feet—as much as 6500 feet—to climb the eastern escarpment of the Sierra or to climb out of the deep canyons of the Kings and Kaweah rivers. We deemed all such trips strenuous.

The authors' subjective consideration also carries over to the evaluation of campsites. Campsites are labeled "poor," "fair," "good" or "excellent." The criteria for assigning these labels were amount of use, immediate surroundings, general scenery, presence of vandalization, availability of water, kind of ground cover and recreational potential—angling, side trips, swimming, etc.

Angling, for many, is a prime consideration when planning a trip. The reports in this book are the result of (1) on-the-trail sampling, (2) on-the-trail observation of fish populations and feeding habits, (3) on-the-trail interviews with other anglers, (4) research into California Department of Fish and Game's trout program, and (5) reading other literature, such as Charles McDermand's *Yosemite and Kings Canyon Trout* and *Waters of the Golden Trout Country*. An up-to-date book on fishing in the High Sierra is Ralph Cutter's *Sierra Trout Guide*. Like the campsites, fishing was labeled "poor," "fair," "good" or "excellent." These labels refer to the quantity of fish in the stream or lake, not the fishes' inclination to take the hook. Experienced anglers know that the size of their catch relates not only to quantity, type and general size of the fishery, which are given, but also to water temperature, feed, angling skill, and that indefinable something known as "fisherman's luck." Generally speaking, the old "early and late" adage holds: fishing is better early and late in the day, and early and late in the season.

Deciding when in the year is the best time for a particular trip is a difficult task because of altitude and latitude variations. Low early-season temperatures and mountain shadows often keep some of the higher passes snowbound until well into August. Early snows have been known to whiten alpine country in late July and August. Some of the trips described here are low-country ones, designed specifically for the itchy hiker who, stiff from a winter's inactivity, is searching for a "warm-up" excursion. These trips are labeled "early season," a period that extends roughly from late May to early July. "Midseason" is here considered to be from early July to late August, and "late season" from then to mid-October.

Most of the trails described here are well maintained (the exceptions are noted), and are adequately signed. If the trail becomes indistinct, look for blazes (peeled bark at eye level on trees) or "ducks" (two or more rocks piled one atop the other). Two other significant trail conditions have also been described in the text: (1) degree of openness (type and degree of forest cover, if any, or else "meadow," "brush" or whatever); and (2) underfooting (talus, granite, pumice, sand, "duff"—deep humus ground cover of rotting vegetation—or other material).

Two other designations used in the descriptive text warrant definition. "Packer" campsite is used to indicate a semi-permanent camp (usually constructed by packers for the "comfort of their clients") characterized by a nailed-plank table, sawn stumps to sit on, and a large, "stand-up" rock fireplace. "Improved" campsite is a U.S. Forest Service designation for places where simple toilets have been installed.

Bridgeless stream crossings are designated either (1) "Wet in early season," indicating that at high water a particular ford is likely to require wading—sometimes through water several feet deep—or (2) "Difficult in early season," indicating that a crossing *may* be dangerous due to fast, deep water, or falls and rapids downstream. A dangerous ford should be attempted only by someone with a rope and the experience to use it properly.

The Care and Enjoyment of the Mountains

The mountains are in danger, particularly the High Sierra. About a million people camp in the Sierra wilderness each year. The vast majority of us care about the wilderness and try to protect it, but it is still threatened with destruction.

Litter is not the problem! Increasingly, wilderness campsites, even when free of litter, have that "beat out" look of over-crowded roadside campgrounds. The fragile high-country sod is being ground down under the pressure of too many feet. Lovely trees and snags are being stripped, scarred, and removed altogether for firewood. Dust, charcoal, blackened stones and dirty fireplaces are accumulating. These conditions are spreading rapidly, and in a few years *every* High Sierra lakeshore and streamside may be severely damaged.

The national park service and the forest service are faced with the necessity for reservation systems, designated campgrounds, restrictions on fire building, increased ranger patrols, and even rationing of wilderness recreation. Not only the terrain but the wilderness experience is being eroded. Soon conditions may be little different from those we wanted to leave behind at the roadend.

The solution to the problem depends on each of us. We must change our habits so as to have as little effect on the terrain as possible. We must try to leave no traces of our passing. This was the rule in the wilderness when Indians and trappers traveled through other people's territory. It is still a good rule today. It does take a little trouble. In an earlier day, that extra trouble was the price of saving one's scalp or load of beaver pelts. Today it is the price of saving the wilderness. A few basic principles of wilderness preservation—particularly aimed at High Sierra conditions but applicable elsewhere too—are offered below.

Learn to go light. This is largely a matter of acquiring wilderness skills, of learning to be at home in the wilderness rather than in an elaborate camp. The "free spirits" of the mountains are those experts who appear to go anywhere under any conditions with neither encumbrances nor effort but always with complete enjoyment. John Muir, traveling along the crest of the Sierra in the 1870's with little more than his overcoat and his pockets full of biscuits, was the archetype.

Modern lightweight equipment and food are a convenience and a joy. The ever-practical Muir would have taken them had they been available in his day. But a lot of the stuff that goes into the mountains is burdensome, harmful to the wilderness, or just plain annoying to other people seeking peace and solitude. Anything that is obtrusive or that can be used to modify the terrain should be left at the roadend: gigantic tents, gas lanterns, radios, saws, hatchets, firearms (except in the hunting season), etc.

Pick "hard" campsites, sandy places that can stand the use. The fragile sod of meadows, lakeshores and streamsides is rapidly disappearing from the High Sierra. It simply cannot take the wear and tear of campers. Its development depends on very special conditions. Once destroyed, it does not ordinarily grow back.

Be easy with the trees! In the timberline country, wood is being burned up faster than it is being produced. The big campfires of the past must give way to small fires or no fires at all. Wood is a precious resource; use it sparingly. Where it is scarce use a gas stove, not a saw or hatchet. Trees, both live and dead, are part of the scenery. They should never be *cut*. The exquisite golden trunks left standing after lightning strikes should be left completely alone. Sadly, in some popular areas they have already been destroyed for firewood, and you would never know they *were* there. We recommend that you carry a stove and fuel (preferably liquid), and always use it when you are above 10,000 feet or in a place where wood is scarce.

In established, regularly used campsites a single, small substantial fireplace should serve for both cooking and warming. If kept scrupulously clean it should last for many years. Unfortunately, fireplaces (and campsites) tend to become increasingly dirty and to multiply. There are now, by actual survey, a hundred times as many fireplaces as are needed in the High Sierra. The countless dirty fireplaces should be eradicated. Many campsites situated at the edge of water should be entirely restored to nature and not used again. It is a noble service to use and clean up established campsites where they are present, and to restore them to nature where called for.

Elsewhere build a small fireplace, if one is legal, and always eradicate it and restore your campsite to a natural condition before you leave. This is facilitated if you build with restoration in mind; two to four medium-sized stones along the sides of a shallow trench in a sandy place. When camp is broken the stones are returned to their places. The coals are thoroughly burned down and pulverized under a heavy foot until nothing is left but powder. The trench is filled with clean sand. *Fires should never be built against cliffs or large boulders.*

Protect the water from soap and other pollution. In many areas the water is unsafe to drink, even apart from the *Giardia* it may contain.

Giardia is not new to the Sierra but it has recently become a widespread problem. This protozoan (*Giardia lamblia*) can cause acute gastrointestinal distress, as anyone who has had it can tell you. The illness is treatable, but prevention is best. There is giardia in the water in most of the popular areas, and the Park Service and the Forest Service recommend that you treat all water to be sure, as giardia can be anywhere. Among the methods used to treat water (for giardia) are commerical and home-made iodine preparations, filters and boiling. It is hard to say which method is the most effective. In popular areas, we use 1 oz. of saturated iodine solution (in water) for every liter of water that is not boiled for 5 minutes, as in cooking. We have never contracted giardia. Some hikers say they never treat their water and have never contracted giardia. It is likely that most people can ingest some giardia without any problem, and some people are probably immune to giardia. But anyone can be a carrier, whether they have symptoms or not. It takes 2–3 weeks for symptoms to appear after exposure.

Maps and Profiles

Today's Sierra traveler is confronted by a bewildering array of maps, and it doesn't take much experience to learn that no single map fulfills all needs. There are base maps (U.S. Forest Service), shaded relief maps (National Park Service), artistically drawn representational maps (California Department of Fish and Game), aerial-photograph maps, geologic maps, three-dimensional relief maps, soil-vegetation maps, etc. Each map has different information to impart (some have more information than others), and the outdoorsman contemplating a back-country trip is wise to utilize several of these maps in his planning.

For trip-planning purposes, the reader will find a plan map in the back of this book. Trails and trailheads used in the following trip descriptions are indicated on this map in red, and all the access roads are delineated in brown.

The profile of each trip in this book gives a quick picture of the ups and downs. All profiles are drawn with the same *ratio* of horizontal miles to feet of elevation, in which the vertical scale is exaggerated by 25 times. Since carrying a pack up a hill gets to be very gruelling sometimes, this exaggeration is probably appropriate.

On the trail most backpackers prefer to use a topographic ("topo") map, because it affords a good deal of accurate information about conditions of terrain and forest cover. Topo maps come in a variety of sizes and scales, but there are three kinds that are useful to hikers. The first is the US Geological Survey's (USGS) fifteen-minute (15') quadrangle series. These maps have an 80-foot contour interval in the Sierra, cover an area about 14 x 17 miles, and are at a scale of about 1 inch = 1 mile, or 1:62,500. These maps have been the standard among hikers as they have been available since the '50s, are easy to carry, and cover most trips on a single quad. The second kind is the new ('80s) seven-and-one-half-minute (7½') series. These maps have a 40-foot contour interval in the Sierra, are the most detailed at a scale of 1:24,000, and cover an area about 7 x 8½ miles. The pertinent quadrangles from each series are listed at the beginning of each trip. Several 15' topos in the area of *Sierra*

South are published by Wilderness Press: *Mt. Whitney, Mineral King, Mt. Goddard* and *Triple Divide Peak*. These four maps are much more accurate and up-to-date than the USGS topos, and are printed on waterproof tear-resistant plastic. At the start of a trip where they apply, they are indicated by "W.P.V." (Wilderness Press version). The third kind of useful topo is a US Forest Service (USFS) topo titled "John Muir Wilderness, Sequoia-Kings Canyon Backcountry." This map, also at scale of 1′ = 1 mile, is printed on three sides of 2 large sheets of paper.

HOW TO ACQUIRE YOUR MAPS

USFS base maps:

U.S. Forest Service,
630 Sansome St.,
San Francisco, CA 94111
Maps are $2 each.

USGS Topo maps:

U.S. Geological Survey,
Box 25286, Federal Center,
Denver, CO 80225
$2.50 each
A state index map is free.

Topo maps plus free state index maps can be obtained *in person* Monday through Friday 8 a.m. to 4 p.m. from USGS offices located at:

7638 Federal Building
300 North Los Angeles Street
Los Angeles, CA

504 Custom House
555 Battery Street
San Francisco, CA

345 Middlefield Road
Menlo Park, CA

All maps are available by mail, by phone or in person from **The Map Center,** 2440 Bancroft Way, Berkeley, CA 94704. Phone (415) 841-MAPS. This store carries a complete line of California 15′ and 7½′ topo maps, National Forest maps, road maps and a variety of other useful maps. In the South Bay area there is another **Map Center** at 63 Washington St., Santa Clara, 95050. Phone (408) 296-6277.

Near the national-forest trailheads, USFS, USGS and Wilderness Press topos are usually available at Forest Headquarters—e.g., Inyo National Forest HQ in Bishop and District Ranger Stations—e.g., Shaver Lake. Topos are often available at trailhead ranger stations or wherever else wilderness permits can be obtained (see the next chapter, "Wilderness Permits and Quotas"). Similarly, in Sequoia and Kings Canyon national parks, books and maps are usually available wherever wilderness permits are—e.g., Cedar Grove Visitors Center.

Wilderness Permits
and Quotas

The wilderness traveler will need a permit from the Forest Service (for most federally designated wilderness areas) or from the National Park Service (for national-park backcountry). You may obtain a permit at a Park Service or Forest Service ranger station or office by indicating where you are going and when you will be there. The Forest Service requires a permit for an overnight backpacking trip. The two services will reciprocally honor each other's permits for trips that cross a boundary between the two types of wilderness. Forest Service permits and reservations for permits are also available by mail, and reservations for permits for the Sequoia-Kings backcountry are available by mail from March 1 through Sept. 15. There is a reservation fee of $3/person for permits in Sierra and Inyo national forests and in the Bridgeport District of Toiyabe National Forest.

If you don't know the address of the nearest Forest Service office or station to your destination, write the Regional Forester, 630 Sansome St., San Francisco, CA 94111. The address of Sequoia-Kings Canyon National Park is Three Rivers, CA 93271.

Wilderness permits are available on the road to or near some trailheads. On the west side of the Sierra, from north to south, permits can be obtained at the following locations: Shaver Lake Ranger Station, just west of the town of Shaver Lake on State Route 168. The station issues permits for the trailheads at Lake Edison, Bear Diversion Dam, Florence Lake, Courtright Reservoir, Wishon Reservoir and the Crown Valley Trailhead. In Kings Canyon National Park at Cedar Grove. In Sequoia National Park at Giant Forest, Lodgepole and Mineral King. On the east side, all the trailheads are in Inyo National Forest. South of Bishop you can get permits at Forest Service offices in Big Pine, Lone Pine, Whitney Portal and Horseshoe Meadow. The Forest Service has also set up "entrance stations" on two east-side access roads leading to High Sierra trailheads—on the roads to Bishop Creek (9.8 miles from US 395) and Rock Creek (0.2

miles from US 395). Information and permits—if you make the quota—are available there, if a shrinking federal treasury hasn't forced them to close.

Quotas have been established for high-use areas in the region covered by this book, including all of Sequoia-Kings Canyon National Park. For example, in a recent year, 30 persons per day were allowed to go up the Bubbs Creek Trail from Cedar Grove, on a first-come, first-served basis. Those who didn't "make the cut" either had to wait until they could be one of the 30 or had to choose an alternative trip. Group size anywhere in the wilderness is limited, and camping is not allowed within 100 feet of lakes and streams. There are some special regulations for particular places. For example, a person may camp only one night at each of the three Rae Lakes. Some places are closed to wood fires, such as the Kearsarge Lakes, and some places are entirely closed to camping, such as Mirror Lake on the Mt. Whitney Trail and Bullfrog Lake, near the John Muir Trail south of Glen Pass. Wood fires are prohibited above 10,000' in Kings Canyon, above 11,200' in the Kern drainage and above 9000' in the Kaweah drainage. Copies of all these special regulations are available from the government agencies that issue Wilderness permits.

A Word About Bears

Since the first edition of this book, more and more people have taken up backpacking. One result has been more and more unnatural food for bears—the food brought in by backpackers. Since this food is attractive to bears, and all too often easily available, the animals have developed a habit of seeking it and eating it. They patrol popular campsites nightly. As the bears have become more knowledgeable and persistent, backpackers have escalated their food-protecting methods. From merely putting it in one's pack by one's bed at night, and chasing away any bear that came, backcountry travelers switched to hanging the food over a branch of a tree. But bears can climb trees, and they can gnaw or scratch through the nylon line you tie around a tree trunk. When they sever the line, the food hanging from the other end of the line of course falls to the ground. This happens all too often in the High Sierra.

To avoid food loss due to line severance, you can learn the *counterbalance* method of "bearbagging." First, put all your food in a stuff sack or other bag. Then tie two pots or metal cups to the bag that will tinkle and alert you if a bear should disturb them. Then tie a small stone to the end of a 30-foot length of nylon line (⅛" or so in diameter) as a weight to hurl up and over a likely branch. The branch should be at least 16 feet up, and long enough that the line can rest securely at a point at least 6 feet from the tree trunk. When you have the line over the branch, tie a rock that weighs about the same as your bag of food to one end of the line. (Instead of a rock, you could tie a bag containing half the food, if you have two appropriate bags.) Now pull the rock up to the branch that the line passes over. Then tie your food bag to the other end of the line, as high as you can conveniently reach, and stuff any extra line into the mouth of the food bag. Now push up on the food bag with just enough force—you hope—that the system will come to rest with the rock and the bag equally high. If they aren't equally high, take a long enough stick, preferably forked, and push up the lower of the two until they are even. If a 6-foot person could reach them standing on tiptoes, they are too low. Try again. Next morning, push up either rock or bag until one descends enough that you can reach it.

Anti-bear cables have been installed between trees at some popular camping areas in Sequoia-Kings Canyon National Park, as have food storage lockers, also called "bear boxes." If there's one of either where you camp, use it, following the instructions provided by the Park Service.

REMEMBER: If a bear does get your food, he will then consider it his, and he will fight any attempts you make to retrieve it. Don't try! Remember also never to leave your food unprotected even for a short while during the daytime.

A Word About Theft

Stealing from and vandalizing cars are becoming all too common at popular trailheads. You can't ensure that your car and contents will be safe, but you can increase the odds. Make your car unattractive to thieves and vandals by disabling your engine (your mechanic can show you how), hiding everything you leave in the car, closing all windows and locking all doors and compartments. Get and use a locking gas-tank cap. If you have more than one car, use the most modest one for driving to the trailhead.

Mono Creek to Glacier Divide

Part of the 600,000-acre John Muir Wilderness, this region towers between Mono Creek and the northern boundary of Kings Canyon National Park. It is a roadless vastness of incredibly rugged alpine beauty, a wilderness that beckons to all who hear of it. Barren summits rise above a dense mat of green conifers, and the landscape is stippled with a thousand blue-green lakes bound by connecting silver ribbons of mountain streams. Encompassing a small area of roughly 500 square miles, this section nevertheless contains enough trails and cross-country routes to satisfy the most dedicated backcountry traveler for several summer seasons.

The profile of this region is classic. It boasts the typical short, steep eastern escarpment, and the typical long, gradual western slope. The west side is cut by the drainages of Mono, Bear and Piute creeks—all tributaries of the South Fork of the San Joaquin. And the east side is cleft by the precipitous, hurrying waters of Rock Creek, Pine Creek and the North Fork of Bishop Creek—all tributaries of the Owens River. These watersheds are separated by spectacular divides, which, together with the main Sierra crest—if one uses a little imagination—form an interesting plan view. Seen from the air, the main crest and the ancillary divide spurs of this section take on the aspect of a very large frog: the head centers on Mt. Mills; Mono Divide and the Mt. Morgan/Wheeler Ridge make the forelegs; and the Mt. Hooper/Mt. Senger complex and the Mt. Tom/Basin Mountain divide are the two lower limbs. Naturalists would hasten to render this absurd analogy more "authentic" by pointing out that the frog's back is covered with warts (17 summits exceeding 13,000'), and that this mountainous region should therefore be analogized to a toad. The reader is free to make his own Rorschach of the topography, but in any case it is vitally important—particularly in cross-country travel—for him to have a working map knowledge of the country and its terrain.

One soon learns, however, that his map knowledge never does justice to the country. This awareness comes with one's first glimpses of the majestic prominences and the awesome, blue-hazed canyons. With awareness comes wonder—a pause to ponder the colossal forces required to move, pluck and sculpt the rock on such a scale. Clarence King, a member of the famous Brewer Survey party of 1864, was among the first white men to look at this part of the Sierra and record his thoughts: "I believe no one can study from an elevated lookout the length and depth of one of these great Sierra canyons without asking himself some profound geological questions." Indeed, how did it happen? The answer has much to do with water, in both liquid and solid forms. The deep canyons were carved primarily by stream erosion, but they have been scoured out and widened periodically by glaciers during many "ice ages" in the Pleistocene Epoch, from 2 million to 10,000 years ago. In this part of the Sierra, glaciers covered over 1500 square miles at different times during the Pleistocene. The small glaciers that exist today were all formed within the last few hundred years. Glaciers are very sensitive to changes in climate; a major "ice age" could be initiated by worldwide cooling of only a 2–3°C.

The huge U-shaped valleys mark the courses of the main glaciers, while the smaller side valleys mark the flows of tributary glaciers. Usually suspended high above the main valleys, they are called *hanging valleys*. At the head of a side valley is an amphitheatrelike *cirque* where a glacier originated. In cirques and just below them are where you typically find lakes in the Sierra.

Other glacial features include glacial polish, where bedrock (especially granitic) was wet-sanded to a smooth sheen by grains of pulverized rock at the base of a glacier. In these scoured areas one also finds grooves and crescentic marks where rocks in the glacier base gouged the bedrock. Rocks—from huge boulders to particles of silt—that a glacier picks up along the way are deposited as moraines at the glacier margins.

The landscape here is still changing. Streams have cut through sediments left by glaciers. Avalanche chutes and frost nivations flute near-vertical peak facades, and accumulations of scree and talus slope away at their feet. Subtler forms of weathering continue to attack the talus, reducing that rock to granules, which then provide a suitable habitat for hardy plants. One can observe this ecological progression while walking the trails around timberline.

The presence of an ample and healthy plant life is necessary to animals, and one is sure to see many animals in this region's heavily wooded drainages. Birds are particularly plentiful, and the lakes and streams abound with fish. Among the most commonly seen mammals are mule deer. Early-season hikers working their way up Bear Creek are almost sure to come upon a grazing doe, and with some luck, perhaps a pair of brand-new, spotted-back fawns.

It should be noted that any wild-animal observation requires "freezing"—not necessarily stealth, but quietness and immobility. There isn't a naturalist observer worth his salt who hasn't experienced the dilemma of a hovering mosquito and a "once in a triptime" wild-animal observation opportunity. In early and mid-season, both does and bucks have reddish coats, which are replaced in the fall with longer, gray hair. Because the buck is much warier, a sighting of him is rarer. One will also make trailside, passing acquaintance with the numerous squirrels that populate the heavily wooded areas, especially the fir belt. Easily recognizable because of the dual stripes running down his coppery-red back is the tiny golden-mantled ground squirrel. He is, perhaps, the most familiar squirrel, and is found in both the lodgepole and subalpine belts. His less distinguished cousin, the California ground squirrel, will be seen near the trailheads—generally below 8000 feet—and the Belding ground squirrel, or "picketpin," is seen in most of the meadows of this section. Constant companions to the high-country hiker are the cony, a small, rabbitlike creature, and the beaverlike marmot. Found in talus and other rocky areas, these somnolent rodents pipe and chirp excitedly whenever approached.

Other, less common, but consequently more exciting, sightings that one may make are of black bear, mountain coyote, porcupine, flying squirrel and mountain lion. The black bear, contrary to impressions one might well have gathered in heavily camped national-park areas, is not often observed in the backcountry. The notable exception to this rule occurs when one leaves food lying about untended. (See page 10 for how to deal with this problem.)

The mountain lion, the coyote and the flying squirrel are more often heard than seen, and the happy occasion of hearing one of these animals usually occurs while one is busy setting up camp, bedding down or cooking a daybreak breakfast. A coyote's "singing" is a familiar sound to anyone who has watched a western movie, but the habitual birdlike whistling of a mountain lion is usually unrecognized because it seems totally out of character. This cat rarely screams, but he does meow, spit and growl in unmistakable feline fashion. Hearing a flying squirrel, contradictory as it may seem, is a fairly common occurrence. It takes place at night (the squirrel is nocturnal), usually with a whhhist . . . splat sound that characterizes his "flight" from one tree to another.

The most commonly seen animal in this region is man. He is usually quite domesticated, and is exceedingly easy to approach. A query like "Where've you been?" can bring forth a stream of information and friendly advice. In the perspective of geologic time, this animal has been on the scene but a moment, and his written history consumes only a fraction of a second. But despite his relative newness, his effect has been great, and the mark of his passage is on the land—temporarily.

In this section, man's trails, usually following those of other animals, are plentiful, clearly marked and well maintained. The trail following Mono Creek and crossing Mono Pass, and the one following the South Fork of the San Joaquin River and branching over Piute pass are old trade routes of the Mono Indian tribes. Paralleling these ancient trails is the relatively newer Italy Pass trans-Sierra crossing, and bisecting all three of these routes is the renowned John Muir Trail, which traverses the west slopes in a north-south direction.

There are seven trailhead entry points to this country that are used for trips in this book.

Mosquito Flat (10,250'). From Tom's Place (24 miles north from Bishop on U.S. 395) go 11 miles on paved road to road's end at Mosquito Flat beside Rock Creek.

Pine Creek Roadend (7580'). Go 10 miles northwest from Bishop on U.S. 395 and then 10 miles on paved road through Rovana to a signed parking area beside Pine Creek.

Lake Sabrina (9130'). Go 18 miles southwest from Bishop on State Highway 168 to the backpackers' parking area below the lake, at the North Lake turnoff.

North Lake (9200'). Go 18 miles from Bishop on State Highway 168 almost to Lake Sabrina and turn right on a dirt road.

After a few hundred feet turn right again and go 2 miles to a backpacker's parking area just west of North Lake. You must walk the last ½ mile to the trailhead beyond the campground.

Vermilion Campground (7650'). Go east from Clovis (near Fresno) 81 miles on State Highway 168 to the Florence Lake/Lake Edison junction, then 8 miles north on a mostly paved road to Vermilion Campground.

Bear Dam Junction (7010'). Go 2½ miles north from the Florence Lake/Lake Edison junction described above, to where the jeep road to Bear Diversion Dam leaves the paved road.

Florence Lake (7350'). Go 6 miles east from the Florence Lake/Lake Edison junction described above.

Sign at Bear Dam Junction

Bear Dam Junction to Twin Falls

TRIP   From Bear Dam Junction to Twin Falls (round trip). Topo maps *Kaiser Peak, Mt. Abbot* 15'; *Mt. Givens, Florence Lake* 7½'. Best early or late season; 11 miles.

Grade	Trail/layover days	Total recommended days
Leisurely	2/0	2
Moderate	....	....
Strenuous	....	....

HILITES   Few creeks in the Sierra possess the simple, primitive appeal of Bear Creek. Never constant, it cascades, chutes and then tumbles down its rocky course, interrupted at graceful intervals by deep, slow-moving, sandy-bottomed pools. Fine brown- and ·golden-trout angling makes this trip a good fisherman's choice early or late season.

DESCRIPTION (Leisurely trip)

1st Hiking Day (**Bear Dam Junction** to **Twin Falls**, 5½ miles): Lichen-covered, glacially scoured granite surrounds the trailhead for this trip. The rock, fractured in many places not by nature but by man, is more precisely granodiorite, which is typically black-flecked because it contains the minerals biotite and hornblende. The first two miles (to the Bear Diversion Dam) follow an un-maintained Southern California Edison Co. jeep road. After the jeep road leaves the Mono Hot Springs/Lake Thomas A. Edison road (7,000') it swings first east and then south, undulating gently as it traverses the long granite field that marks the south-east end of Bear Ridge. Rounding Bear Ridge, the jeep road ascends gently, and then drops down to the Bear Diversion Dam spillway.

     This particular stretch of road overlooks the gorge of the river to the south, and gives the traveler a fine opportunity to watch the abundant population of birds that frequent these broken slopes.

Among the birds one is most likely to see are Steller jays, mountain chickadees, juncos, dusky and olive-sided fly-catchers, cliff and barn swallows, red-tailed hawks, and a variety of sparrows. Where the jeep road starts to descend to the spillway, one can see southeast to Ward Mountain and Mt. Shinn, and east to Bear Dome and the barren glacial cirques above. This route also offers the traveler on foot a chance to absorb the feeling of this glacially scoured country. It is a feeling of openness that is emphasized by the scattering of the forest cover. The mountain juniper and Jeffrey pine occur in moderate stands amid broad expanses of granite, where they have taken root in the granular sand swales that have accumulated as a result of mechanical weathering. In turn, the sprouting of roots from pine, willow, ceanothus and manzanita accelerates the continual process of granite breaking up.

Beyond the parking area above the reservoir is a sign marking the beginning of the trail up Bear Creek. After the trail leaves the roadend area, it doesn't take one long to realize he has left that feeling of openness behind. The canyon walls close in, and the forest cover becomes moderate to dense.

Should one desire to try the fair-to-good fishing along the stream (they come in sizes up to 15"), he will also more than likely encounter small stands of water-loving cottonwood and aspen en route, as well as some lodgepole, oak, and the first fir. Near the creek, wildflower fanciers will relish the luxuriant growth of penstemon, lupine, paintbrush, monkey flower, and cinquefoil.

Bear Creek, in the stretch immediately above the reservoir, is a rock-bottomed, briskly flowing stream with a surprising penchant for suddenly eddying out into broad, emerald-green pools. Fortunately, the trail is never far from the creek's banks, and one can make several worthwhile forays to the water's edge without too much loss of trail time. For 1½ miles above the reservoir, the trail ascends very gradually, and then as the canyon narrows it begins to ascend more steeply. The duff trail gives way to rocky underfooting, which prevails for the rest of the trip, and about ½ mile farther this route encounters the boundary of the John Muir Wilderness. At the boundary, one can catch his first V-notched glimpse of Recess Peak directly up-canyon. The trail drops down for a short distance and then begins a steady, rocky ascent. Several good campsites dot the nearby banks of Bear Creek, and the traveler can take his choice of any of these primitive sites. Though the emerald-green pools occur less often, they stand in dramatic contrast to the plunging white water.

In this country slight changes in altitude entail significant changes in the plant and animal life. For example, as the trail ascends steeply, fishermen find golden trout as well as brown in their catch, and exploring naturalists discover that the predominant forest cover is now Jeffrey pine and the shrubs are now mostly gooseberry and snow bush. Arrival at the packer site is presaged by several "corduroy" bridge crossings of marshy sections, and a stock-drift fence. At the improved packer camp-site (8,000′) there is a fine, large pool offering good fishing for brown and golden trout (8″–15″). Campers in this canyon are frequently serenaded by coyotes who range Bear Ridge. Swimming in mid or late season is excellent.

2nd Hiking Day: Retrace your steps, 5½ miles.

Recess Peak over Lake Edison

2 Bear Dam Junction to Upper Bear Creek

TRIP
From Bear Dam Junction to Upper Bear Creek (round trip.) Topo maps *Kaiser Peak, Mt. Abbot 15', Mt. Givens, Florence Lake, Mt. Hilgard 7½'*. Best early or late season; 27 miles.

Grade	Trail/layover days	Total recommended days
Leisurely	4/1	5
Moderate	3/1	4
Strenuous	....	....

HILITES
This trip ascends Bear Creek beyond the densely forested flats at the site of Old Kip Camp. The angler seeking varied sport will find good fishing from the time he first sees Bear Creek at Bear Diversion Dam. Brown trout, a particular favorite of the serious fisherman, populate the lower waters of this trip, and justly famous golden trout inhabit the upper waters and nearby lakes.

DESCRIPTION (Leisurely trip)

1st Hiking Day: Follow trip 1 to **Twin Falls**, 5½ miles.

2nd Hiking Day (**Twin Falls** to **Upper Bear Creek**, 8 miles): An improved packer campsite marks the point where the trail veers north away from cascading Bear Creek. As you ascend steadily up the north wall of the canyon, you have good views of the jumbled cirque crest on the opposite side of the canyon to the southeast. Though rocky, this trail is well maintained as it rises above the floor of the valley. The moderate-to-dense forest cover of the creek bottom thins as the trail climbs to the slight granite-ribbed saddle that marks the start of the descent to a reunion with Bear Creek.

The floral display along this stretch of trail includes penstemon, larkspur, monkshood, lupine, goldenrod, paintbrush and western mountain aster. The descent reveals a marked change in the forest cover in that the predominant Jeffrey of the lower canyon has given way to lodgepole and juniper. Where the views during the ascent were of the down-canyon Bear Creek drainage, you now have views of the Mono Divide.

After descending from a low granite ridge, the trail meanders through dense forest cover and soon arrives at the flats of Old Kip Camp. The forest cover is now predominantly lodgepole, with some fir and aspen in the wetter areas and along the creek on the right. Now the trail begins climbing and soon we arrive at a junction with the John Muir Trail (9000'). Our route turns right onto this famous trail and ascends steadily along the east side of tumbling Bear Creek. Then we swing south through thinning forest on a moderate ascent that stays close to the stream, passing several campsites near the creek. About 2 miles beyond the Muir Trail junction our trail passes the Lake Italy Trail and soon fords the several branches of Hilgard Creek. About 1 mile beyond this creek are several good campsites far enough from Bear Creek to be legal stopping places.

3rd and 4th Hiking Days: Retrace your steps, 13½ miles.

Mono Creek country　　　　　　　　　　*U.S. Forest Service*

3

Bear Dam Junction
to Vermilion Campground

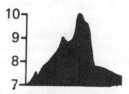

TRIP   From Bear Dam Junction to Vermilion Campground via Quail Meadows (shuttle trip). Topo maps
*Kaiser Peak, Mt. Abbot 15'; Mt. Givens, Florence
Lake, Graveyard Peak, Sharktooth Peak 7½'*. Best
early or late season; 21 miles.

Grade	Trail/layover days	Total recom- mended days
Leisurely	4/1	5
Moderate	3/1	4
Strenuous	2/1	3

HILITES   Varied scenery that ranges from the intimate confines of Bear Creek to the open expanses on Bear
Ridge gives this long-weekend trip a universal
appeal. The trek circumnavigates Bear Ridge,
visiting the Bear and Mono Creek drainages, and the
close proximity of the beginning and the end of this
horseshoe-shaped route makes it a potential loop.

DESCRIPTION (Moderate trip)

1st Hiking Day: Follow trip 1 to **Twin Falls,** 5½ miles.

2nd Hiking Day (**Twin Falls** to **Quail Meadows,** 10 miles): Follow the
2nd hiking day, trip 2, to the John Muir Trail and turn left. Our
route follows the Muir Trail as we traverse northward toward
Bear Ridge. The trail soon makes a steady climb to top Bear
Ridge. Views back into the Bear Creek drainage are excellent,
including Recess Peak, Mt. Hilgard and Seven Gables. At the
rocky summit of Bear Ridge, we pass a trail that goes west to
Mono Hot Springs.

As the trail begins the steep series of 70 switchbacks that drop into the Mono Creek watershed, the traveler is treated to excellent views of the Silver Divide, the immediate Mono Creek watershed, and Lake Thomas A. Edison. When the trail finally levels off, we ford a tributary of Mono Creek and soon reach a bridge crossing of the creek. Several good campsites line the north side of Mono Creek near Quail Meadows (7760'), several hundred yards west. Additional campsites can be found along the south side of the creek.

3rd Hiking Day (**Quail Meadows** to **Vermilion Campground**, 5½ miles): Our route leaves the John Muir Trail (which turns northeast as we turn southwest) and proceeds downstream toward Lake Thomas A. Edison. The first mile of level going sometimes parallels the magnificent chutes and rapids that precede Mono Creek's absorption by the Lake Edison reservoir. These white waters are periodically interrupted by sandbottomed granite potholes that offer excellent swimming to the mid or late season traveler. One can easily imagine the members of the famous Brewer Survey Party of 1864 stopping here for a few moments of relaxation and refreshment. Shortly after we leave John Muir Wilderness, we reach a junction with a path that branches off to the left and leads to the boat landing at the northeast tip of the lake. Here a boat-taxi service operates during the summer months, and it can save us up to 6½ miles of walking. Vermilion Valley Resort operates the boat-taxi and offers food-drop and mail pick-up services for hikers. Write: P.O. Box 258, Lakeshore, CA 93634 (enclose a SASE).

Those choosing to use the trail along the north side of Lake Edison will find that the route first undulates along the north wall of Vermilion Valley. The point where our trail passes the Goodale Pass Trail marks the beginning of relatively level going. Along these more level stretches the forest cover of fir and pine becomes somewhat denser. In one of the denser stands of lodgepole, a few yards from the Goodale Pass Trail junction, our route meets a second boat-landing trail. Continuing westward, our trail crosses the Cold Creek bridge, passes the trail lateral to Devils Bathtub, and climbs to meet the former road—now a trail—that leads us to the trailhead at Vermilion Campground (7650').

4

Bear Dam Junction to Lake Italy

TRIP From Bear Dam Junction to Lake Italy (round trip). Topo maps *Kaiser Peak, Mt. Abbot,* 15′; *Mt. Givens, Florence Lake, Mt. Hilgard* 7½′. Best mid or late season; 37 miles.

Grade	Trail/layover days	Total recom- mended days
Leisurely	6/1	7
Moderate	4/1	5
Strenuous	3/1	4

HILITES This trip is tailor-made for the traveler who wants to experience the high, alpine country of the mid Sierra without having to contemplate cross-country walking. Lake Italy, the aim of this trip, is a frequently used base camp for climbers, and a fine trip selection for the photographer.

DESCRIPTION (Leisurely trip)

1st Hiking Day: Follow trip 1 to **Twin Falls**, 5½ miles.

2nd Hiking Day (**Twin Falls** to **Hilgard Branch**, 7½ miles): Follow the 2nd hiking day, trip 2, to the Lake Italy Trail and turn left onto it to ascend steadily on rocky underfooting under moderate-to-dense lodgepole pines. In ½ mile the trail levels out and soon forest gives way to large expanses of meadow. Good campsites can be found at the lower end of this meadow.

3rd Hiking Day (**Hilgard Branch** to **Lake Italy**, 5½ miles): In the long meadow just beyond the campsites, one is apt to see much violet-colored Indian paintbrush. Then our route enters lodgepole forest and ascends moderately over rocky underfooting to the outlet of Hilgard Lake. Beyond, the trail swings southeast and traverses a long talus field where the traveler may see fat marmots sunning themselves atop large talus blocks. Beyond the talus, the trail crosses a very wet, meadowy area where seepage emanating from the base of Mt. Hilgard saturates the trail all season long, and it is very difficult to keep one's feet dry. The trail disappears in this area, but is easily recovered once you reach drier ground.

Before the canyon turns east, the trail veers away from Hilgard Branch and begins a steep, rocky, switchbacking ascent. At the top of this climb the trail swings into a narrow canyon and follows the creek's course on a jumbled ascent high on the precipitous slope above crashing Hilgard Branch. Then the ascent becomes gentle and the trail enters meadowy sections with scattered clumps of whitebark pine. The stream flows relatively slowly here, but its velocity increases as the canyon floor steepens and the trail becomes fainter. When the trail nears the creek one will see an enormous willow patch on its south side. There is a fairly clear line where the west side of the willow patch ends and sparsely forested slopes continue. Ford the creek at the edge of the patch and climb the south canyon wall. Our route crosses the top of the willowy area and ascends gently through meadow to a ford of the outlet from Teddy Bear and Brown Bear lakes. The trail then passes clumps of whitebark pine, emerges above timberline, and stays closer to the creek as it crosses long granite ledges that alternate with grassy patches to the outlet of Lake Italy (11,202'). This large lake (124 acres) derives its name from its similarity to the European peninsula.

Rounding the curve of the lake just above the outlet, one can easily see the cirque basin where the feeder glacier had its beginnings. At the east end of the cirque, Bear Creek Spire marks the division between the western and eastern directional flows of the old glaciers. There are a number of fair exposed campsites along the turfy south shore of the lake near the outlet. However, the granitic scenery surrounding this large lake compensates for the lack of forest cover. To the west towers Mt. Hilgard; to the north Mt. Gabb; and to the east are Bear Creek Spire and Mt. Julius Caesar. To the immediate north of Bear Creek Spire, filling the distant skyline, are Mts. Dade and Abbot. A mountaineer's heaven: every peak bordering on this lake towers well over 13,000 feet. The golden-trout fishery (8"–12") in Lake Italy is

fair-to-good—a classification that applies to the surrounding
Toe, Jumble, Brown Bear and Teddy Bear lakes as well.

4th, 5th and 6th Hiking Days: Retrace your steps, 18½ miles.

Spotted sandpiper's nest with egg   *Jeff Schaffer*

Bear Dam Junction to Lake Italy

5

TRIP   From Bear Dam Junction to Lake Italy via Hilgard Branch, return via Vee Lake, East Fork Bear Creek (semiloop trip). Topo maps *Kaiser Peak, Mt. Abbot* 15'; *Mt. Givens, Florence Lake, Mt. Hilgard* 7½'. Best mid or late season; 41½ miles.

Grade	Trail/layover days	Total recommended days
Leisurely	7/2	9
Moderate	5/2	7
Strenuous	4/2	6

HILITES   For intermediate and experienced backpackers only, this varied and exciting cross-country trip seeks the kind of high country that is the exclusive province of the backpacker.

DESCRIPTION (Leisurely trip)

1st, 2nd, and 3rd Hiking Days: Follow trip 4 to **Lake Italy**, 18½ miles.

4th Hiking Day (**Lake Italy** to **Vee Lake**, 5 miles, part cross country): Our route skirts the south side of Lake Italy, following the ducked and sometimes faint Italy Pass Trail. As the trail ascends on the west side of the outlet stream from Jumble Lake, one has excellent views northeast along the Sierra Nevada crest. The trail then fords the stream, and about ¼ mile above Jumble Lake our route branches south away from the Italy Pass Trail and, going cross-country, traverses the granite slope above Jumble

Lake. The route levels off before we reach the rocky saddle that dents the ridge above White Bear Lake. At this saddle, one can see the clear division that this ridge made between two small glaciers which once fed the main *mer de glace* that flowed down Bear Creek canyon. By virtue of having come "through the back door," the hiker has the opportunity to trace the old glacier's path from its inception all the way to the main trunk. Anglers will probably want to try the fair-to-good golden-trout fishing at White Bear and Black Bear lakes before proceeding, but as a rule of thumb the fishing gets better as one descends into the East Fork drainage.

At the saddle a faint trail begins, and it continues to Big Bear Lake. The descent to White Bear Lake is not difficult if one doesn't stray too far west, where there are cliffs. Follow the west shore of White Bear Lake to its outlet, where the trail becomes more evident, and follow it down the intermittent stream to Big Bear Lake. At Big Bear Lake and Ursa Lake, just east of it, the angler will find the biggest fish of the trip—golden trout, rainbow trout and golden-rainbow hybrid (to 16").

To keep from getting lost, it is best to follow the rocky outlet stream from Big Bear Lake to Little Bear Lake. The route passes high above Little Bear Lake on its south side, and then turns southwest over a low granite ridge and gently descends to the northwest shore of Vee Lake. A trail on this shore leads to the outlet, where a treeless but pleasant campsite is found. The views from here include Royce Peak and "Feather Peak" (Peak 13242) to the east, and Seven Gables to the west. Vee Lake makes an excellent base for exploring the upper part of the basin, and it also offers good fishing for golden trout (to 15").

5th Hiking Day (**Vee Lake** to **Upper Bear Creek**, 4½ miles): Keeping to the west side of the outlet stream, our route descends steeply to the Seven Gables Lakes basin. The intimate falls and chutes found along this outlet stream are a pleasant contrast to the brooding heights of Seven Gables peak to the west. At the confluence of the outlet creek and the Seven Gables branch of East Fork Bear Creek, our route turns downstream. However, anglers electing to first test the good fishing for golden trout at the largest of the Seven Gables Lakes will alter their route upstream—½ mile of gentle ascent. Those continuing downstream will find a faint trail on the east side, but travel here isn't much better than on the west side, and route-finding abilities may come in handy.

Descending steadily, the route continues northwest for a short quarter mile, then crosses by a shallow wade where the canyon narrows, and continues northwest to reach an obvious trail down the canyon which soon turns west. This steady descent encounters timberline just north of Seven Gables peak, and witnesses the typical hemlock-lodgepole-fir spectrum as it follows the length of a narrow canyon and emerges into the wide, more open expanses of Bear Creek canyon. Turning northward, the trail meets and turns right onto the John Muir Trail. Your descent becomes moderate to gentle as the trail winds through alternating meadows and lodgepole stands to the campsites on upper Bear Creek.

6th Hiking Day (**Upper Bear Creek** to **Twin Falls**, 8 miles): A mile of gentle descent leads to the fords of multibranched Hilgard Creek. A few yards beyond these fords the trail meets the Hilgard Branch Trail and then retraces most of the 2nd hiking day, trip 2.

7th Hiking Day: Retrace the steps of the 1st hiking day, 5½ miles.

6

Bear Dam Junction to Sandpiper Lake

TRIP   From Bear Dam Junction to Sandpiper Lake (round trip). Topo maps *Kaiser Peak, Mt. Abbot 15'; Mt. Givens, Florence Lake, Mt. Hilgard 7½'*. Best mid or late season; 33 miles.

Grade	Trail/layover days	Total recom- mended days
Leisurely	5/1	6
Moderate	4/1	5
Strenuous	3/1	4

HILITES   This trip provides an unusual opportunity to trace a river's course from its inception. Much of this route follows the famous John Muir Trail, but most of our campsite recommendations avoid that trail's heavily used stopover places.

DESCRIPTION (Moderate trip)

1st Hiking Day: Follow trip 1 to **Twin Falls**, 5½ miles.

2nd Hiking Day (**Twin Falls** to **Sandpiper Lake**, 11 miles): Follow the 2nd hiking day, trip 2, to the campsites on upper Bear Creek. (This is a long uphill hiking day, and some people may want to stop somewhere on upper Bear Creek and continue on to Sandpiper Lake the next day.) The ascent is still gentle-to-moderate as it passes along open granite slab sections with meadowy breaks, and arrives at the trail junction where the Vee and Seven Gables Lakes Trail branches left (east). This junction is just a few yards short of a Bear Creek ford—a wade-across ford that is hazardous during high water. The trail then ascends steeply by switchbacks to the corduroy bridge crossing of West Fork Bear Creek at Rosemarie Meadow.

At an obvious junction, our route branches left, off the John

Muir Trail, eastward over an easy ridge to Lou Beverly Lake. (This well-established trail is not shown on the 15' map.) The moderate forest cover of lodgepole through which the trail winds shows the effects of the higher altitude. The two-needled trees take on a stunted appearance, and one begins to see clumps of red mountain heather. Lou Beverly Lake (10,100') is a tiny (5 acre), shallow, moderately forested lake with campsites at the southwest end. Fishing for golden (to 14") is good to excellent, which should be adequate reason for anglers to try their luck. For the camper who prefers a more protected and timbered lake, Lou Beverly is a fine alternative place to end this hiking day.

For the camper who prefers a high alpine feel to his campsite, the choice should be Sandpiper Lake. The trail to that lake crosses the marshy inlet of Lou Beverly Lake and ascends along the north and east side of the stream connecting the two lakes. This ascent, over rough, unmaintained trail, is steady until it reaches the abrupt granite face just below Sandpiper Lake, where the going becomes very steep. The waterfall outlet of Sandpiper Lake (10,500') makes a musical accompaniment to end the climb by, as one arrives at the good campsites near the outlet and along the west side of the lake. This fair-sized lake (about 25 acres) has a very sparse forest cover of stunted lodgepoles but the view of the surrounding granitic peaks is excellent—particularly from the granite shoulder just south-west of the lake. Despite fairly heavy fishing pressure, angling for golden (to 13") is often good, and this lake makes an excellent base camp for fishing and hiking excursions to the surrounding lakes on the headwaters of Bear Creek. The morning and evening sounds of Pacific tree frogs and Yosemite toads are welcome background music for the hustling cook at his chores.

3rd and 4th Hiking Days: Retrace your steps, 16½ miles.

7 Bear Dam Junction to Little Moccasin Lake

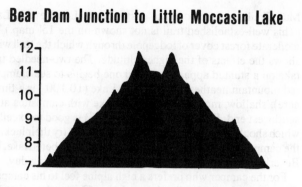

TRIP
From Bear Dam Junction to Little Moccasin Lake via Sandpiper Lake, cross-country return via West Pinnacles Creek drainage, Three Island Lake (semi-loop trip). Topo maps *Kaiser Peak, Mt. Abbot* 15'; *Mt. Givens, Florence Lake, Mt. Hilgard* 7½'. Best mid or late season; 47 miles.

Grade	Trail/layover days	Total recom- mended days
Leisurely	....	....
Moderate	....	....
Strenuous	6/2	8

HILITES
Loop trips that include the variety of this country this one does are rare. From the confines of Bear Creek, this route climbs above timberline and circles two rarely visited watersheds. The cross-country work is often difficult, and this trip is recommended for highly experienced hikers only.

DESCRIPTION (Strenuous trip)

1st and 2nd Hiking Days: Follow trip 6 to **Sandpiper Lake**, 16½ miles.

3rd Hiking Day (**Sandpiper Lake** to **Little Moccasin Lake**, 6½ miles cross country): Our rugged cross-country loop begins by rounding the west side of Sandpiper Lake (10,500') and fording the inlet stream coming from Medley Lake. From here the route ascends southeast by means of granite ledge systems. Following the south fork of the east inlet stream of Medley Lake, your route ascends steeply over smoothed, barren granite slabs and grassy pockets to reach the upper drainage of the north fork of the east inlet stream. Climbing eastward, you cross a saddle at 12,000′+, pass the lake east of it, and then cross another saddle directly east. Views during the course of this climb include Medley Lake, Mts. Senger and Hooper, and Seven Gables. Just short of this saddle, one has superlative views to the west, and these views are matched to the east and north when the crest of the saddle is reached, for from the saddle one can see Mts. Hilgard, Abbot, Gabb, Dade, Bear Creek Spire, Julius Caesar, Royce, Humphreys and Gemini.

Route-finding on these rugged talus slopes is difficult at best, but the hiker will find the traverse around the steep north slope of Gemini a moderate one that descends to a broad saddle and down to the unnamed, scree-ridden lake just north of Aweetasal Lake. This traverse offers excellent views down into the Seven Gables Lakes cirque until it crosses a saddle. The rock cairn at the saddle marks a point from which one can see the crest as it dwindles away to the southernmost skyline, including Glacier Divide, Emerald Peak, and Mts. McGee, Henry and Goddard. Immediately on the right are the twin peaks of Gemini and the spectacular jumbled crest of The Pinnacles. It is the latter that dominate the views to the west for the remainder of this hiking day's progress down the East Pinnacles Creek drainage. Descent into this drainage is first moderate (to the first unnamed, talus-cluttered lake), and then steeper as one drops down to shallow Aweetasal Lake.

Typical of most of the lakes on this drainage, Aweetasal has poor fishing and virtually no timber, but tundralike grassy spots between granite slabs. This rugged and somewhat sterile land is the alpine Sierra at its best. Here, despite the harsh, exposed environment, tough yet delicate grasses grow. Near the streams one can rediscover the yellow columbine that is found only in these rarified heights. There are, of course, the usual whorled penstemon, paintbrush, yellow cinquefoil and shooting star, but all are dwarfed, clinging close to the turf, as though they were foreign to this clime. Here the margin for life is slim, and the hardiest backpacker finds himself imitating the plant life. When he rests or seeks sleep in the comfort of his bedroll, he instinctively curls up to conserve his precious body heat. This is perenially ice-touched land, always cold, and yet a place where one can get a severe sunburn.

Harsh and uninviting as the land seems, the hiker soon finds a beauty to wonder at as he progresses down the drainage. Only those who dare this harshness manage to view The Pinnacles from the east side, and that rugged, spiring rock mass towers on the right as one scrambles down the alternately moderate and steep granite slabs between Aweetasal and Jawbone lakes.

Following the outlet stream from Jawbone Lake, one arrives at shallow, grassy Council Lake. Here route-finding becomes simpler as the going levels off, and by a series of grassy benches one passes Poacha and Negit Lakes, and, rounding a granite shoulder, comes to Big Moccasin Lake. Stunted and solitary whitebark pines dot the rock fringes of this shallow lake. From Big Moccasin Lake it is an easy descent to Little Moccasin Lake, where one has fine views of the Piute Creek drainage. Above its U-shaped valley one can see Pilot Knob and the complex of avalanche chutes on the north face of Mt. Henry to the south. Majestic Mt. Humphreys dominates the Sierra crest, and the adjacent subrange is crowned by Emerald Peak. From this viewpoint, our route veers due west, descending a grassy chute to the campsites along the outlet streams from the upper lakes. These campsites (10,850′) are good, with excellent views.

4th Hiking Day (**Little Moccasin Lake** to **Sandpiper Lake**, 7½ miles cross country): From the west fork of East Pinnacles Creek this cross-country route swings around the south end of The Pinnacles on a long talus-and-boulder traverse to a point just north of Pemmican Lake. This scrambling traverse offers the views described in the 3rd hiking day until the drainage of West Pinnacles Creek is reached. A slight descent past several tarns leads to Spearpoint Lake, which, unlike the lakes of the East Pinnacles Creek drainage, is deep, and populated by a few small golden trout (6–8″). The rugged terrain around the edges of Spearpoint Lake determines the best feasible route to be over the easy granite ridge separating Spearpoint and Pendant lakes, and thence north across the marshy section separating Pendant and Big Chief lakes. After skirting the east side of shallow Big Chief Lake, this route ascends on a moderate grade from the meadowed north end of the lake to Old Squaw Lake. This lake is barren of trout, but it offers some of the best views of The Pinnacles to be obtained on this trip. Glacially smoothed granite slabs line the lake's edge on all sides, and progress is fairly easy along the east shore. Following the inlet stream, the route ascends steadily to Wampum Lake, where anglers may try their luck for the fair fishing (golden 6–8″).

At Wampum Lake the twin peaks of Gemini once more come into view, and one has reached the cirque-basined headwaters of West Pinnacles Creek. This bowl-like cirque presents route-picking problems, and some care should be excercised in crossing the sometimes steep west wall, which divides the West Pinnacles Creek drainage from the South Fork Bear Creek drainage. From the head of Wampum Lake, the route goes westward. At the top of this wall one has a panoramic vista of Seven Gables, Gemini, The Pinnacles, Emerald Peak, Mt. Henry, Mt. Senger, Mt. Hooper and the Bear Creek drainage.

Descent from this ridge presents no problems to the accomplished rock-climber, but the easiest route is to pick one's way westward around above the head of the Three Island Lake cirque to the saddle just east-southeast of Sharp Note Lake, and then traverse down the steep slopes on the west side of Three Island Lake. Anglers will find fair-to-good golden-trout fishing in this large (80-acre) lake. These rockbound, deep waters provide a classic glacial setting for high-country enthusiasts, and they are a favorite of camera-carrying visitors. Following the outlet stream at the north end of Three Island Lake past Medley Lake, an easy descent along a ledge system of granite leads to the inlet of Sandpiper Lake, the beginning for this cross-country loop.

5th and 6th Hiking Days: Retrace the steps of the 2nd and 1st hiking days, 16½ miles.

8   Bear Dam Junction to Florence Lake

TRIP
From Bear Dam Junction to Florence Lake via Sandpiper Lake, Selden Pass, Blaney Meadows (shuttle trip). Topo maps *Kaiser Peak, Mt. Abbot* 15′; *Mt. Givens, Florence Lake, Mt. Hilgard, Ward Mtn.* 7½′. Best mid or late season; 34 miles.

Grade	Trail/layover days	Total recommended days
Leisurely	5/1	6
Moderate	4/1	5
Strenuous	3/1	4

HILITES
This popular shuttle trip circles the Mt. Hooper complex and visits some of the best creek and lake fishing in the Sierra. Part of this trip's popularity stems from the near proximity of the trailhead to the conclusion of the trip—making the shuttle fairly simple.

DESCRIPTION (Moderate trip)

1st and 2nd Hiking Days: Follow trip 6 to **Sandpiper Lake**, 16½ miles.

3rd Hiking Day (**Sandpiper Lake** to **Lower Blaney Meadows**, 10 miles— 2 miles cross country): The first 2 miles of this hiking day are cross country. Starting from the campsites along the west side of Sandpiper Lake, this route ascends the easy, tarn-dotted swale at the southwest end of the lake and leads around the granite-slabbed nose of the ridge descending north from Mt. Senger. From this nose, one has excellent views down the Bear Creek drainage to Bear Ridge, and beyond to the barren tops of the Silver Divide. Immediately below is Lou Beverly Lake, and in its mirrorlike green surface one sees the reflection of Recess Peak. Looking north, views from left to right include Mt. Hooper, the Bear Creek drainage, and Lou Beverly Lake; and beyond, Graveyard Peak, Mt. Izaak Walton and Red and White Mountain. Given a clear atmosphere, one can see all the way north to the Minarets and the Mammoth Crest. To the immediate right is the bouldery crest of Mt. Hilgard, and to the right of that towers multipeaked Seven Gables, with Mt. Gabb peeking over its left shoulder. Turning toward the south, one looks into the immense cirque basin capped by Mt. Senger.

From the top of this ridge, it is a moderate descent west to large, granite-lined Marie Lake, where our route skirts the meadowy northern edge. Walking the turfy fringes of the lake, one will find elephant heads and western mountain aster mixed among the heather. This lake is at timberline, and as our route turns south on the west side of Marie Lake, the mixed sparse forest is left behind. At the outlet of Marie Lake, our route rejoins the John Muir Trail as it winds along the west banks of the lake. From the south end of the lake, the trail ascends on a gentle-to-moderate grade to Selden Pass (10,873'). Breather stops on this climb offer fine views back to Mt. Hilgard and the granitic Marie Lake cirque.

From Selden Pass the trail descends over short, steep switchbacks to Heart Lake. This rockbound, heart-shaped lake has meadow-turfed fringes delicately colored with heather, primrose and yellow columbine. Continuing the moderate descent from Heart Lake along its outlet stream, the trail arrives at Sally Keyes Lakes. This short walk is lined with a great abundance of wildflowers, where in season one can see corn lily, Indian paintbrush, Douglas phlox, shooting star, yellow cinquefoil, yarrow milfoil, penstemon, lupine, red heather, wallflower, nude buckwheat and western mountain aster.

The trail crosses the short stream joining the two Sally Keyes Lakes and then descends on duff and sand through a thickening forest cover of lodgepole. There are several good, though heavily used, campsites at the outlet and along the west shore of the lower of the two lakes. In 1979 the main trail was rerouted around the large meadow that lies ¼ mile south of the lower lake, so you will have to find the old main trail southbound or go to this meadow via cross country to reach the start of the shortcut trail (not shown on the 7½' map) down to the South Fork San Joaquin

River. Although this unmaintained trail is dusty and steep, one can enjoy an unusual cross section of Sierra flora in the course of a 3000-foot descent. At first, altitude-loving whitebark pines are mixed with the dense forest cover of lodgepole pines, but within a few miles the whitebarks disappear and fir makes a brief appearance, only to be replaced by Jeffrey pine at lower altitudes. Juniper is found in both the high and low altitudes; quaking aspen is not seen until the trail nears Senger Creek, near the foot of a descent. The dry canyon walls are generally brush-covered, with heavy manzanita around the middle of the descent, but with some surprise the trail traveler will also find many wildflowers along these same stretches. In the drier regions are Douglas phlox, streptanthus and Mariposa lily; in the wetter sections are shooting star, red columbine, corn lily, cinquefoil and penstemon; almost everywhere are lupine, white Mariposa, Bigelow sneezeweed, golden brodiaea and groundsel.

The switchbacking descent ends above Blayney Meadows (visible from the trail) and then this route turns right onto the Florence Lake Trail. From this junction the duff trail soon descends through a moderately dense mixed forest cover of lodgepole, juniper, Jeffrey and quaking aspen. Just before the boundary of the Muir Trail Ranch a trail branches left. Shortly down it, another left-branching trail leads to some overused campsites on both sides of the river. About 150 yards southwest of them is a natural-spring hot pool. Nearby is an unnamed lake good for a swim.

The trail through the Muir Trail Ranch is on a public right-of-way through private property. Stay on the trail, and do not camp here. Beyond the ranch we soon arrive at Lower Blayney Meadows and the public campground (7650'). Several fair campsites, including two improved packer sites, are available. Fishing in South Fork San Joaquin River for brown trout (to 12") is fair to good—mostly downstream.

4th Hiking Day (**Lower Blayney Meadows** to **Florence Lake,** 7½ miles): Following the well-used route west from Lower Blayney Meadows the trail ascends steadily over sand and rock to the footlog ford of the creek just east of Double Meadow. Here, the trail has been rerouted around the fringes of the grassland. Damage to fragile meadows like these, particularly during the wet early-summer months, has made a sufficient impression on the Forest Service and the National Park Service that they are now deemed worthy of appropriate conservation measures to guarantee their survival. As the trail rounds the north side of the meadow, it affords excellent views of Ward Mountain and high, pointed Mt. Shinn, and then it makes a moderate descent through a forest cover of Jeffrey, juniper and white fir over granite slabs to an improved campground above the head of Florence Lake. From here a bridge leads over South Fork San Joaquin River, just above the southeast end of Florence Lake. Crossing the smooth granite west of the bridge, this trail passes a short lateral branching right to the edge of Florence Lake, and a heavily used campground. At Boulder Creek the trail crosses by means of a log footbridge.

This route then passes an unsigned lateral to Thompson Lake and commences a series of moderate ups and downs through a mixed forest cover of Jeffrey and juniper, with occasional aspen, white fir and lodgepole. We skirt the west side of Florence Lake, sometimes ascending to granite ledges 150 feet above the lake's surface. About halfway around the lake we pass a signed junction with the Thompson Lake/Hot Springs Pass Trail. Views to the southeast always include Mt. Shinn and Ward Mountain and glimpses up the South Fork San Joaquin River drainage. To the north are the granite walls of Florence Lake's basin, foregrounded by its blue waters.

Our route leaves John Muir Wilderness, meets the Southern California Edison dam road (no public auto travel), and descends to the travelable roadend. From here we continue on the road uphill through a picnic area to the trailhead parking lot. (A boat-taxi shuttles from the head of Florence Lake to the roadend in summertime. Write Muir Trail Ranch, Box 176, Lakeshore, CA 93634 for details. Enclose an SASE.)

Bear Dam Junction to Vee Lake

TRIP   From Bear Dam Junction to Vee Lake via Sandpiper Lake, cross country to Vee Lake, return via
cross-country route to Lake Italy, Hilgard Branch
(semiloop trip). Topo maps *Kaiser Peak, Mt. Abbot
15'; Mt. Givens, Florence Lake, Mt. Hilgard 7½'.*
Best mid or late season; 45 miles.

	Grade	Trail/layover days	Total recommended days
Leisurely		....	....
Moderate		7/2	9
Strenuous		5/2	7

HILITES   A fine fishing trip including a rugged cross-country
segment, this route should appeal to the skilled
backpacker who likes to eat trout.

DESCRIPTION (Moderate trip)

1st and 2nd Hiking Days: Follow trip 6 to **Sandpiper Lake,** 16½
miles.

3rd Hiking Day (**Sandpiper Lake** to **Vee Lake,** 5 miles cross country):
Our rugged cross-country hike begins by rounding the west side
of Sandpiper Lake (10,500') and fording the inlet stream coming
from Medley Lake. From here the route ascends southeast by
means of granite ledge systems. Following the south fork of the
east inlet stream of Medley Lake, your route ascends steeply
over smoothed, barren granite slabs and grassy pockets to reach
the upper drainage of the north fork of the east inlet stream.

Climbing eastward, you cross a saddle at 12,000'+, pass the lake east of it, and then reach another saddle directly east. Views during the course of this climb include Medley Lake, Mts. Senger and Hooper, and Seven Gables.

At the saddle one has unmatched views to the north and east. Besides the immediate summits of Seven Gables and the twin spires of Gemini, one can see Mts. Hilgard, Abbot, Gabb, Dade, Julius Caesar, Royce and Humphreys and Bear Creek Spire. Every one of these peaks towers over 13,000 feet. Also from this saddle, one can spy out the natural route to the southernmost of the Seven Gables Lakes. Though steep, this descent is made mostly over glacially smoothed rock. Route-picking, however, is sometimes made difficult by interruptions of talus and scree slides.

The upper lakes of the Seven Gables chain are talus-bound, shallow bodies of water having no fish, but anglers will want to try the good fishing on the lower lakes (golden trout to 12") before making the final ascent to Vee Lake. These lower lakes and the intersecting stream are a fly fisherman's paradise. The ascent to Vee Lake is made over granite and talus along the outlet stream from that lake. The ascent terminates at the turfy east end (11,120'), where there are fair campsites. (Hikers who do not care for the high, alpine kind of camping should plan on ending their day at the lowest of the Seven Gables Lakes, where there are several good campsites.) Fishing on large Vee Lake (50 acres) is good to excellent for golden (to 15"). Views from the campsites on the east and north sides of the lake are excellent of the striking, white-granite faces of Royce and Merriam peaks.

4th Hiking Day (**Vee Lake** to **Lake Italy**, 5 miles cross country): Beginning at the north side of the north arm of Vee Lake, this hiking day's route ascends a granite shoulder to the string of rockbound tarns just south of Little Bear Lake. This moderate ascent is accomplished over a granite ledge system broken by talus. Fishing on tiny Little Bear Lake for golden is fair to good, and this evaluation holds for Big Bear and White Bear lakes upstream. Following the inlet stream of Little Bear Lake, the route ascends to the outlet of Big Bear/Ursa/Bearpaw Lake basin, crosses the stream joining Big Bear and White Bear lakes, and ascends steeply along the east side of this stream. Above the abrupt northeast side of White Bear Lake, one can make out the obvious saddle that separates the drainage of East Fork Bear

Creek from that of Hilgard Branch. Our route crosses this saddle, traverses the southeast end of the Jumble Lake cirque, and strikes the Italy Pass Trail (not shown on the 7½'map), where it turns left.

The saddle and the traverse offer unusual end-on views of Mts. Julius Caesar, Dade, Abbot, and Mills and Bear Creek Spire. Descending the moderate-to-steep slopes above Jumble Lake, one cannot help feeling awed by the forces that carved this basin. The smoothed rock is mute testimony to the grinding action of the glaciers that had their start here, and, as the trail continues to descend along the north shore of Jumble Lake, one pursues the course of the glacier as it forged its way into the much larger Lake Italy cirque. This descent fords the stream that joins Jumble Lake and Lake Italy and drops down to the shores of the latter about a mile above the outlet (11,202'). This very large lake (124 acres) is granite-enclosed, with narrow, meadowed fringes. Fair campsites that are quite exposed can be found along the south shore near the outlet, and there are superlative views of the surrounding peaks. Fishing for golden (8–12") is fair.

5th, 6th and 7th Hiking Days: Reverse the steps of trip 4, 18½ miles.

Douglas phlox

Bear Dam Junction to Second Recess   **10**

TRIP
From Bear Dam Junction to Second Recess via Hilgard Branch, Lake Italy, cross-country route to Lower Mills Creek Lake, Second Recess, return via Fish Camp, Quail Meadows (semiloop trip). Topo maps *Kaiser Peak, Mt. Abbot 15′*; *Mt. Givens, Florence Lake, Mt. Hilgard, Mt. Abbot, Graveyard Peak 7½′*. Best late season; 48½ miles.

Grade	Trail/layover days	Total recom- mended days
Leisurely	....	....
Moderate	7/2	9
Strenuous	5/2	7

HILITES
Another fine partly cross-country route, this trip is frequently used by climbers making ascents of the cluster of peaks that line the route. Anglers, photographers, naturalists and garden-variety trail-pounders will all find something to excite them en route. Because of the cross country, this route is recommended for experienced backpackers only.

DESCRIPTION (Moderate trip)

1st, 2nd and 3rd Hiking Days: Follow trip 4 to **Lake Italy**, 18½ miles.

4th Hiking Day (**Lake Italy** to **Lower Mills Creek Lake**, 5 miles cross country): This scenic cross-country route rounds the granite-bound north side of Lake Italy to Toe Lake, and then ascends the increasingly steep north cirque wall to 12,250-foot Gabbot Pass (the saddle between Mt. Gabb and Mt. Abbot). The ascent involves a strenuous workout, but does not require rock-climbing skills. As a reward, the hiker acquires some of the finest views obtainable in this part of the Sierra. This route is generally considered a climber's access route for ascents of Mts. Gabb and Abbot, and is seldom used by casual hikers. Parts of it are slippery in early summer. Peaks in line of sight during the ascent and at the pass include, to the west, Mts. Hilgard and Gabb; to the south, Mt. Julius Caesar, Royce Peak and "Feather Peak"; to the east, Mts. Dade, Abbot and Mills, and Bear Creek Spire; and to the north, the crest of the Silver Divide.

From the pass, this ducked route descends just east of the Mt. Gabb glacier to the steep headwall of the Upper Mills Creek Lake cirque. Traversing the east side of this cirque, the route becomes a trail as it continues down the east side of the cascading creek between the lakes to the good campsites at the timberlined outlet of Lower Mills Creek Lake (10,840'), an outstandingly pretty lake. Both Upper and Lower Mills Creek lakes are meadow-fringed, though mostly rockbound, and offer good-to-excellent golden-trout fishing (to 13"). Views from the campsites are excellent of the Mono and Silver divides.

5th Hiking Day (**Lower Mills Creek Lake** to **Quail Meadows**, 9½ miles): Staying on the east side of Mills Creek, a faint fisherman's trail descends the sparsely timbered slopes below Lower Mills Creek Lake past two small lakelets (good fishing for golden to 10"). At the final drop into Second Recess Creek canyon, this faint, often washed-out trail switchbacks down steeply to the confluence of the two creeks. The forest cover alters during the course of this descent from stunted lodgepole and some whitebark to flat-needled fir, lodgepole pine, and occasional quaking aspen and Jeffrey pine.

Our route, now following a distinct trail, descends on a moderate slope along the east side of Second Recess Creek. As one nears the brink of Mono Creek canyon, one gets a clear picture of the glacial story that left these spectacular landforms. It is evident that the valley of the Second Recess was a secondary (or feeder) arm of the greater ice mass that once filled deeper Mono Creek canyon. After accomplishing the moderate-to-steep descent to the log crossing of Mono Creek, the traveler can look back whence he came and fully understand the nature of the geologic term "hanging valley." The greater ice mass of the main trunk ground deeper, leaving these valleys literally hanging.

At Fish Camp this route passes several improved packer campsites and turns left (west) onto the Mono Creek Trail. This creekside trail descends moderately, offering between-the-trees views into First Recess, and of the abrupt, dark north face of Volcanic Knob. Frequent groves of quaking aspen line this route, and late season sees the banks of Mono Creek clad in golden hues. At the point where the canyon walls appear to be closing in, about 3 miles below Fish Camp, the trail veers away from the creek on a steep, switchbacking ascent that crosses the long-nosed ridge that separates the North Fork from the main canyon of Mono Creek. On the west side of this ridge, our route descends a short distance to the John Muir Trail junction, and turns left along the east side of North Fork Mono Creek. The trail then switchbacks down steeply to ford the North Fork a few yards above its confluence with the main stream. From this ford it is less than a mile of relatively level going through a dense lodgepole forest cover to the good campsites at Quail Meadows (7760').

6th and 7th Hiking Days: Reverse the 2nd and 1st hiking days, trip 3, 15½ miles.

Running Mono Creek below Quail Meadows   *Jeff Schaffer*

11 Mosquito Flat to Second Recess

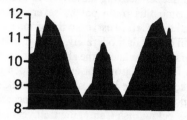

TRIP   From Mosquito Flat (on Rock Creek) to Second Recess via Mono Pass (round trip). Topo maps *Mt. Tom, Mt. Abbot* 15'; *Mt. Morgan, Mt. Abbot* 7½'. Best mid or late season; 32 miles.

| | Trail/layover | Total recom- |
Grade	days	mended days
Leisurely	6/2	8
Moderate	5/2	7
Strenuous	4/2	6

HILITES   The exciting eastern escarpment makes the first part of this trip a memorable experience. On this escarpment, the trail to Mono Pass offers sweeping vistas that vie for the traveler's consideration with the intimacy of the beautiful, cirque-bound lakes of Second Recess.

DESCRIPTION (Leisurely trip)

1st Hiking Day (**Mosquito Flat** to **Ruby Lake**, 2½ miles): The magnificent Sierra crest confronts the traveler at the very onset of this trip. From the trailhead at Mosquito Flat (10,230') the wide, rocky-sandy trail starts southwest toward the imposing skyline dominated by Mts. Mills, Abbot and Dade and Bear Creek Spire. A short distance from the trailhead, we come to a junction with the Little Lakes Valley Trail. Here our route branches right (west) and ascends steeply on rocky switchbacks. In the course of this switchbacking ascent, we see the moderate-to-dense forest cover of whitebark and lodgepole diminish in density as we near timberline. Views during the climb include the glacier-fronted peaks named above, and, midway up the ascent, imposing Mt. Morgan in the southeast. Immediately below to the east, the deep blue of Heart and Box lakes and some of the Hidden Lakes reflects the sky above, and the viewer looking at the panorama of the valley can readily comprehend the glacial history that left these "puddles" behind.

Near the meadowed edge of the outlet stream from Ruby Lake is a junction, where we turn left. It becomes apparent that a cirque basin is opening up, although one cannot see Ruby Lake, which completely fills the cirque bottom, until one is actually at water's edge (11,000'). This first breathtaking view of the lake and its towering cirque walls makes the climb worth the effort. Sheer granite composes the upper walls of the cirque, and the crown is topped by a series of spectacular pinnacles, particularly to the west. To the north, also on the crest, a notch indicates Mono Pass, and close scrutiny will reveal the switchbacking trail that ascends the south ridge of Mt. Starr. The lower walls of the cirque are mostly made up of talus and scree that curve outward to the lake's edge, and it is over this jumbled rock that ambitious anglers must scramble to sample the fair fishing for brook, rainbow and brown (to 12"). Good campsites can be found below the outlet of the lake.

2nd Hiking Day (**Ruby Lake** to **Fish Camp**, 9 miles): First retrace your steps ¼ mile to the Mono Pass Trail. Following a general east-to-west course, the trail climbs by long, steady switchbacks up the north wall of the cirque, and after a long, steady traverse veers northward by steeper switchbacks to the summit of Mono Pass (12,000'). The best views from the pass area are obtained by climbing the easy granite shoulder of Mt. Starr, to the east. Views from this shoulder include Mts. Stanford, Huntington, Crocker and Hopkins and Red and White Mountain to the north; and Mts. Abbot, Dade, and Humphreys and Bear Creek Spire to the south.

The trail continues north from the pass, descending steadily over granite. It traverses the west side of rockbound Summit Lake, and then descends more steeply to the slopes above Trail Lakes. The westward descent around Trail Lakes turns northward, and the trail drops to a Golden Creek ford. Here this route re-enters forest cover, and it continues to descend as it passes the lateral to Pioneer Basin and the lateral to Fourth Recess Lake. Serious anglers may wish to alter their hiking plan with a rewarding excursion to the excellent brook (some rainbow and golden) fishing obtainable at the lower Pioneer lakes. Fishing at nearby Fourth Recess Lake is good for brook (to 14"). Beyond these laterals, the trail fords the outlet streams from Pioneer Basin.

Mono Rock towers on the left as our route passes the Third Recess Trail lateral, and, about a mile farther, the lateral to Hopkins Lakes and Hopkins Pass. Anglers who wish to sample the good fishing for brook, rainbow and occasional golden in Mono Creek will find many fine, deep holes along this stretch of trail. For the most part, Mono Creek rushes along briskly, but occasional potholes and level stretches in the stream bed contribute to the good spawning areas that any good Sierra trout stream requires. Anglers and hikers alike will appreciate the abundance of quaking aspens that line Mono Creek. For those with color film in their cameras, the best time to capture the aspen color is usually late September or early October. This route then passes the Grinnell Lakes lateral, and descends to the good improved campsites on both sides of a log spanning Mono Creek at Fish Camp (8550').

3rd Hiking Day (**Fish Camp** to **Lower Mills Creek Lake**, 4½ miles): Retrace the steps of part of the 5th hiking day, trip 10.

4th, 5th and 6th Hiking Days: Retrace your steps, 16 miles.

Fishing in Rock Creek at Mosquito Flat

Pine Creek Roadend to Honeymoon Lake **12**

TRIP   From Pine Creek Roadend to Honeymoon Lake (round trip). Topo maps *Mt. Tom* 15'; *Mt. Tom* 7½'. Best midseason; 11 miles.

Grade	Trail/layover days	Total recommended days
Leisurely	2/1	3
Moderate	2/0	2
Strenuous	day	....

HILITES   The steep, winding ascent to Honeymoon Lake offers breathtaking over-the-shoulder views of the Pine Creek watershed, and the Honeymoon Lake campsite views of the Sierra crest make this one of the best choices for a base camp location on the east side of the Sierra.

DESCRIPTION (Moderate trip, but 3000' elevation gain)

1st Hiking Day (**Pine Creek Roadend** to **Honeymoon Lake**, 5½ miles): The trailhead (7400') is located at the pack station just south of Pine Creek. The dusty duff trail ascends steeply from the pack station through a dense, mixed forest cover of Jeffrey pine, juniper, red fir, quaking aspen and birch, and fords several branchlets of an unnamed creek that feeds Pine Creek. These fords are decorated by plentiful blossoms of wild rose, columbine, tiger lily and Queen Anne's lace. About ⅓ mile beyond these fords, the trail emerges from the forest cover, directly opposite the Union Carbide tungsten mill, and then merges with a recently rebuilt mining road for access to the Brownstone Mine, where new drilling was carried on in 1974. Although the slope into the Pine Creek canyon is steep, the road's grade is, for the most part, moderate, and this route segment is simply a matter of slog-and-pant. Three welcome streams break the monotony of the climb, and the view (despite the ugly roadcut that scars Morgan Creek) is spectacular. Through the Pine Creek valley that slopes away to the northeast, one can look across the Owens River drainage to the volcanic tableland and White Mountain (14,242') on the skyline. The road ends just above the scraps of metal marking the site of the Brownstone Mine.

There is one advantage to the presence of the mining activities in this canyon—and that is the dramatic contrast between industrial and recreational use of wilderness country. Coincident to this is the contrasting tempi of the lower and upper parts of the valley. One has only to watch the antlike scurrying of trucks and people across the way to fully appreciate the slow, peaceful pace of the wilderness traveler. From the mine, the trail ascends over talus and scree by short, steep switchbacks. Along this ascent one sees juniper, limber pine and lodgepole pine, and the juniper have left beautiful, weathered snags of a dramatic golden hue that are a constant delight to color photographers.

With the steepest part of the ascent behind, the trail fords another unnamed tributary, switchbacks past a sign at the boundary of the John Muir Wilderness, and veers north to join Pine Creek ⅓ mile below Pine Lake. Here, the creek alternates cascades, falls and chutes in a riot of white water. The trail fords the stream via logs and boulders, and amid a moderate forest cover of lodgepole pines arrives at the northeast end of Pine Lake. This medium-sized lake (16 acres) is a popular overnight camping place (campsites along the northeast shore), and fishermen may wish to tarry here to sample the fair fishing for brook (to 12"), but fishing is generally better at Upper Pine Lake.

Our trail skirts the rocky northwest side of Pine Lake and ascends through forest to the outlet stream from Birchim Lake, which we cross via logs. After climbing over a small ridge, the trail parallels the outlet stream from Upper Pine Lake and arrives at the north side of the lake (10,200'). Anglers will find that brook and rainbow (to 12") frequent these waters, and angling is good. After skirting the meadowy areas at the north side of the lake, the trail crosses the multibranched inlet stream via boulders. Then, after a moderate ½-mile ascent, we arrive at the Pine Creek Pass/Italy Pass junction. Our route turns right, away from the Pine Creek Pass Trail and onto the Italy Pass Trail, and soon turns right again on the short lateral to the outlet of Honeymoon Lake (10,400'). This moderate-sized lake (10 acres) has good campsites near the outlet stream and excellent sites above the head of the waterfall on the inlet stream, reached by following the trail up from the lake's south end. Fishing for brook and rainbow (to 10″) is good. This lovely lake makes an excellent base camp for side excursions to 40 surrounding lakes in four drainages, or for climbing five nearby peaks that exceed 13,000′ in elevation.

2nd Hiking Day: Retrace your steps, 5½ miles.

Bear Creek Spire

13

Pine Creek Roadend to Moon Lake

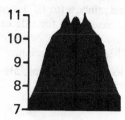

TRIP   From Pine Creek Roadend to Moon Lake via Pine Creek Pass (round trip). Topo maps *Mt. Tom* 15′; *Mt. Tom* 7½′. Best midseason; 20 miles.

Grade	Trail/layover days	Total recommended days
Leisurely	4/1	5
Moderate	3/1	4
Strenuous	2/1	3

HILITES   The snarling trucks that surround the trailhead belie the primitive country that lies beyond the first climb. Pine Creek, from its lower aspen-clad banks to its tundra-meadow birthplace, is a kind of stream that hiker, angler, photographer and naturalist can take a fancy to. At Moon Lake the visitor will experience memorable open, alpine surroundings at their finest.

DESCRIPTION   (Leisurely trip)

1st Hiking Day (**Pine Creek Roadend** to **Upper Pine Lake**, 5 miles): Follow most of the 1st hiking day, trip 12.

2nd Hiking Day (**Upper Pine Lake** to **Moon Lake**, 5 miles): From the junction of the Italy Pass and Pine Creek Pass trails, our route bears left on a steady ascent toward Pine Creek Pass. Originally a Mono Indian trading route, this route and pass have been used by man for almost five hundred years. The moderate forest cover of lodgepole and then whitebark thins as the trail climbs. Tiny, emerald-green, subalpine meadows break the long granite slabs, and wildflower fanciers will find clumps of color that include wallflower, shooting star, penstemon, lupine, primrose and columbine. The trail comes to a small creek that is the headwaters of Pine Creek and ascends a long swale between two granite walls, before making the final steep, rocky climb to Pine Creek Pass (11,100') on the Sierra Crest. From the vicinity of the pass, one has excellent views to the north of Bear Creek Spire, to the northwest of Merriam and Royce peaks; to the south of Pilot Knob and Glacier Divide, and to the southeast of Mt. Humphreys. From the pass, the trail descends to a fairly level, rocky meadow, and then drops to French Canyon over lupine-dotted ledges. Soon our route meets the fisherman's trail branching left to Elba and Moon lakes.

Our route leaves the main trail, following this fisherman's trail as it ascends the fairly steep south wall of French Canyon. This 300-foot climb brings one to fair-sized Elba Lake. Typical of these high, montane lakes, Elba seems virtually devoid of vegetation and life. It is understandable that the first-time visitor to this country often refers to it as "moon country," but those who come to know and love the high country soon discover the beauty that hides close beneath the near-sterile veneer. Spots of green between the tumbled talus blocks indicate grassy tundra patches or clumps of willows, and occasionally the weathered landscape is broken by a dwarfed lodgepole or whitebark pine. Steady, silent scrutiny will usually discover movement that indicates animal life. A bird is usually the first to be detected, and most likely it will be either a rosy finch or a hummingbird. Four-footed movement among the rocks is most likely a cony or a marmot, or it just might be a wolverine or a bushy-tailed wood rat. Fishermen will soon find life in the lake, for Elba Lake has a good population of golden and golden hybrids (to 12").

Following the inlet stream, our route then ascends steadily to larger Moon Lake (10,998'). Fair campsites can be found along the southeast side of the lake. Fishing for golden (to 12") is excellent, and, using Moon Lake as a base, anglers can explore eight more fishing lakes sharing this same bench system.

3rd and 4th Hiking Days: Retrace your steps, 10 miles.

14 Pine Creek Roadend to Bear Dam Junction

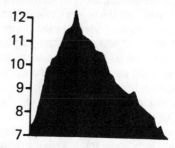

TRIP From Pine Creek Roadend to Bear Dam Junction via Honeymoon Lake, Italy Pass (shuttle trip). Topo maps *Mt. Tom, Mt. Abbot, Kaiser Peak 15'*; *Mt. Tom, Mt. Hilgard, Florence Lake, Mt. Givens 7½'*. Best mid or late season; 30 miles.

Grade	Trail/layover days	Total recommended days
Leisurely	6/2	8
Moderate	5/1	6
Strenuous	3/1	4

HILITES This is one of the best and shortest routes for an ambitious intermediate backpacker desiring to get the "feel" of a trans-Sierra crossing, for the route embraces the steep eastern escarpment, the barren, glaciated granite of the Sierra crest, and the long, densely wooded slopes of the west side.

DESCRIPTION (Moderate trip)

1 Hiking Day: Follow trip 12 to **Honeymoon Lake**, 5½ miles.

2nd Hiking Day (**Honeymoon Lake** to **Lake Italy**, 6 miles): The trail to Lake Italy may require some route-finding skills, for it is almost nonexistent in places. A faint trail rounds the south shore of Honeymoon Lake and crosses an inlet in a willow patch just above the lake, and another one a few dozen yards above the foot of a small meadow (excellent campsites). From here the trail winds up the jumbled valley, sometimes steeply, on the north side of the creek that drains Granite Park. The route passes many lovely little swales and crosses sparkling creeks four times as it ascends through thinning whitebark pines. If you lose the trail, look for it in places with soil, since it mostly avoids crossing bedrock or talus. Where it does cross these, look for ducks.

The trail arrives in Granite Park in a lovely meadow at timberline where the brook-trout-filled stream momentarily flows slowly. The trail fords the creek here and then doubles back to cross it again at the highest stand of whitebark pines. Then the route winds up the open, rocky expanses of upper Granite Park, where the ducked trail is very faint at times. Soon we come to the northeast shore of the highest lake, and the hiker can admire the views to the east before beginning the last, straightforward climb to Italy Pass (12,400′). Views from the north side of this saddle are excellent, including—clockwise from the east—Mt. Tom, Mt. Humphreys, the Palisades, Seven Gables, Mt. Hilgard, Mt. Gabb, and, nearby in the north, Mt. Julius Caesar.

From the pass, the faint, ducked trail descends around the north side of a cirque and, after following a creek here for a short distance, drops down to the slopes above the north shore of Jumble Lake. Crossing this talus-covered slope to the edge of the hanging valley above Lake Italy, the trail may become lost amid boulders, but it becomes better defined as it winds down to the south shore of Lake Italy (11,202′). This large lake (124 acres) lies in a majestic basin surrounded by four of the highest peaks in this part of the Sierra. It was named Lake Italy by the USGS in about 1907 because of its resemblance to that country in shape. After skirting the lake's south shore (difficult when snow lingers late), our route arrives at the fair campsites near the outlet. Although the population of golden trout is somewhat depleted, their size (sometimes up to 12″) makes this a fair lake for angling.

3rd, 4th and 5th Hiking Days: Reverse the steps of trip 4, 18½ miles.

15 Pine Creek Roadend to Sandpiper Lake

TRIP
From Pine Creek Roadend to Sandpiper Lake via Honeymoon Lake, Italy Pass, Selden Pass, Hutchinson Meadow, French Canyon, Pine Creek Pass (loop trip). Topo maps *Mt. Tom, Mt. Abbot, Blackcap Mountain* 15′; *Mt. Tom, Mt. Hilgard, Florence Lake, Ward Mtn.* 7½′. Best mid or late season; 53½ miles.

Grade	Trail/layover days	Total recommended days
Leisurely	....	....
Moderate	7/2	9
Strenuous	5/2	7

HILITES
The intermediate trail traveler will find this long trip a rewarding choice. After leaving beautiful Pine Creek, this trail route tours Granite Basin and Italy Pass, and then joins the John Muir Trail. Traveling south, this singular trail crosses Selden Pass and ascends the South Fork San Joaquin River watershed. Leaving the Muir Trail at Piute Creek, this route then loops back to rejoin the Pine Creek Trail via Pine Creek Pass.

DESCRIPTION (Moderate trip)

1st and 2nd Hiking Days: Follow trip 14 to **Lake Italy,** 11½ miles.

3rd Hiking Day: (**Lake Italy** to **Sandpiper Lake,** 11½ miles): The trail descends along the east bank of Hilgard Branch past the low ridge behind which lie Teddy Bear and Brown Bear lakes and then switchbacks down steeply to a ford of the creek. Then the trail levels out as it winds through a sparse forest cover of lodgepole. About a mile farther, it descends steeply once more, via rocky switchbacks, and after losing 500 feet levels out. The loss of altitude brings an increase in density of the forest cover— mostly lodgepole—and the individual trees no longer appear gnarled and stunted. The route then fords the outlet stream draining Hilgard Lake, and presently we make a final switch-backing drop into the main canyon of Bear Creek. Here we turn left on the Muir Trail and follow the second part of the 2nd hiking day, trip 6.

4th Hiking Day (**Sandpiper Lake** to lower **Sally Keyes Lake**, 5 miles): Follow the first part of the 3rd hiking day, trip 8.

5th Hiking Day (**Lower Sally Keyes Lake** to **Hutchinson Meadow**, 12½ miles): An early start for this hiking day is advisable in order to complete the long, sometimes steep, always dusty descent into the South Fork San Joaquin River drainage. From Sally Keyes Lakes (10,200'), the duff trail descends through heavy stands of lodgepole interspersed with tiny meadows. Colorful wild-flowers, often in patches, dot this stretch of trail: Indian paint-brush, Douglas phlox, shooting star, yellow and white cinque-foil, penstemon, lupine, red heather, western wallflower, buck-wheat, and western mountain aster. This route swings eastward, and crosses two terminal moraine ridges.

The sometimes rocky trail then descends to ford Senger Creek in a lovely forested flat, where it leaves the heavy concentra-tions of lodgepole behind. Alternately steep and moderate descents characterize the southeastward course of the trail, and the traveler soon finds that he is entering a drier area of manzanita and fractured granite. Views are excellent to the south and west of the resistant granite slopes of Mt. Shinn and Ward Mountain. To the southeast, the skylined peaks of the LeConte Divide and Emerald Peak dominate the view until the trail passes the lateral to Blaney Meadows, and then makes the final descent to a junction with the main Florence Lake Trail. A prelunch swim in the nice holes on the South Fork San Joaquin River to the west of the junction is in order, and fishermen will find fair fishing for brook in the same vicinity. Several fair-to-good primitive campsites and one packer campsite are near the junction.

From this junction, our route continues east on a duff-and-granite-sand trail through a mixed forest cover of Jeffrey pine and juniper interspersed with occasional red and white fir. The trail crosses an easy series of ridges and descends past several good campsites to the Piute Canyon Trail junction, where our route branches left, away from the John Muir Trail. Sporadic appearances of quaking aspen (in the wetter spots) line our rocky ascent up Piute canyon. The trail keeps to the west side of briskly flowing Piute Creek, and fords multibranched Turret Creek. This climbing, rocky trail affords excellent views of highly fractured Pavilion Dome and the surrounding, unnamed domes composing the west end of Glacier Divide. The trail then swings east through a narrowing canyon, fords tiny West Pinnacles Creek, and pursues a rocky course until it enters a moderate lodgepole forest cover before reaching the East Pinnacles Creek ford. Views of the cascading tributary streams are frequent along this trail section. From the ford, the trail ascends gently to beautiful Hutchinson Meadow (9439'), where travelers will find excellent campsites near the Pine Creek Pass Trail junction. Fishing for golden and brook is good-to-excellent (to 9"). The lovely meadow setting provides excellent campsite views of several granite peaks (Pilot Knob and Peak 12432) to the east and west.

6th Hiking Day (**Hutchinson Meadow** to **Upper Pine Lake**, 8 miles): This hiking day's route leaves the Piute Pass Trail and ascends moderately up French Canyon. Rocky stretches alternate with the soft underfooting of grassy sections. Fishing along these upper reaches of French Canyon Creek is good to excellent, despite the diminishing size of the stream. The trail crosses several unnamed tributaries draining the east and west slopes of Royce and Merriam peaks, and soon climbs above timberline. The character of the canyon walls reflects the increase in altitude. Barren granite, mostly white and heavily fractured, scoops away to the east, making a broad-headed, typical cirque basin. The footing becomes very rocky as the trail passes the faint fisherman's trail to Moon Lake, and then veers north, climbs steeply, and crosses a long granite bench. From the bench, it is but a short, easy climb to the summit of Pine Creek Pass, where there are excellent views of Bear Creek Spire, Royce and Merriam peaks, Pilot Knob, the Glacier Divide and Mt. Humphreys.

Directly ahead, the trail descends a long, talus-ridden swale. This descent soon enters a sparse forest cover of lodgepole, winding between large slabs of granite. Tiny subalpine meadows fill the gaps in the rock, and the traveler is sure to encounter western wallflower, shooting star, penstemon, lupine, primrose and columbine. The trail veers away from the trickling Pine Creek headwaters, crosses a slight rise, and then drops to the hard-to-see junction with the Italy Pass Trail. Our route keeps to the right, fords North Fork Pine Creek just above the cascading inlet to Upper Pine Lake, and arrives at the excellent campsites along the west side of the lake and below the outlet (10,200'). Good fishing for brook, rainbow, and some golden (to 12") can be had on Upper Pine Lake.

7th Hiking Day: (**Upper Pine Lake** to **Pine Creek Roadend**, 5 miles): Retrace most of the steps of the 1st hiking day, trip 12.

Mt. Humphreys   *E. P. Pister*

16 North Lake to Piute Lake

10
9

TRIP From North Lake to Piute Lake (round trip). Topo maps *Mt. Goddard* 15′; *Mt. Darwin* 7½′. Best mid or late season; 7 miles.

Grade	Trail/layover days	Total recommended days
Leisurely	2/0	2
Moderate	....	....
Strenuous	day	....

HILITES This trip offers an easy walk into the high country and a lake with large trout. It is an excellent choice for beginning backpackers who want to sample the high country with only a modest effort.

DESCRIPTION (Leisurely trip)

1st Hiking Day: (**North Lake** to **Piute Lake**, 3½ miles): Shortly after leaving the trailhead (9360′), this route enters the John Muir Wilderness and then ascends gently along slopes dotted with meadowy patches, aspen groves and stands of lodgepole pine. In season the traveler will find a wealth of wildflowers in these little meadows and in the sandy patches among the granite slabs, including paintbrush, columbine, tiger lily, spiraea and penstemon. After the trail fords and quickly refords North Fork Bishop Creek, the ascent becomes moderate. Aspen is left behind, the lodgepole becomes sparse, and some limber pine is seen. The glaciated canyon is flanked by slab-topped Peak 12691 on the south and 13,118-foot Mt. Emerson on the north. The newcomer to the High Sierra will marvel at how the great granite slabs maintain their precarious perches atop Peak 12691, seeming to be almost vertically above him. But they all topple eventually, due to the action of frost wedging, and add to the piles of talus at the foot of the peak.

Approaching Loch Leven, the trail levels off, and the angler may wish to try the lake waters for brook, rainbow and brown trout (to 10″). The trail then ascends moderately again, through a cover of sparse lodgepole and whitebark, winds among large, rounded boulders, and skirts a small lake before arriving at the next bench up the canyon, which contains this day's destination, Piute Lake (10,950′). The traveler may wish to consider the wind in selecting a campsite, as it often blows stiffly in this Piute Pass country. There are overused campsites on the north side close to the trail. Fishing for brook and rainbow is fair (to 18″). Those who would go out of their way to find seclusion may elect to scramble southeast up a fairly steep slope to granite-bound Emerson Lake.

2nd Hiking Day: Retrace your steps, 3½ miles.

Duck on glacial erratic

17

North Lake to Hutchinson Meadow

TRIP
From North Lake to Hutchinson Meadow via Piute Lake, Piute Pass (round trip). Topo maps *Mt. Goddard, Mt. Tom, Mt. Abbot* 15′; *Mt. Tom, Mt. Darwin, Mt. Hilgard* 7½. Best mid or late season; 22 miles.

Grade	Trail/layover days	Total recommended days
Leisurely	4/1	5
Moderate	3/1	4
Strenuous	2/0	2

HILITES
Hutchinson Meadow is one of the finest meadows in the High Sierra, and the trail to it beside Piute Creek takes the traveler through several miles of wild mountain "lawns" and gardens, where Sierra wildflowers are at their best. Add the views of dominating Mt. Humphreys and the spectacular Glacier Divide, and this trip becomes one of the most scenic in all the Sierra. Yet Humphreys Basin is equally famous for its golden trout.

DESCRIPTION (Moderate trip)

1st Hiking Day: Follow trip 16 to **Piute Lake**, 3½ miles.

2nd Hiking Day: (**Piute Lake** to **Hutchinson Meadow**, 7½ miles): From Piute Lake the trail ascends an open, rocky slope to timberline, and switchbacks up to the last traverse before Piute Pass (11,423′). Here the traveler in midsummer will probably pass through a "road cut" in a snowbank, created by packers using sand and shovels. At the pass there are grand views west to the canyon of South Fork San Joaquin River, south to Glacier Divide (the north boundary of Kings Canyon National Park) and north to Mt. Humphreys, highest peak this far north in the Sierra. (If it could acquire 14 feet from somewhere, Bishop residents would have their own 14,000-foot Sierra peak.) The rocky trail curves along the north side of the Summit Lake cirque and then strikes off northwest into the great, high lake bowl called Humphreys Basin, with 31 lakes that have golden trout.

In this basin the sandy trail contours through alpine grasses, crosses some streamlets draining the high lakes below Mt. Humphreys, and passes the unmarked use trail northward to Little and Big Desolation lakes at a point where our main trail is above and north of a small lake with a green island. The main trail then descends to ford the outlet stream of the Desolation Lakes. If you miss the use trail, follow that outlet—last reliable water before Hutchinson Meadow in a dry year—upstream to the lakes. There is good fishing in Big Desolation for golden to 20″. Or the angler may wish to sample the waters of heavily used Golden Trout Lake, south of the trail, for the fair fishing for golden (to 10″). Several trails strike off toward Golden Trout Lake, and the main trail itself has several alternative branches in this area. Heading down-valley well above the creek will keep you on course. Entering timber, the route begins a moderate descent on a rocky trail through sparse lodgepole which soon becomes moderate.

About 4 miles from Piute Pass the display of flower-studded green "lawns" begins (in a normal year), and from here to Hutchinson Meadow the traveler is seldom out of sight of these subalpine gardens. The amateur botanist will discern paintbrush, shooting star, fleabane, swamp onion, red mountain heather, buttercup, cinquefoil, penstemon, buckwheat, yarrow milfoil, groundsel and Douglas phlox, along with Labrador tea, lemon willow and alpine willow. Rollicking Piute Creek is often close at hand, lending its music to complete this scene of mountain beauty.

Beyond a drift fence, the trail levels out and fords the distributaries of French Canyon Creek, arriving at the good campsites at forested Hutchinson Meadow (9439′). Here beneath Pilot Knob and Peak 12402 the angler will find the riffles of Piute Creek good-to-excellent fishing for brook and some golden (to 9″), or he may cautiously approach the little pools on the distributaries of French Canyon Creek, which spread out through the east side of the meadow and offer equally good fishing.

3rd Hiking Day: Retrace your steps, 11 miles.

18

North Lake to Florence Lake

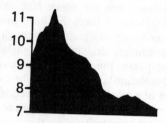

TRIP

From North Lake to Florence Lake via Piute Lake, Piute Pass, Hutchinson Meadow, Lower Blaney Meadows (shuttle trip). Topo maps *Mt. Goddard, Mt. Tom, Mt. Abbot, Blackcap Mountain 15'; Mt. Darwin, Mt. Tom, Mt. Hilgard, Mt. Henry, Ward Mtn., Florence Lake 7½'*. Best mid or late season; 27½ miles.

Grade	Trail/layover days	Total recommended days
Leisurely	4/1	5
Moderate	3/1	4
Strenuous	3/0	3

HILITES

Following an old Indian trade route, this trip tours nearly every life zone and type of forest belt found in the Sierra. Well suited to foot or stock travel, the trail crosses Piute Pass and descends the west slopes via the San Joaquin drainage. Good angling in the Humphreys Basin waters, fine views of the Sierra crest and Glacier Divide, and well-maintained trails make this a good, solid trip for the beginner who has spent a few nights in the wilderness.

DESCRIPTION (Leisurely trip)

1st and 2nd Hiking Days: Follow trip 17 to **Hutchinson Meadow,** 11 miles.

3rd Hiking Day: (**Hutchinson Meadow** to **Lower Blayney Meadows,** 9 miles): Staying on the north side of Piute Creek, the alternately duff and rocky trail descends gently through a moderate forest cover of lodgepole. After the easy ford of East Pinnacles Creek, the timber thins, and the precipitous valley walls begin to close in. There are excellent views of the cascading tributaries, and the green rock around Pavilion Dome in the southwest is but one of many beautiful parts of these canyon walls. Meadowy patches of grass lace the rockier sections of trail, and it drops over a moderate slope to a tiny lakelet that interrupts the brisk, bouncing flow of Piute Creek. Although the fish are somewhat smaller than in the lakes passed on the 2nd hiking day, they are plentiful, and anglers may wish to sample some of these pan-sized golden.

Our route then swings west to ford West Pinnacles Creek, and south as it approaches the ford of multibranched Turret Creek. Crossing the easy granite nose protruding from the west wall of the canyon, the trail descends over steep and then moderate slopes to a junction with the John Muir Trail. Here our route turns rights (west), and undulates via rocky trail down the South Fork San Joaquin River canyon. The mostly sparse forest cover has changed from a predominance of lodgepole to Jeffrey, juniper, some red and white fir, and the seepage-loving quaking aspen. The underfooting of this trail exhibits the effects of both chemical and physical weathering of the granite walls, with its deep pockets of heavy, coarse, quartz sand. Where this sand has mixed with alluvial deposits, trees and shrubs have taken root, and along these stretches the ground is frequently carpeted with a shallow layer of duff.

The trail junction where our Florence Lake route leaves the John Muir Trail, which goes to the right, makes an excellent lunch or swimming stop. In a forest cover that has become heavy, the trail from the junction continues by a series of moderate ups and downs to a junction with a trail climbing north, where signs indicate the Muir Trail is 1½ miles away, both to the east and to the north. In 200 yards you come to an unsigned trail on the left which leads south ¼ mile down to riverside campsites. From the campsites on the south side of the river a faint trail goes 150 yards southwest to a natural hot-spring pool. The fence right by this pool encloses the Muir Trail Ranch, and several of the outbuildings of this commercial establishment are in view as, back on the main trail, we skirt its boundary.

Soon we ford the noisy branchlets of Senger Creek and wind through the heavy forest cover surrounding Blayney Meadows.

Then our trail continues around the fringes of the meadow to the fair campsites at Lower Blaney Meadows (7650'). Fishing for brown trout is fair to good (mostly downstream).

4th Hiking Day: (**Lower Blaney Meadows** to **Florence Lake**, 7½ miles): Follow the 4th hiking day, trip 8.

Florence Lake

Lake Sabrina to Emerald Lakes   **19**

TRIP   From Lake Sabrina to Emerald Lakes (round trip). Topo maps *Mt. Goddard* 15′; *Mt. Darwin* 7½′. Best mid or late season; 8 miles.

Grade	Trail/layover days	Total recom-mended days
Leisurely	2/0	2
Moderate	....	....
Strenuous	day	....

HILITES   The sparkling blue lakes near the head of Middle Fork Bishop Creek, nestled close under 13,000-foot granite peaks, are among the most scenic on the Sierra Nevada's east slope. Of these, Emerald Lakes are some of the loveliest yet some of the most accessible.

DESCRIPTION (Leisurely trip)

1st Hiking Day (**Lake Sabrina** to **Emerald Lakes**, 4 miles): From the designated backpackers' parking area below Lake Sabrina, our route follows the Lake Sabrina road ½ mile to the trailhead, on the left about 100 yards below the Sabrina Dam. The well-used trail, signed SABRINA BASIN TRAIL and BLUE LAKE TRAIL, climbs above Sabrina Dam (9180′) and begins a long traverse of the slope above the blue expanses of Lake Sabrina. The route is initially through lush greenery and over small streams but it soon strikes out across the dry, sunny hillside above the lake, where there is a sparse cover of aspen, Jeffrey pine, juniper, lodgepole pine, silver pine and mountain mahogany. Where the dusty trail crosses talus, we encounter many aspen, indicating a plentiful underground water supply. Views from here are excellent, extending all the way to the Sierra crest. The trail undulates gently until about halfway along the lake, and then ascends steadily to a junction with the George Lake Trail, branching left.

Soon beyond, the trail descends to a precarious log ford of the cascading outlet from George Lake, where we find our first water and shade since the north end of Lake Sabrina.

From here the trail switchbacks steeply through a moderate cover of lodgepole pine, crosses a small stream, and climbs onto the ridge north of Blue Lake. Then our rocky trail climbs over this shadeless ridge and swings south. The remaining ascent to Blue Lake is up a quiet ravine that heads just above the lake's north shore. A short descent through overused campsites brings one to the outlet of picturesque Blue Lake (10,388'; no camping within 300 feet). This spot is a photographer's delight, with lodgepoles along the uneven shoreline and rugged Thompson Ridge towering above the clear waters of the lake.

From the rock-and-log ford of the outlet, the trail winds through granite outcrops on the west side of the lake. About midway along this side is a signed trail junction, where going straight would head to Donkey Lake. Our route turns right toward Dingleberry Lake. The winding trail passes over a low saddle, down across a rocky slope and back up granite ledges into a grassy valley spotted with lodgepole pines. Soon our route reaches the shaded outlet of the lowest of the Emerald Lakes. Although these lakes are closer in size to ponds, they are indeed little gems. It is a short distance to the next larger of these lakes, where there are good campsites. More secluded camping can be found at the largest and westernmost Emerald Lake, reached by ascending southwest from the second lake for ¼ mile over broken granite. The fishing in these lakes is fair-to-good for brook to 8".

2nd Hiking Day: Retrace your steps, 4 miles.

Thompson Ridge over Blue Lake

Lake Sabrina to George Lake

TRIP   From Lake Sabrina to George Lake (round trip). Topo maps *Mt. Goddard* 15'; *Mt. Thompson* 7½'. Best mid and late season; 6.4 miles.

Grade	Trail/layover days	Total recom- mended days
Leisurely	2/0	2
Moderate	day	....
Strenuous	day	....

HILITES   Few lakes reachable by trail and so close to a road offer as much solitude as George Lake. After the day-hiking fishermen leave, you may have the lake to yourself.

DESCRIPTION (Leisurely trip)

1st Hiking Day (**Lake Sabrina** to **George Lake**, 3.2 miles): Follow trip 19 to the George Lake Trail junction and turn left, uphill, onto that trail. This steep path switchbacks up an open, exposed hillside for more than ½ mile before it reaches the first clumps of welcome whitebark pines. When you come to the first stream, cross it and almost immediately recross it to continue on switchbacks up the steep hillside. As the forest cover grows thicker, the steep grade abates, becoming mild and then, very soon, level. At the head of a meadow, cross the stream to the right side and continue up the valley. Then the trail veers left to cross a sloping, willowed meadow, in the middle of which a guiding duck sits atop a house-size boulder. Beyond this meadow, the sandy trail rises steeply for about 100 vertical feet, and then suddenly you are at George Lake (10,700'). There are good campsites near the trail on the east side of the lake, and fishing is good for brook and rainbow (to 12").

21   Lake Sabrina to Tyee Lakes

TRIP   From Lake Sabrina to South Lake Road via Tyee
Lakes (shuttle trip). Topo maps *Mt. Goddard* 15′;
Mt. Thompson 7½′. Best mid or late season, 7.7
miles.

Grade	Trail/layover days	Total recom- mended days
Leisurely	2/0	2
Moderate	....	....
Strenuous	day	....

HILITES   The views from the plateau atop Table Mountain
give one an ineffable feeling of grandeur that is not
soon forgotten. Beyond and below, the numerous
Tyee Lakes offer hundreds of bays and bowers to
swim and picnic in.

DESCRIPTION (Leisurely trip)

1st Hiking Day (**Lake Sabrina** to **George Lake,** 3.2 miles): Follow the
1st hiking day, trip 20.

2nd Hiking Day (**George Lake** to **South Lake Road,** 4½ miles): Before
reaching the upper end of George Lake, the trail turns left (northeast) up slopes of granite sand dotted with whitebark pines.
Although the tread is not always distinct on this slope, the route
is well-ducked. Switchbacking up the increasingly steep trail,
you have increasingly good views of George Lake and the Sierra
crest beyond. Near the summit is a small stream that runs till
midsummer, and one could camp beside it. The trail becomes
nearly level before reaching its high point, and on this barren-
seeming, rocky plateau grow many clumps of white phlox and
lavender whorled penstemon.

Beyond the summit we head down the east side of a tributary of Tyee Lakes creek and, following ducks, enter corn-lily country. The flowering plant that looks like a cornstalk grows profusely in dozens of soggy hillside gardens here. Where the little valley narrows and steepens, a trail becomes obvious on the right side of the creek. Just before this creek drops into a gorge there is a beautiful lunch spot beside the stream with a commanding view of the fifth and largest Tyee Lake. Then the trail winds down to that lake, which has fair campsites on its north side under groves of whitebark pines. After we cross the outlet stream, the trail becomes more distinct, and it remains so to the end of this trip. We circle the fourth lake, keeping some distance from its shore until we near the outlet. Beside the outlet are some well-developed but otherwise good campsites near a very picturesque, rock-dotted pond.

Beyond these campsites the trail again crosses Tyee Lakes creek and then winds down-canyon far from the third lake, seen in the east, to the shores of small, partly reed-filled lake #2, whose campsites are poor. Lake #1 has practically no campsites, and we skirt its swampy west edge, then veer away from its outlet to begin a moderate descent through increasingly dense forest. In ½ mile the trail crosses Tyee Lakes creek, and then it switchbacks in a generally eastward direction, crossing another refreshing stream soon after. The descent continues on dusty switchbacks down an often steep hillside, finally ending at a bridge across South Fork Bishop Creek just downstream from a parking area on the South Lake road 5.0 miles up the South Lake road from the Lake Sabrina road.

A Tyee Lake

22   Lake Sabrina to Baboon Lakes

TRIP   From Lake Sabrina to Baboon Lakes (round trip).
Topo maps *Mt. Goddard* 15′; *Mt. Thompson* 7½′.
Best mid or late season; 9 miles.

Grade	Trail/layover days	Total recom-mended days
Leisurely	2/0	2
Moderate	....	....
Strenuous	day	....

HILITES   Sooner or later, everyone who returns to the High
Sierra will want to try a little cross-country hiking.
This fairly short trip is a fine choice for the traveler
who has reached that point in his career.

DESCRIPTION (Leisurely trip)

1st Hiking Day (**Lake Sabrina** to **Baboon Lakes**, part cross country,
4½ miles): Follow the 1st hiking day, trip 19 to the trail junction
on the west shore of Blue Lake. Here we go straight and walk
through granite-slab terrain under a forest of lodgepole pine,
passing the south end of Blue Lake (not visible) and crossing a
seasonal tributary. Not much farther on we meet and climb
beside the main stream. Just before the trail crosses it, our
obscure trail takes off up beside the stream. The trail is almost
nonexistent, but is marked by a line of ducks. The route is not
difficult, however, as the country is open granite slabs dotted
with lodgepoles and a few whitebark pines. Bearing southwest
for a half mile, we reach the bouldery north shore of lower
Baboon Lake and some fine open campsites. Upper Baboon
Lake is a short, easy scramble to your left (southeast). One mile
southeast, cross-country, is icy-cold Sunset Lake, close under
the glaciated ramparts of Mts. Powell and Thompson. Fishing in
Baboon Lakes is fair-to-good for rainbow trout (to 12″).

2nd Hiking Day: Retrace your steps, 4½ miles.

Florence Lake to Lost Lake

23

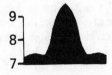

TRIP   From Florence Lake to Lost Lake (round trip). Topo
              maps *Mt. Abbot, Blackcap Mountain* 15'; *Florence
              Lake, Ward Mtn.* 7½'. Best early or mid season; 18
              miles.

Grade	Trail/layover days	Total recom-mended days
Leisurely	....	....
Moderate	2/0	2
Strenuous	....	....

HILITES   Almost every "Lost Lake" in the Sierra Nevada is
              somewhat lost in the sense that there is no regular,
              maintained trail to it, and the Lost Lake of Florence
              Lake country is no exception. This trail situation
              always makes for seclusion and solitude, which are
              becoming ever more valuable.

DESCRIPTION (Leisurely trip)

1st Hiking Day (**Florence Lake** to **Lost Lake,** 9 miles): From the foot
of Florence Lake, the hiker has a choice of walking the trail
around the west side of the lake or taking the ferry to the
lakehead. (Write Muir Trail Ranch, Box 176, Lakeshore, CA
93634 for details. Please enclose SASE.) The description in this
book covers the trail route from the parking area at the foot of the
lake.

Leaving the parking area, the route follows a maintenance
road (closed to public vehicles) for ⅛ mile as it skirts the west
side of the lake, before giving way to a trail which veers off to the
right and undulates over granite ridges that form a series of
spines down to the lake. The trail rolls through a mixed forest of
Jeffrey pine, juniper, aspen, white fir and lodgepole pine.
Previews of the kind of country to come are provided by

views southeast of Ward Mountain and Mt. Shinn, and north-ward of the granite walls across the lake, and glimpses of the San Joaquin drainage to the east. Now in John Muir Wilderness, about halfway to the head of the lake this route passes a junction with a Thomson Lake/Hot Springs Pass Trail (not main-tained). Just before the ford of Boulder Creek, a second, unsigned lateral to Thomson Lake takes off to the right (south), and it is our trail. From the west side of the log-bridge crossing of Boulder Creek this trail climbs steeply up a hot, manzanita-covered hillside under a sparse-to-moderate forest cover of Jeffrey pine, mountain juniper and a few firs and lodgepoles. The trail comes momentarily alongside the welcome creek and then swings away and climbs moderately to steeply through thinning forest. As the trail tops the canyon wall, one can obtain good views of Mts. Hooper, Senger and Shinn, and the valley of the South Fork San Joaquin River. Just beyond, we ford small, brook-trout-inhabited Boulder Creek and then climb moder-ately as the forest cover slowly increases with the additions of silver pine and mountain hemlock. Soon the trail rounds a shallow ridge and then climbs steadily to the Lost Lake Trail branching left. Our route crosses the outlet stream from Thompson Lake and then parallels the outlet of Lost Lake to the campsites on the lake's northern edge.

2nd Hiking Day: Retrace your steps, 9 miles.

Florence Lake

Florence Lake to Courtright Reservoir

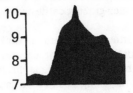

24

TRIP   From Florence Lake to Courtright Reservoir (shuttle trip). Topo maps *Mt. Abbot, Blackcap Mountain 15'; Florence Lake, Ward Mtn., Courtright Reservoir 7½'*. Best early or mid season; 21 miles.

Grade	Trail/layover days	Total recom-mended days
Leisurely	....	....
Moderate	2/0	2
Strenuous	....	....

HILITES   Those who hate to retrace their steps are always looking for good trips that have a roadhead at both ends. This mid-Sierra shuttle should be a valuable addition to their collections.

DESCRIPTION (Moderate trip)

1st Hiking Day: Follow trip 23 to **Lost Lake**, 9 miles.

2nd Hiking Day (**Lost Lake** to **Courtright Reservoir**, 12 miles): We begin this hiking day by contouring at 9,600 feet from Lost Lake west to the outlet of Thomson Lake. A packer campsite is located at the outlet, and the meadows around the lake show signs of grazing cattle. Angling southeast, our trail climbs steeply toward Thomson Pass under a moderate-to-dense forest cover of lodgepole and silver pines. At the top of this climb, views of the Silver Divide and the Ritter Range improve as we pass a few small springs which may offer a welcome draught, depending on the amount of recent bovine activity in the area. At Thomson Pass views are poor, and it's worth walking north a few hundred yards to the top of a small ridge, where you get magnificent views to the north. From this pass our trail descends moderately through dense lodgepole forest to a meadow crossing of West Fork Burnt Corral Creek. Then the trail makes a long, gentle descent through thick lodgepole forest where the forest floor is a lovely carpet of grass. This descent can be very pleasant and quiet unless summer-grazing cattle are mooing somewhere nearby.

About 35 yards northeast of where the trail fords West Fork Burnt Corral Creek for the second time, several very cold springs provide a refreshing reason for the thirsty hiker to pause before continuing down to the Long Meadow/Chamberlain's Camp junction. Taking the right fork at this junction, we make a gentle-to-moderate ascent to serene Hobler Lake, where good campsites can be found among the giant red firs and the lodgepole pines. Ascending gently, the trail then leaves the Muir Wilderness, crosses the outlet of a tiny lake to the west, and meets the Courtright/Blackcap Basin Trail on a ridge above Chamberlain's Camp. From here we retrace part of the 1st hiking day, trip 25.

Glacier Divide to Bubbs Creek

This area is bounded by Glacier Divide on the north, Owens Valley on the east, Courtright and Wishon reservoirs on the west, and Bubbs Creek on the south, and it contains the greatest single block of unbroken wilderness in the southern Sierra. Still untainted by roads, the core of it enjoys the protection of National Park status, and the adjacent peripheral zones to the west, north and east are declared Wilderness Areas. Spread out over an area of roughly 1200 square miles, it boasts some of the most remote and scenic sections of the Sierra, and it is replete with scores of peaks that soar above 13,000 feet, hundreds of lakes and thousands of miles of sparkling streams. Were the hiker able to take every trip suggested in this section, he would have a solid sampling of four life zones ranging in altitude from 5000 feet to well over 12,000 feet. Further, he would have crossed ten major divides, visited three major watersheds, and enjoyed a wilderness experience perhaps unequaled anywhere in the world.

Topographically, the country divides neatly into three disparate types: the west slopes, Kings Canyon National Park, and the eastern escarpment. The Park, the heart of the high country, was established in 1940 when the Congress recognized the obvious need to protect this fragile wilderness from the increasing encroachment of stockmen and local, shortsighted business interests. Although the Park makes up the largest part of this section, the potential visitor should not ignore trips into the wilderness areas on the east and west sides of the Park.

The Park "heartland" is the rugged, comparatively barren, mostly alpine zone that lies between the Sierra crest and the LeConte/White Divide. Here are the headwaters of the South Fork of the San Joaquin and the Middle and South Forks of the Kings River. The latitudinal watershed divides, within the Park, are Goddard Divide (separating the South Fork of the San Joaquin River from the Middle Fork of the Kings River), and the Monarch/Cirque Crest divide (splitting the watersheds of the

Middle Fork and the South Fork of the Kings River). Within the Park are several longitudinal divides that serrate the topography into a complex ridge-chasm conformation. Most outstanding among these secondary divides are White Divide, Ragged Spur, Black Divide and King Spur.

In contrast to the west side, the eastern escarpment rises steeply to the crest. The escarpment from Rock Creek to Horseshoe Meadows is severe and forbidding, and the stretch between Big Pine Creek and Onion Valley is particularly lacking in heavily used roadheads and trails. Most of the many eastside streams flow into the Los Angeles Aqueduct, and they are separated by towering spur ridges that protrude from the backbone of the crest. Peculiar also to the east side is the lower juniper woodland belt, replete with the scattered grasses, pinon pine, Utah juniper and brush plants associated with the Great Basin. Fortunately, for those who enjoy and would preserve the east escarpment's native primitive appeal, the higher elevations are protected by a long, narrow belt of wilderness designation.

Similarly, the western slopes (west of the Park boundary) enjoy this immunity. The terrain of these western slopes is remarkable for its absence of outstanding peaks. In general it is a gradual, steady ascent to the LeConte/White Divide and the timbered rise of Kettle Ridge. The pleasant, rolling landscape of Woodchuck Country and the several alpine basins nestled at the foot of the LeConte Divide make up the headwaters of North Fork Kings River.

Looking at topo maps of this section (*Blackcap Mountain, Mt. Goddard*) one can readily ascertain the comparative heavy forestation of the region west of the LeConte Divide. Travelers working their way up any one of the various dendritic tributaries of North Fork Kings River will discover for themselves the magnificent spectrum of Sierra flora that attends these westside entries to the high country. Beginning in the lower elevations around 6500 feet are the stately mixed conifers such as sugar pine, ponderosa pine and incense-cedar. Ponderosa pine, with its distinctive bark plates and its long needles, is frequently mistaken for its close cousin Jeffrey pine, which is usually of a higher elevation but sometimes found in the same locale. There are many distinguishing characteristics, but the surest is the difference in their cones. The naturalist's rule of thumb is, "If you

can comfortably catch a tossed cone, it is a cone of Jeffrey pine."
This differentiation arises from the fact that the prickle found on
the end of each scale of the Jeffrey cone is turned inward,
whereas the prickle on the ponderosa cone turns outward. But
the most distinctive cone of all belongs to the sugar pine. Sometimes as long as a man's arm, it is an impressive fruit whether it
can be found on the ground or seen hanging in clusters at the ends
of massive branches.

Climbing a little higher, one enters the fir belt. First comes the
white fir, along with occasional groves of Jeffrey pine, and
finally the noble stands of red fir. Being rather brittle, red firs are
frequently associated with a heavily littered forest floor that is
noticeably void of ground-cover species. Standing in a cathe-
dral-like grove of red firs, it is the easiest thing in the world to
empathize with John Muir's bitterness when he wrote:

> Any fool can destroy trees. They cannot run away; and if they could,
> they would still be destroyed—chased and hunted down as long as fun
> or a dollar could be got out of their bark hides, branching horns, or
> magnificent bole backbones. Few that fell trees plant them; nor would
> planting avail much toward getting back anything like the noble
> primeval forests. During a man's life only saplings can be grown, in
> the place of the old trees—tens of centuries old—that have been
> destroyed. It took more than three thousand years to make some of the
> trees in these Western woods—trees that are still standing in perfect
> strength and beauty, waving and singing in the mighty forests of the
> Sierra. Through all the wonderful, eventful centuries since Christ's
> time—and long before that—God has cared for these trees, saved
> them from drought, disease, and avalanches, and a thousand straining,
> leveling tempests and floods; but he cannot save them from fools—
> only Uncle Sam can do that.*

*Our National Parks, by John Muir.

The "gentle country" of the trees continues as the trails wind
upward through dense groves of the two-needled lodgepole pine.
Near treeline the slim lodgepole pine no longer appears in tall,
dense stands—now its trunk is bent to the unchecked winds of
alpine country. Occasional clumps of whitebark pine and mountain hemlock dot those spaces among the granite that are not
already filled with the tender-yet-tough grasses of an alpine
meadow.

This, then, is the land and the forests of the west slopes—an
environment that has nurtured and awed man since his first

acquaintance with it. It is an often-ignored fact that the first visitor to these slopes was the North American, and there is adequate evidence to show that he was leaching his ground acorn meal at the sites of Simpson and Zumwalt meadows long before Europeans had settled the eastern shores of America. While Englishmen and Spaniards fought sea battles for supremacy of ocean trade routes, the Indians of Mono and Monache groups were peacefully plying their primitive trade routes over Piute, Bishop and Kearsarge passes. Using laurel-wood bows and cane arrows that were dipped in a poison concoction of crushed, rattlesnake-venomed deer liver, Indian hunting parties ranged the upper watersheds of the Kings and San Joaquin rivers—this, while the white man was establishing the first Presidio-Mission complexes in Alta California. In Philadelphia, civilized men of 1776 used a bird feather and decomposed animal fat to paint their names on a piece of wood pulp—historians now refer to it as an historic document. At almost the same time, in Tehipite Valley, an unknown Indian artisan using a similar stain produced a series of amebalike figures—and today's archeologist-historian refers to them as primitive graffiti.

The first meetings of these original inhabitants and exploring white men had the seeds of disaster. Gabriel Moraga, among the first white men to penetrate this country, was called "the greatest pathfinder and Indian fighter of his day." Subsequent incursions by trappers, pioneer settlers and gold seekers brought the inevitable confrontation, and, to the white man's discredit, the inevitable eradication of the red man. Like the grizzly bear, he was judged a nuisance, and was considered "fair game." Today, both species are extinct in this region.

Early exploratory ventures from west to east into the heartland of this region were so arduous as to render their continuation impractical. This is quite understandable, as any examination of the topography will show. Numerous divides, nearly all exceeding 12,000 feet, cross-hatch the landscape, making passage even to this day lengthy and arduous. John C. Frémont, in December 1845, endeavoring to carry out a rendezvous with Theodore Talbot and Joseph Walker on the westside river they called "Lake Fork," led an unsuccessful sally into the reaches of North Fork Kings River. He was turned back by snow and "impossible" going. Jedediah Smith's party, in an earlier attempt during spring, had suffered the same travails, and the subsequent annals of the Brewer Survey parties of 1864 and 1870 tell a similar story.

The actual trail-blazers of currently used trails were, however, not the Spaniards or the trappers. The earliest trails were usually those of the sheepherders who grazed their flocks in the backcountry during the last half of the 19th century. Among the better known of these sheepherders were Bill Helm and Frank Dusy, whose early exploratory efforts on the west slopes culminated in the discovery of Tehipite Valley and in the building of the Tunemah Trail. W. Baird, operating in the same vicinity, established what is now known as the Hell-for-Sure Pass Trail, and although the 1864 Brewer Survey party was the first to visit the area, it is assumed that Portuguese sheepmen were the first to establish the current western access route to the Evolution region.

Wood fires are *prohibited* above 10,000' in Kings Canyon National Park and in Onion Valley from the road end to the Park boundary. *Use a gas stove.*

The locations of the trailheads for this part of *Sierra South* are given below.

South Lake (9760'). Go 15½ miles southwest from Bishop on State Highway 168 to the South Lake turnoff, and then 7 miles to the South Lake parking area.

Taboose Creek Roadend (5460'). Turn west on a dirt road that leaves U.S. 395 12 miles south of Big Pine. Go right at a fork at 1.7 miles, pass through a gate at 2.4 miles, and continue to the roadend at 5.8 miles.

Sawmill Creek Roadend (4600'). Turn west on a dirt road that leaves U.S. 395 18 miles south of Big Pine and go west on Sawmill Creek Road 0.8 mile to a junction. Turn north and follow Old U.S. 395 1.2 miles to Division Creek Road, leading west. Follow this road 2.1 miles to the trailhead.

Oak Creek Roadend (6040'). Turn west from U.S. 395 2.3 miles north of Independence onto the paved Fish Hatchery Road and go 1.3 miles to a junction. Go right here, passing Oak Creek Campground, 5.8 miles to the roadend.

Onion Valley (9200'). Drive west from Independence 15 miles to the roadend parking lot.

Courtright Reservoir (8200'). Drive northeast 42 miles from Clovis (near Fresno) on State Highway 168 and in Shaver Lake turn right onto the Dinkey Creek Road, following it 26 miles to the Courtright/Wishon **Y**. Courtright Reservoir is 7½ miles north, and there is a large parking area (the "Maxson Trailhead") across the dam and around a bedrock ridge.

Wishon Reservoir (6720'). Follow the directions above to the Courtright/Wishon **Y** and from there drive east 4 miles to a parking lot (the "Woodchuck Trailhead") just past Wishon Dam.

Crown Valley Trailhead (6750'). From Wishon Village go 6 miles south on paved road almost to the roadend, to a large parking lot on the west side of the road.

You will need to pay a national-park entrance fee or have an equivalent pass to get to these two trailheads:

Lewis Creek Trailhead (4580'). Go 77 miles east from Fresno on State Highway 180, to a parking area about ¼ mile east of the national park boundary (and 1½ miles west of Cedar Grove).

Cedar Grove Roadend (5035'). Go 85 miles east from Fresno on State Highway 180 to the roadend 6 miles east of Cedar Grove.

Mt. Brewer over East Lake

Courtright Reservoir to Post Corral Meadows   **25**

TRIP   From Courtright Reservoir to Post Corral Meadows
(round trip). Topo map *Blackcap Mountain* 15';
Courtright Reservoir, Ward Mtn. 7½'. Best early to
mid season; 16 miles.

Grade	Trail/layover days	Total recom-mended days
Leisurely	2/0	2
Moderate	....	....
Strenuous	day	....

HILITES   A fine weekend selection, this two-day trip visits
enchanting Long and Post Corral Meadows. The
dense forests of fir and lodgepole that line the route
are a pleasant habitat for a variety of wildlife. This
trip is an excellent selection for the beginner.

DESCRIPTION (Leisurely trip)

1st Hiking Day (**Courtright Reservoir** to **Post Corral Meadows**, 8 miles):
From the Maxson trailhead your route follows the paved road
north ⅓ mile to a green steel gate, where pavement ends and a
sign says CLOSED TO MOTOR VEHICLES. Now on a dirt road, you
make a short descent and then ascend gently under moderate
lodgepole-pine forest. After 1 mile the dirt road veers left and
your trail goes right at a sign declaring NO MOTOR VEHICLES
beyond. Across a meadow the trail passes a sign: WILDERNESS
PERMIT REQUIRED AHEAD. The shaded trail now ascends
moderately on the west side of a flower-lined creek and then
levels off to ford it at the foot of Maxson Meadows. Staying east
of the meadows, you pass Chamberlain's Camp and climb 500
feet to a signed junction with a trail to Burnt Corral Meadows.
Here, your trail veers right, crosses a seasonal creek and then
descends to the head of aptly named Long Meadow. For ¾ mile
the sandy trail winds along the margins of the nearly level
meadow, which is drained by a small stream. You then boulder-

hop the stream and swing away from the meadow, passing through dense stands of ubiquitous lodgepole pine. Soon a gentle descent leads to the grassy environs of Post Corral Meadows and you pass a faint trail leading to a privately owned cabin on leased Forest Service land. Most of Sierra National Forest, including parts of the John Muir Wilderness, is grazed by cattle, as Forest Service multiple-use land policy provides for cattle grazing.

It's another mile to the ford of Post Corral Creek (wet in early season) but you can avoid the often crowded camping there by finding good campsites nearby between the trail and the creek. Post Corral Meadows support a variety of plants and animals. Wildflowers found here include paintbrush, Fendler's meadow rue and streamside marsh marigolds. Bird life makes itself readily known. Groups of small, black-and-white dark-eyed juncos flit from branch to branch in search of insects. Robins are common, but you might also see a great horned owl or a Cooper's hawk. Post Corral Creek has a subaqueous ecosystem ruled by the brook trout, which isn't a true trout but a char imported from the eastern United States. Fishing is fair-to-good (to 7″).

2nd Hiking Day: Retrace your steps, 8 miles.

Along Post Corral Creek

Courtright Reservoir to North Fork Kings **26**

TRIP From Courtright Reservoir to North Fork Kings River via Post Corral Meadows (round trip). Topo maps *Blackcap Mountain* 15'; *Courtright Reservoir, Ward Mtn., Blackcap Mtn.* 7½'. Best early to mid season; 24 miles.

Grade	Trail/layover days	Total recommended days
Leisurely	4/1	5
Moderate	3/1	4
Strenuous	2/0	2

HILITES The winding, horseshoe-shaped route-plan of this trip tours magnificent backcountry meadows and lush forests, and terminates alongside the racing, pothole-dotted North Fork Kings River. Good fishing and easy terrain make this a good trip selection for the beginner desiring maximum wilderness experience for a minimum of hiking.

DESCRIPTION (Leisurely trip)

1st Hiking Day: Follow trip 25 to **Post Corral Meadows**, 8 miles.

2nd Hiking Day (**Post Corral Meadows** to **North Fork Kings River**, 4 miles): On the east side of the ford of Post Corral Creek (wet in early season) you pass the Hell-for-Sure Pass Trail branching left, but your trail heads south through dense stands of lodgepole pine. After crossing an unnamed creek, the sandy, almost level trail winds through forest and small meadows for 2 miles before climbing over a ridge. From the ridgetop you have a good view of the granitic North Fork Kings River canyon. The entire valley was covered with glacial ice many times during the past million years, and the most recent glacier retreated up-canyon only about 11,000 years ago. Many more glacial advances are likely, as our earth seems to be in the midst of a series of ice ages.

At this point it is interesting to speculate on the route followed by Capt. John C. Frémont, the "Pathfinder". Historians are unsure of the exact route, but they do agree that Frémont's party got lost high in this drainage. They were caught in an early winter storm, were forced to eat their saddle stock, and finally retreated. After descending an open hillside to slabs near the river, the trail turns east and climbs gently to a forested flat. Just before you cross Fleming Creek, you can turn right and find good campsites near the river (8029′) a short distance away. Fishing along the river is good for brook, brown and rainbow trout (to 8″).

3rd and 4th Hiking Days: Retrace your steps, 12 miles.

Glacial erratic beside North Fork Kings River

Courtright Reservoir to Rae Lake

TRIP   From Courtright Reservoir to Rae Lake via Post Corral Meadows (round trip). Topo maps *Blackcap Mountain 15'; Courtright Reservoir, Ward Mtn., Blackcap Mtn. 7½'.* Best mid to late season; 27 miles.

	Grade	Trail/layover days	Total recommended days
	Leisurely	4/2	6
	Moderate	3/1	4
	Strenuous	2/1	3

HILITES   Rae Lake, an alpine gem surrounded by meadows on two sides and tumbled granite slopes on the other two, has long been a favorite of anglers and other high-country visitors. Situated beneath Fleming Mountain, this lake's innate beauty and its proximity to 25 other lakes and the intervening streams make it a choice base camp for discovery exploration of Red Mountain Basin.

DESCRIPTION (Leisurely trip)

1st Hiking Day: Follow trip 25 to **Post Corral Meadows**, 8 miles.

2nd Hiking Day (**Post Corral Meadows** to **Rae Lake**, 5½ miles): Just east of the ford of Post Corral Creek (wet in early season) your route leaves the Blackcap Basin Trail and takes the Hell-for-Sure Pass Trail up the ridge separating Post Corral Creek and Fleming Creek. At first the ascent is moderate under shady lodgepole pines, but in less than a mile the grade steepens and the trail crosses several sections of dynamited slabs. To dynamite these granite slabs is a policy decision—an unfortunate and unrepresentative policy that sees the Forest Service maintaining backcountry trails for horses and pack animals when the overwhelming use of the trails is by hikers on foot.

As you near the top of the ridge, the trail crosses a small, forested flat, and then switchbacks the last few hundred feet to the ridgetop. Turning northeast, you soon begin a gently rolling ascent up the forested north side of Fleming Creek canyon. After 1½ miles you swing north and ascend steep, rocky switchbacks to the meadows surrounding small Fleming Lake. Now the country takes on a definite subalpine character: the lodgepole pines are fewer and more stunted, and one may see bright mountain bluebirds perched on top of small trees.

The trail crosses the outlet at Fleming Lake and soon meets a junction with the Hell-for-Sure Pass Trail at the foot of a long, flower-dotted meadow. Here you turn left and then climb to a shaded hillside junction with the spur trail to Rae Lake. Turning left onto it, you climb over a moraine and come to Rae Lake (9889'). There are excellent campsites under trees on the north side of this meadow-fringed lake. Fishing is good for brook trout (to 9"). Rae was originally named Wolverine Lake, but it is unlikely that there are any wolverines left in the area. Several nearby lake basins offer a variety of good day-hiking options.

3rd and 4th Hiking Days: Retrace your steps, 13½ miles.

Devils Punchbowl   *U.S. Forest Service*

Courtright Reservoir to Devils Punchbowl **28**

TRIP   From Courtright Reservoir to Devils Punchbowl;
return via Meadow Brook and North Fork Kings
River (semiloop). Topo maps *Blackcap Mountain*
15'; Courtright Reservoir, Ward Mtn., Blackcap
Mtn. 7½'. Best mid to late season; 35½ miles.

Grade	Trail/layover days	Total recommended days
Leisurely	6/2	8
Moderate	5/2	7
Strenuous	4/2	6

HILITES   Traveling what was originally known as the "Baird
Trail" (an old sheepherder's trail that remained for
years the primary access to the Evolution Valley
country), this route culminates at regal Devils
Punchbowl. The leg of this trip along Meadow
Brook can kindle an appreciation for preserving
delicate subalpine meadows.

DESCRIPTION Leisurely trip

1st and 2nd Hiking Days: Follow trip 27 to **Rae Lake**, 13 miles.

3rd Hiking Day (**Rae Lake** to **Devils Punchbowl**, 4 miles): Descending from Rae Lake (9894'), our trail meets and joins the trail from Lower Indian Lake, and a few hundred yards farther (in the meadow) joins the Hell-for-Sure Pass Trail. Here your route turns left, then fords Fleming Creek and ascends a tree-covered slope. At first you cross meadowy sections that often boast paintbrush, daisies and fireweed, but soon the soil becomes dry and sandy. Near the top of this 500-foot ascent you can look back on much of the country surrounding the Fleming Creek drainage. The extensive forests you see have grown on a thin layer of soil that has formed in the 10,000 years since the last glaciers covered this basin. From the ridgetop the trail crosses open meadows and several seasonal creeks and then, by a tall, gray stump, meets a junction with the trail to Devils Punchbowl.

Turning right at this junction, your route descends gently past a small, meadow-fringed lake and then drops 300 feet to the grassy environs of East Fork Fleming Creek. Beyond a rock ford, (wet in early season) you make a moderate ascent for 300 feet to the low ridge on the north side of large, deep Devils Punchbowl (10,098'). Good campsites can be found to the left on the east side of the lake. This lake is heavily used, so please try to make a minimal impact. Fishing is good for brook trout (to 13"). Anglers spending layover days may wish to explore Red Mountain Basin, all of whose main lakes have been planted. For anyone who loves rugged, alpine country, the basin merits investigation.

4th Hiking Day (**Devils Punchbowl** to **North Fork Kings River**, 6½ miles): On the north side of the lake you join the trail and head south along the granitic ribs that dam the lake. Midway along the lake you get a bird's-eye view, from the edge of the escarpment, of the two lakes to the west. At the southwest corner of Devils Punchbowl the trail makes several short switchbacks up to a low saddle. The following 2000-foot descent to the North Fork Kings River starts with a sandy 200-foot slope to the lush meadows at the head of Meadow Brook. For the next mile the trail skirts the forest-meadow margin where dry, sandy soil borders the wet, organic-rich soil of the meadow. With these meadows in the foreground you get beautiful vistas of the far side of the North Fork Kings River drainage. The pond in the upper meadow is often the summer home for a family of mallards, and the flowers that bloom here include lavender shooting star, purple Sierra gentian and several species of monkey flowers. Cattle may or may not be run in this drainage in a given year, but if present they definitely detract from the appeal of meadows like these. Sierran meadows evolved in the absence of cattle; their grazing and sharp hooves damage turf and their by-products pollute both trails and streams.

For over a mile your trail follows the lush meadows along Meadow Brook. Then the grade steepens and the trail swings away from the creek, angling down a forested moraine. When the trail levels off temporarily, it crosses a seasonal stream and again nears Meadow Brook. Soon the trail begins to switchback, and the last 1000 feet to the canyon floor are marked by the appearance of red fir, Jeffrey pine, Sierra juniper and quaking aspen. At the bottom of the grade you cross slabs to a junction with the Blackcap Basin Trail. Turning right, you soon reach a California Cooperative Snow Survey cabin by a waterfall and a large pool in the river. For ½ mile you stay close to rock outcrops on the right before descending to ford multi-branched Fleming Creek on logs. Beyond the ford you can turn left to the good campsites along North Fork Kings River. Fishing is good for brook, brown and rainbow trout (to 8″).

5th and 6th Hiking Days: Reverse the steps of trip 26, 12 miles.

Devils Punchbowl—another view

29   Courtright Reservoir to Guest Lake

TRIP

From Courtright Reservoir to Guest Lake via Post Corral Meadows, North Fork Kings River (round trip). Topo maps *Blackcap Mountain* 15'; *Courtright Reservoir, Blackcap Mtn.* 7½'. Best mid to late season; 37 miles.

Grade	Trail/layover days	Total recommended days
Leisurely	6/1	7
Moderate	5/1	6
Strenuous	4/0	4

HILITES

Of the three lake basins lying close under towering LeConte Divide, Bench Valley is the least known and least visited. This is surprising in view of the excellent angling at McGuire Lakes and Guest Lake. The other lakes of this basin are among the most picturesque in the Sierra, and the angler with an inclination to visit stirring subalpine scenery en route should give this trip serious consideration.

DESCRIPTION (Leisurely trip)

1st and 2nd Hiking Days: Follow trip 26 to **North Fork Kings River**, 12 miles.

3rd Hiking Day (**North Fork Kings River** to **Guest Lake**, 6½ miles): Reverse the last part of the 4th hiking day, trip 28, to the junction with the trail up Meadow Brook. Heading up-canyon from the junction, you first cross multi-branched Meadow Brook and then swing near a large pool in the river. The trail ascends gently for about a mile and then makes 4 switchbacks to gain the top of a bench. The grade is again easy to the rock-and-log ford of the several channels of Fall Creek (wet in early season). About 350 yards beyond the last channel of Fall Creek is an unsigned junction with a trail climbing left to Bench Valley. We take this faint, ducked trail, which climbs steeply up the rocky hillside on the south side of cascading Fall Creek.

After gradually levelling off into dense lodgepole forest, the trail meets a trail ascending from North Fork Kings River above Big Maxson Meadow. Soon our route winds along the luxuriantly foliaged banks of Fall Creek, where shooting stars, penstemon, larkspur, monkshood, monkey flower, columbine, wallflower and paintbrush nearly fill the valley floor.

After traveling a short distance beside the creek, our trail climbs steeply for a short time and then moderately for a while, to reach the outlet from McGuire and Guest lakes. Here the trail begins a series of short switchbacks which soon become rocky and steep, but soon also we arrive at the outlet of meadow-fringed lower McGuire Lake. The lake's waters appear suddenly only a few feet from the precipitous drop-off, and from this point one can indeed ascertain the true meaning of the term "hanging valley." Our route passes several primitive and packer campsites as it rounds the north side of lower and upper McGuire Lakes. Both of these lakes afford excellent fishing for brook (to 15"). Through moderate-to-sparse timber, the trail crosses an easy ridge to the fisherman's lateral that turns off the main trail and leads to Guest Lake (10,160'). Good packer and primitive campsites with unobstructed views of Blackcap Mountain line the north shore of this lovely granite-lined lake, and it is a fine choice as a base camp for excursions to 20 nearby lakes in this basin. At Guest Lake fishing for brook trout (to 12") is good. Fishing in the lakes of the upper Bench Valley Basin varies from good to excellent, and offers the angling sportsman a creel of both brook and rainbow trout.

4th, 5th and 6th Hiking Days: Retrace your steps, 18½ miles.

30 Courtright Reservoir to Guest Lake

TRIP
From Courtright Reservoir to Guest Lake via Post Corral Meadows, North Fork Kings River; return via cross country to Devils Punchbowl, then by trail to North Fork Kings, Post Corral Meadows (semi-loop trip). Topo maps *Blackcap Mountain 15'*; *Courtright Reservoir, Ward Mtn., Blackcap Mtn. 7½'*. Best mid or late season; 43½ miles.

Grade	Trail/layover days	Total recom- mended days
Leisurely	....	....
Moderate	7/1	8
Strenuous	4/1	5

HILITES
This looping trip traverses two of the finest angling basins on the west side of the Sierra. The rugged cross-country route between the basins makes it a choice limited to experienced hikers, and the grand vistas encountered along this route more than compensate for the demands on skill and energy.

DESCRIPTION (Moderate trip)

1st 3 Hiking Days: Follow trip 29 to **Guest Lake,** 18½ miles.

4th Hiking Day (**Guest Lake** to **Devils Punchbowl** via cross country, 6½ miles): The trail from Guest Lake is a fisherman's trail that joins the main Bench Valley Basin Trail ascending to Horsehead Lake. This ascent winds north through a moderate cover of whitebark pines and passes Colt Lake before it descends to the southeast shore of Horsehead Lake, where there is an improved packer campsite. After the trail arrives at the grassy fringes above Horsehead Lake, the traveler has excellent views to the east and northwest of the barren crest of LeConte Divide. From this lake's open shores one can readily see that he has surmounted a series of hanging valleys, and that this hanging-valley chain continues in the tiny cirques carved out of the granite divide to the east and northeast.

Beyond the marshy inlet to Horsehead Lake, this route rounds the east side of the lake, fords the east inlet (from Filly Lake), and parallels the north inlet steam as it ascends. Faint fisherman's routes crisscross this drainage, and the conflicting ducks placed by misguided but well-meaning visitors should be taken with a grain of salt. Anglers passing through this country will be able to sample the brook and rainbow (to 10") at Horsehead Lake; brook (to 8") at Roman Four Lake; rainbow (to 11") at West Twin Buck Lake (East Twin Buck Lake is barren); and rainbow (to 7") at Schoolmarm Lake.

From the west side of Twin Buck Lakes we ascend northward to the outlet of Schoolmarm Lake. From the outlet our trail climbs northwest and emerges above timberline in a high, rolling valley. After crossing two small creeks, our route ascends steeply to the saddle just north of Peak 11398 (11404 on the 7½' map). From this point, the route contours around to the notch just to the northwest and makes a rather steep descent into the cirque just above Devils Punchbowl. This descent should be undertaken only by experienced hikers with rudimentary climbing skills. Our route passes a small, golden-trout-filled lakelet and then makes another less steep descent down to the first of the two little lakes above Devils Punchbowl, called Little Shot and Big Shot. After descending past Big Shot Lake, our route arrives at the moderate-to-dense forest cover at the east side of Devils Punchbowl. There are several good campsites here, and fishing for brook (to 13") is good. This lake is a perennial choice among anglers as a base camp for side trips into Red Mountain Basin.

5th Hiking Day (**Devils Punchbowl** to **North Fork Kings River**, 6½ miles): Follow the 4th hiking day, trip 28.

6th and 7th Hiking Days: Reverse the 2nd and 1st hiking days, trip 26, 12 miles.

31

Courtright Reservoir to Portal Lake

TRIP   From Courtright Reservoir to Portal Lake (Blackcap Basin) via Post Corral Meadows, North Fork
Kings River (round trip). Topo maps *Blackcap Mtn.*
15′; *Courtright Reservoir, Ward Mtn., Blackcap*
Mtn. 7½′. Best mid or late season; 45 miles.

Grade	Trail/layover days	Total recom- mended days
Leisurely	6/1	7
Moderate	5/1	6
Strenuous	4/1	5

HILITES   Portal Lake lives up to its name. It is indeed the door
to Blackcap Basin, a beautiful, austere, granite
basin forming the headwaters of North Fork Kings
River. This trip boasts an encompassing look at
west-slope ecology over a 2500-foot elevation span.

DESCRIPTION (Leisurely trip)

1st Hiking Day: Follow trip 25 to **Post Corral Meadows**, 8 miles.

2nd Hiking Day (**Post Corral Meadows** to **Big Maxson Meadow**, 8
miles): Follow the 2nd hiking day, trip 26, to North Fork Kings
River. Then proceed to the junction of the trail to Bench Valley as
described in the 3rd hiking day, trip 29. From this junction, the
Blackcap Basin Trail continues south along North Fork Kings
River. Fishing along the river continues to be good for brook and
rainbow (to 12″), and occasional pools, usually located at the
foot of a chute or a fall, make for fine late-season swimming. The
narrowing canyon walls open briefly as the trail reaches wide Big
Maxson Meadow (8480′). Formerly a sheepherders' camp, and
more recently grazed by cattle, this meadow offers fair-to-good
campsites at its northwest end. If used as a base-camp location,

these meadow campsites are central for side trips to Halfmoon Lake and to the alpine lakes of upper Bench Valley. The trail to Halfmoon Lake, not shown on the 15′ topo map, leaves the meadow right across the river from the cabins.

3rd Hiking Day (**Big Maxson Meadow** to **Portal Lake**, 6½ miles): As the trail leaves the open flats of the meadow, the traveler has excellent views east-southeast to the glacially smoothed, narrowing walls of the canyon. Immediately beyond a drift fence at the southeast end of the meadows, you can turn right to reach a fair campsite. Bearing in the direction of these canyon narrows, our duff trail passes the main Bench Valley Trail. The louder river sounds on the right reflect the steepening slopes as our trail returns to riverside near some fine campsites under lodgepole pines with views of beautiful pools in the North Fork. Very soon, the trail veers away from the stream again, then leads southeast for about ⅔ mile before once more approaching the river across some expansive granite slabs. Beyond these boulder-dotted slabs we traverse a bog for about 100 yards to a ford of the North Fork which is difficult in early season. Immediately beyond the ford is a junction with the Blackcap Basin Trail, coming over from Halfmoon Lake.

Beyond this junction the trail swings east, following the North Fork, and passes a campsite with a table and a label "Snowslide Camp." This gentle-to-steady ascent through moderate-to-dense lodgepole forest traverses some areas that have been swept by avalanches and the lodgepoles replaced by willows. The North Fork on our left, sometimes near and sometimes far, sometimes meandering slowly through meadows and sometimes tumbling down large slabs, contains an adequate population of golden, brook and brown trout.

About 1½ miles beyond Snowslide Camp the trail steepens, veers south toward Portal Lake, and joins its outlet stream. The trail climbs to a meadowy area where there is an improved packer campsite on the right beside the junction with the Crown Basin Trail. Just beyond this campsite is the easy-to-miss rock ford (difficult in high water) of the outlet from Portal Lake. Beyond the ford, our trail climbs via short switchbacks to the poor-to-fair campsites on the north shore of jewellike Portal Lake. Other campsites may be found by following the trail a short ½ mile to the unnamed lake northeast of Portal Lake.

4th, 5th and 6th Hiking Days: Retrace your steps, 22½ miles.

32   Courtright Reservoir to Florence Lake

TRIP From Courtright Reservoir to Florence Lake via Post Corral Meadows, Hell-for-Sure Pass, John Muir Trail, Blaney Meadows (shuttle trip). Topo maps *Blackcap Mountain, Mt. Abbot* 15'; *Courtright Reservoir, Blackcap Mtn., Ward Mtn., Florence Lake* 7½'. Best mid or late season; 39½ miles.

Grade	Trail/layover days	Total recommended days
Leisurely	6/2	8
Moderate	5/2	7
Strenuous	4/1	5

HILITES Crossing the LeConte Divide at Hell-for-Sure Pass, this fine shuttle trip tours the headwaters of two major Sierra drainages—North Fork Kings River and South Fork San Joaquin. Unparalleled scenery and excellent angling recommend this trek for hiker and angler.

DESCRIPTION (Moderate trip)

1st and 2nd Hiking Days: Follow trip 27 to **Rae Lake**, 13 miles.

3rd Hiking Day (**Rae Lake** to **Lower Goddard Canyon**, 11 miles): This is a very long day on sometimes-poor trails, with considerable elevation gain and loss and with great scenery to enjoy, so an early start is in order. Proceed to the Devils Punchbowl Trail junction as described in the 3rd hiking day, trip 28. From this junction our trail ascends steadily above the meadowed basin to the sparsely wooded bench north of Disappointment Lake. Far from being a disappointment, anglers will find the brook-trout fishing in this lake to be good to excellent (to 15″).

The trail then fords the outlet of Chagrin Lake (10,440′—just northeast of Disappointment Lake) and ascends gently, then moderately, to the north end of barren Hell-for-Sure Lake. This large (58-acre) lake with its narrow northern meadow fringe is a long-time favorite of people using this century-old former sheep trail. A fine fishing spot for rainbow trout (to 10″), this lake takes up a large part of the upper cirque of Red Mountain Basin. Smoothed and polished slab granite rises from the lake's waters, broken only by an occasional glacial erratic or a small patch of green. Just beyond the slab granite, the broken slopes of talus and scree lead up to abrupt, metavolcanic-topped LeConte Divide. The notch to the northeast of Hell-for-Sure Lake marks Hell-for-Sure Pass (11,297′), and the climb to this saddle is a loose, steep, switchbacking, rocky slog. The climb is not as bad as the name would suggest, and one soon arrives at the wind-swept saddle of Hell-for-Sure Pass. From the pass, Hell-for-Sure Lake and the bold north face of Mt. Hutton make up most of the scenery to the south, but one can see a good part of the way down the Fleming Creek drainage. The most impressive view, however, is that of Goddard Canyon, Emerald Peak, Peter Peak and Mt. McGee to the east and northeast. Made of the dark gray volcanic rock characteristic of the Goddard area, the steep canyon walls plunge uninterrupted nearly 2500 feet to the valley floor below (not visible yet).

This breathtaking view lasts most of the steep, loose, rocky way down—a couple of long zigzags through a steep meadow, a crossing of a small bench, and a switchbacking dive down the canyon wall to the ford of the first unnamed tributary feeding South Fork San Joaquin River. From this ford (about halfway down the vertical distance) the trail traverses the west canyon wall on a long, up-and-down descent that crosses two more tributaries, and meets the Goddard Canyon Trail (turn left, northwest) at a junction where, in 1989, the signs sat in a pile of rocks. On the Goddard Canyon Trail we then double back along the South Fork. The subsequent steady-to-moderate descent stays on the west side of the river and refords the tributaries cited above. The trail crosses over mostly rock, some talus and scree, and occasional meadowy sections. Willow clumps along the river always ensure the presence of birdlife, and the passerby is likely to encounter Brewer blackbirds, hummingbirds, flycatchers, fox sparrows, Lincoln sparrows, nuthatches, robins, and an occasional finch.

We continue the gentle descent through long, lodgepole-dotted Franklin Meadow, separated from the river by a low ridge. At the meadow's north end we pass through one drift fence. The trail passes another drift fence a short way upstream from the John Muir Trail junction, and arrives at the fair-to-good campsites south of the wooden bridge (8640') for the John Muir Trail near the river's confluence with Evolution Creek. Fishing for brook and some rainbow in the river remains fair-to-good despite heavy angling pressure.

4th Hiking Day (**Lower Goddard Canyon** to **Lower Blayney Meadows**, 8 miles): Quickly stepping onto the John Muir Trail, we pass but do not cross the wooden bridge and make a gentle descent on dusty underfooting through stands of quaking aspen, lodgepole and some juniper. Underfoot, gardens of wildflowers line the trail, including sneezeweed, penstemon, yellow cinquefoil, penny-royal, Mariposa lily and lupine. As the trail approaches a wood-and-steel bridge crossing of the South Fork San Joaquin River, the canyon walls narrow and rise V-shaped from the canyon floor. On the north wall one can make out the unmistakable stria-tions carved there by ice-driven rocks in the last glacial stage. Our route passes several more campsites on the right, and then, just before we cross the bridge, a short spur trail leads west to some campsites on the south side of the river. Beyond the bridge, we descend a short, rocky stretch over morainal debris. This steady descent levels out through a densely forested flat ("Aspen Meadow") that is made up of postglacial alluvial deposits. An occasional Jeffrey and juniper add variety to the forest cover as the route leaves the flat and descends steeply on a rocky, dusty trail. Looking back, one has a last look at Emerald Peak, V'd by the steep canyon walls. Our route passes a sign indicating one's exit from Kings Canyon National Park and entry into John Muir Wilderness and then crosses Piute Creek on a wood-and-steel bridge, passing the trail to Piute and Pine Creek passes branching right. From this junction one has good views of the domes to the east, the most notable being Pavilion Dome. This route continues as described in the 3rd hiking day, trip 18.

5th Hiking Day (**Lower Blayney Meadows** to **Florence Lake**, 7½ miles): Follow the 4th hiking day, trip 8.

Courtright to Crown Valley Trailhead

33

TRIP   From Courtright Reservoir to Crown Valley Trailhead via Post Corral Meadows, North Fork Kings River, Blackcap Basin, cross country to Blue Canyon, then by trail to Cabin Creek (shuttle trip). Topo maps *Blackcap Mountain, Mt. Goddard* (W.P.V.), *Marion Peak, Tehipite Dome* 15'; *Courtright Reservoir, Ward Mtn., Blackcap Mtn., Mt. Goddard, Tehipite Dome* 7½'. Best mid or late season; 48 miles.

Grade	Trail/layover days	Total recommended days
Leisurely	....	....
Moderate	8/2	10
Strenuous	6/1	7

HILITES   Employing a challenging cross-country route (*for experienced backpackers only*), this trip joins Blackcap Basin with Blue Canyon. Where it crosses the LeConte Divide, it offers breathtaking views to each side. The trailed segments of this trip touch a full range of flora and fauna representative of the exciting west slopes of the Sierra.

DESCRIPTION (Strenuous trip)

1st 3 Hiking Days: Follow trip 31 to **Portal Lake**, 22½ miles.

4th Hiking Day (**Portal Lake** to **Blue Canyon Cabinsite**, 7 miles cross country): Staying on the north side of the outlet stream from Midway Lake, our route ascends the steep, fractured granite slope above Portal Lake. One can follow ducks and other signs of use up the short headwall to arrive at Midway Lake. After skirting the north shore of this lake, our route follows up its inlet stream past several rocky tarns to medium-sized (32 acres) Cathedral Lake. Fair fishing for rainbow and some brook trout (to 10″) is available here. This high, alpine lake is typical of the lakes of Blackcap Basin: situated in a granite pocket, ringed by cirque walls on three sides, characterized by deep, cold waters, and relieved only by an occasional clump of willow, heather or stunted lodgepole. Our route rounds the north side of the lake, then turns up southeast and climbs talus and steep granite slabs to a jagged notch, the top of a scree slope on the White Divide north of Finger Peak.

From the notch, walk right a few yards down a narrow ledge and descend into the talus-strewn cirque on the north side of Finger Peak. The traverse to Blue Canyon Pass requires little elevation loss but a large amount of boulder-hopping, which should be done with caution. After a good mile of rugged cross-country walking, we arrive at Blue Canyon Pass, the first saddle east of Finger Peak. Views from this saddle are superlative of the White Divide, Goddard Divide and Ragged Spur, and into southern Kings Canyon National Park. Thence our route descends by chutes to the northernmost, unnamed lakes of the Blue Canyon Creek drainage, and follows the southwest course of this drainage over slab granite. The route veers left and drops down to the west side of granite-bound Lake 10364 (on the 15′ topo, the lake just east of Peak 10518 on the 7½′ topo). From the outlet of this lake, our route crosses the stream and descends into lodgepole forest at about the 10,000-foot level, and soon we pick up a trail on the south side of the creek. From the slopes on the left, the hiker is very apt to hear the piping of a marmot as he rounds the turn in the canyon that gives him a view of the lovely, open meadows below. This trail scrambles down to the head of these meadows, skirting the eastern fringe, and arrives at the log ford leading to the good campsites up and downstream from the landmark cabinsite (8430′). Fishing for brook (to 10″) in Blue Canyon Creek is good.

5th and 6th Hiking Days: Reverse the steps of trip 39, 18½ miles.

Wishon Reservoir to Halfmoon Lake

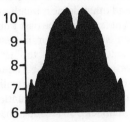

34

TRIP   Wishon Reservoir to Halfmoon Lake (round trip). Topo map *Blackcap Mountain* 15′; *Courtright Reservoir, Blackcap Mtn.* 7½′. Best early or mid season, 24 miles.

Grade	Trail/layover days	Total recommended days
Leisurely	4/1	5
Moderate	3/0	3
Strenuous	2/0	2

HILITES   Halfmoon Lake, beside an unnamed trail, nestled in a cirque below an unnamed peak, can serve as a hideout for the city-dweller who—temporarily—has had it. On the way to this fine lake, Moore Boys Camp offers a campsite where the flora and fauna are plentiful and fascinating.

DESCRIPTION (Leisurely trip)

1st Hiking Day (**Wishon Reservoir** to **Moore Boys Camp**, 6 miles): From the Woodchuck trailhead parking lot your trail heads south up granite benches, gaining several hundred feet. Then you turn east and climb steeply, crossing a dirt road. Soon in shade, your trail passes a spur coming in from a packer's trailhead on the left and then another coming in on the right. After 500 feet of climbing, the trail swings north and begins a traverse high on the forested ridge east of Wishon Reservoir. The trail undulates under lush forest with tall white fir, and as you pass many flower-lined creeks, you can see but probably won't hear the activity at the PG&E base on the west side of the reservoir.

After nearly 2 miles the trail turns east around a ridge into the canyon of Woodchuck Creek. Looking north, you can see granitic Lost Peak and other domes. Much of what you can see was under glaciers at times during the past 1 million years, and as you walk east you are on top of a moraine put here by a glacier. Beyond an aspen-dotted meadow the trail turns left and descends to cross Woodchuck Creek on boulders (wet in early season). From this ford the wide, dusty trail, just downstream from a little gully, ascends gently north under tall conifers and then turns east to switchback 500 feet up a shaded slope. Beyond these switchbacks the grade is easy for over a mile past a ford of the north fork of Woodchuck Creek. A little beyond some campsites along Woodchuck Creek is a short section of new, overconstructed switchbacks and then another gentle ascent. With the introduction of lodgepole pine you pass a signed trail to Chuck Pass branching right at an unnamed creek. Turning north, your trail makes a short but steep ascent over a moraine to the south end of sloping Moore Boys Camp (8710'). There is a California Cooperative Snow Survey course here where measurements of snow depth and water content are periodically taken. Crossing these lush meadows in spring can be wet, but you can skirt the meadow to the east. At the far side of the meadow, beyond 2 collapsing cabins, is a well-used campsite near the creek. Fishing is poor for brook trout (to 6").

2nd Hiking Day (**Moore Boys Camp** to **Halfmoon Lake**, 6 miles): Just beyond Moore Boys Camp is a junction with a trail up-canyon to Woodchuck Lake. Here, you turn east and ascend steeply to a small meadow supporting rangers button, tall mountain helenium and Bigelow's sneezeweed. You are now in Woodchuck Country, named for the many marmots in the area. (Resembling the woodchuck of the eastern United States, marmots were misidentified by people from the East.) After further steep climbing under red fir and silver pine, you pass a second trail to Woodchuck Lake in another meadow. Continuing the climb past outcrops of ancient volcanic mudflows, you cross abrupt boundaries between wet and dry ground; one moment you're walking on dry sand, the next moment you're on mud.

Near a grove of aspens you pass a pond, and then you pass a third trail to Woodchuck Lake branching north. Beyond a second pond the trail levels off on a sandy flat. Here you pass an unmarked trail of use branching left before climbing up slabs.

Ascending a gentle-sided dome, your faint, ducked trail winds between sand and slab, generally heading northeast to cross the shoulder of the 10,500-foot dome ¼ mile southeast of its summit. Only a hiker totally dedicated to pushing on up the trail could pass up the exhilarating panorama from the top of this rock island: an east-west spectrum from the LeConte Divide and Kettle Ridge down to the forested sloped west of Wishon Reservoir, and a north-south range from the Minarets near Mammoth to the high peaks of the Great Western Divide and the Kings-Kern Divide. Seen through a notch in the latter divide, Mt. Whitney doesn't seem to be the highest thing in California, but it is.

From the top of the climb you descend northeast to a junction signed CROWN PASS (10188'), where you meet a trail going south to Crown Lake, and shortly a rough, unmaintained trail going north down Nichols Canyon. Heading east toward Blackcap Basin you wind down a granitic ridge to an overlook of Halfmoon Lake (9422'). The trail then switchbacks down an open slope to the timbered north shore of this lovely lake. Good but heavily used campsites can be found near the trail and on the peninsula bulging into the north side of the lake. Firewood is nonexistent, so please use a stove. Brook trout are plentiful in the lake (to 10").

Marmots live in rocky territory

35 Wishon Reservoir to Portal Lake

TRIP   From Wishon Reservoir to Portal Lake via Half-moon Lake (round trip). Topo maps *Blackcap Mountain* 15′; *Courtright Reservoir, Blackcap Mtn.* 7½′. Best mid season; 37 miles.

Grade	Trail/layover days	Total recom-mended days
Leisurely	6/1	7
Moderate	4/1	5
Strenuous	3/0	3

HILITES   Blackcap Basin is a worthy goal of any vacation trip, but this long route to it offers additional attractions along the way, from the serene forests of Wood-chuck country to the dramatic cliffs surrounding Halfmoon Lake.

DESCRIPTION (Leisurely trip)

1st and 2nd Hiking Days: Follow trip 34 to **Halfmoon Lake**, 12 miles.

3rd Hiking Day (**Halfmoon Lake** to **Portal Lake**, 6½ miles): Along the north side of the lake, our route passes a *TRAIL* sign by the outlet, the trail to Big Maxson Meadow. We cross the creek and head east through lodgepole-pine forest. Soon we climb around a rocky ridge and then turn southeast, winding gently along a forested bench. The trail skirts a number of meadowy areas, and conies and marmots can be heard in the talus at the base of the wall on the right. After a short descent and a ford of the outlet of Maxson Lake this trail meets the North Fork Kings River trail coming up on the left. From this signed junction you follow the latter part of the 3rd hiking day, trip 31, to Portal Lake.

4th, 5th and 6th Hiking Days: Retrace your steps, 18½ miles.

Wishon Reservoir to Crown Lake

36

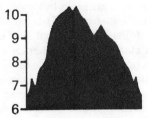

TRIP   From Wishon Reservoir to Crown Lake (semiloop trip). Topo maps *Blackcap Mountain, Tehipite Dome* 15'; *Courtright Reservoir, Blackcap Mtn.* 7½'. Best early or mid season; 24 miles.

Grade	Trail/layover days	Total recommended days
Leisurely	4/1	5
Moderate	3/1	4
Strenuous	2/0	2

HILITES   Everybody wants to get off the beaten path, but if everybody goes to the same unused place, it will be beaten. This guidebook attempts to offer a number of selections for solitude, so that your chances of being alone, when you go to one of them, will be pretty good. This excursion touches a number of such places.

DESCRIPTION (Leisurely trip)

1st Hiking Day: Follow trip 34 to **Moore Boys Camp**, 5½ miles.

2nd Hiking Day (**Moore Boys Camp** to **Crown Lake**, 5 miles): Follow the 2nd hiking day of trip 32 to the junction of the Crown Lake Trail and turn right (south) on it.

From the junction, the trail descends steeply south to the large, lodgepole-ringed meadow of Crown Lake. Viewed from the pass, the lake does have a crownlike shape, but its west side, containing several small pools, can be quite marshy at times, and campsites are best on the east side of the lake, where the trail skirts it.

3rd Hiking Day (**Crown Lake** to **Indian Springs**, 6 miles): The trail becomes somewhat indistinct as it crosses the marshy south end below Crown Lake, but it can easily be located as it follows along the east side of the outlet creek. Here we descend easily in moderate forest, at first lodgepole, but later mixed with silver pine. Intermittent marshy patches interrupt the duff trail as it descends gently south. On the east side of this outlet, our trail descends easily past a junction with the Scepter Lake Trail and then crosses this outlet. Then the trail swings west of Scepter Creek, so that it is out of sight and sound, but returns to creekside at another meadow. Beyond this lovely meadow we cross another and then continue south up to a junction with the Chuck Pass Trail. After turning west on this level trail, we soon ford the sandy-bottomed, unnamed stream that drains Chuck Pass and then climb moderately up the southwest side of the little creek. The string of forest-bordered meadows along the creek's head-waters are, in the mountain springtime, narrow emerald ribbons interspersed with lush gardens—one of the finest series of meadows in the Sierra.

After topping out at Chuck Pass, our rocky trail leads down through heavy, parklike pine forest on a set of steep, dusty switchbacks. Soon the route passes above a rocky, snag-strewn meadow and then it descends to pass a series of sweeping green meadows, where the wildflower population boasts dozens of species. Descending gently, the trail reaches the vicinity of Indian Springs. It skirts the large meadow beside this label on the topo map and arrives at the good campsites just below the meadow on both sides of Woodchuck Creek. Nearby down the trail is a sign INDIAN SPRINGS, but no springs.

4th Hiking Day: (**Indian Springs** to **Wishon Reservoir**, 7½ miles): The trail down the valley of Woodchuck Creek, often soft and muddy from the seepage of springs, penetrates a dense forest of lodgepole pine and reaches a junction with the Hoffman Mountain Trail. Here it veers north and immediately passes the ruins of an old cabin. This sandy forest path then dips west to meet the Wishon/Halfmoon Trail at a junction passed on the first hiking day. From here we retrace the steps of the first part of that hiking day to the roadend.

Crown Valley Trailhead to Cabin Creek   **37**

TRIP   From Crown Valley Trailhead to Cabin Creek (round trip). Topo map *Tehipite Dome* 15'. Best early season, 9 miles.

Grade	Trail/layover days	Total recommended days
Leisurely	2/1	3
Moderate	2/0	2
Strenuous	day	....

HILITES   When the high country is still under snow, you can sample the Sierra springtime, with its millions of wildflowers, on this trip to a small but extremely attractive stream.

DESCRIPTION (Leisurely trip)

1st Hiking Day (**Crown Valley Trailhead** to **Cabin Creek,** 4½ miles): From the trailhead parking lot, this route crosses an easy rise to the east, passing through sugar, lodgepole, Jeffrey, white fir and incense-cedar. Mostly duff, the trail becomes very dusty owing to heavy stock usage as the summer progresses. The trail then fords Little Rancheria Creek, and continues its gentle ascent past the Spanish Lake Trail, where the ascent becomes steeper. Short switchbacks bring one to the lush, wildflower-filled seepage area surrounding Three Springs. Here, fresh, cold water gushes from the ground in a dainty meadow. A dense fir forest pushes against the edges of the lush meadow, and wildlife tracks abound in the vicinity of the spring.

    The ascent eases off gradually before arriving at the Finger Rock Trail, and soon we reach the top of the flat ridge, where tiny tributaries repeatedly cross the trail. At the top of this climb is a lovely wildflower garden that includes lupine, monkey flower, golden brodiaea, currant, gooseberry and larkspur. As the trail turns one has limited views in the southeast of Spanish Mountain, Rodgers Ridge and the Obelisk. The duff trail then descends through a moderate-to-dense forest cover to a ford of a tributary of Cabin Creek. About ½ mile beyond, our trail arrives at the fair campsites on Cabin Creek (8240′). This creek is a tiny stream of water, but its diminutive size does not hide its irrepressible nature as it tumbles down with a riot of sound. Brook trout inhabit this little creek, but fishermen will find them generally very small. The better campsites are just upstream.

2nd Hiking Day: Retrace your steps, 4½ miles.

Under Piute Creek bridge on the John Muir Trail

Crown Valley Trailhead to Crown Creek   38

TRIP   From Crown Valley Trailhead to Crown Creek via
Cabin Creek, Crown Valley (round trip). Topo map
Tehipite Dome 15'; *Tehipite Dome 7½'*. Best early
to mid season; 21 miles.

Grade	Trail/layover days	Total recommended days
Leisurely	4/1	5
Moderate	3/0	3
Strenuous	2/0	2

HILITES   After a few miles in cowgrazing land, this trip
reaches the wilderness precincts of Crown Creek,
where it makes a detour off the main trail to an excellent campsite on this enchanting creek.

DESCRIPTION (Leisurely trip)

1st Hiking Day: Follow trip 37 to **Cabin Creek**, 4½ miles.

2nd Hiking Day (**Cabin Creek** to **Crown Creek**, 6 miles): Leaving
Cabin Creek, the trail climbs steeply and then crosses two easy
saddles and descends past the jeep road to a little meadow where
there is a junction with a trail to Chain Lakes and Hoffman
Mountain. Our route then joins the jeep road and climbs over
another easy ridge, then traverses the slope above Cow Meadow,
leaves the jeep road, and soon comes to a junction with the
Statum Meadow Trail branching right. The red-fir-and-lodge-
pole forest is dense as we pass Summit Meadow (incorrectly
labeled "Wet Meadow" on the topo map). Just beyond a sandy
flat we come to a junction with a trail to Fin Dome and Geral-
dine Lake, branching right. Our duff-and-sand trail winds
through dense timber and passes a lateral on the right leading to
Spanish Lakes before it arrives at the uniquely constructed

Crown Valley Guard Station, where emergency services are usually available. Turning somewhat north, the trail descends to the lupine-infested and ghost-snagged west end of Crown Valley meadows, where we cross a small creek. The trail then winds around the fenced southern edge of the grassland, crossing several corduroy log bridges to arrive at a junction with the Tehipite Valley Trail. Just north of this junction are the half dozen or so buildings of the Crown Valley Ranch. About ⅓ mile beyond the ranch, where the trail to Mountain Meadow branches left, we pass a sign indicating our entrance into John Muir Wilderness, in which the permanent works of man are barred.

From here the trail descends moderately, then steeply, into the drainage of Crown Creek. Occasional tree-shrouded views of Kettle Dome, Monarch Divide and Tombstone Ridge can be had on the upper part of this descent. About 1½ miles from the ranch our trail fords little Deer Creek and then Willow Creek. Then the trail climbs an easy ridge under a dense forest cover and drops down to the campsiteless ford of Bob Creek. Ahead, on the last, steep, sandy slope above Crown Creek is a junction signed CAMP-SITE, from where a lateral trail goes left, up-canyon, ¾ mile and fords Crown Creek (difficult in high water) to arrive at an improved campground (7040'). This is a lovely site; anglers will delight in the good brook and rainbow fishing to be had along the creek, and naturalists will find the natural salt lick just above the ford a superlative spot for quiet wildlife watching.

3rd and 4th Hiking Days: Retrace your steps, 21 miles.

Crown Valley Trailhead to Blue Canyon **39**

TRIP From Crown Valley Trailhead to Blue Canyon via Cabin Creek, Crown Creek, Kettle Ridge (round trip). Topo maps *Tehipite Dome, Marion Peak, Mt. Goddard* (W.P.V.), 15′; *Tehipite Dome* 7½′. Best mid or late season; 37 miles.

Grade	Trail/layover days	Total recom- mended days
Leisurely	7/2	9
Moderate	6/1	7
Strenuous	4/1	5

HILITES This trip winds through magnificent stands of fir and lodgepole before crossing lofty Kettle Ridge to Blue Canyon. Wildflowers abound around the many tributary crossings, and fishing is excellent.

DESCRIPTION (Leisurely trip)

1st 2 Hiking Days: Follow trip 38 to **Crown Creek**, 10½ miles):

3rd Hiking Day (**Crown Creek** to **Kettle Dome Campsite**, 4½ miles): Retrace your steps to the main trail, and turn left toward Crown Creek. After descending a few yards from this junction, the trail fords Crown Creek and continues eastward in fairly level fashion. As the trail nears the foot of Kettle Ridge, Kettle Dome comes into view as a granite finger. The trail crosses several small run-off streams (not all are indicated on the topo; fill your water bottle at the third stream), and at the Kings Canyon National Park boundary begins a steady climb. For those who are interested, the 7600-foot contour marks the best place to begin a side excursion to ascend Tehipite Dome. It is an interesting historical sidelight that Frank Dusy, a local sheepherder, around the turn of the century pursued a wounded grizzly bear approximately along this route. Further exploration by Dusy for grazing areas resulted in the blazing of this crossing of Kettle Ridge and the old Tunemah Trail (leading to Simpson Meadow). It is interesting to note that the lower slopes have some sugar pine, John Muir's favorite Sierra tree.

The trail soon becomes very steep, with exceptionally few switchbacks, and this poor trail construction results in the trail's being heavily washed—a condition not helped by the heavy stock traffic it suffers. As the trail ascends, the forest cover thins somewhat, but still includes sugar pine, red fir, lodgepole and Jeffrey. The underbrush, for the most part, is manzanita and snowbrush.

Eventually you reach the top of the ridge; it is time well spent to detour off to the right of the trail for the unsurpassed views of the Monarch Divide, Cirque Crest, the Middle Fork Kings River watershed, and a large part of eastern Kings Canyon National Park. The panorama of the Monarch Divide encompasses Goat Crest, Slide Peak, Kennedy Mountain and Hogback Peak. Slide Peak, with its clearly defined avalanche chutes, is particularly interesting, and above the canyon's blue haze one can trace the glacial paths on the far side that left the remarkable, unnamed, finlike ridge to the east-southeast. The trail then descends steeply from the top of the ridge, and this descent offers a different set of views, including Burnt Mountain, a little bit of Blue Canyon, Marion Peak, parts of Cirque Crest, Goat Crest and some of the Monarch Divide. The descent levels off in a meadowed bench containing a small tributary stream (unnamed), where there are several good primitive campsites around the meadow above the ford (8200'). These campsites are due east of Kettle Dome, and about 1000 feet above the Blue Canyon floor. The creek here, though small and isolated, has a fairly large population of rainbow trout.

4th Hiking Day (**Kettle Dome Campsite** to **Blue Canyon Cabinsite**, 3½ miles): The dusty and rocky trail descends by steady, steep switchbacks the remaining 1000 feet to the canyon floor. This descent meets the tributary on which the campsites for the previous hiking day were situated and then swings up-canyon as it nears Blue Canyon Creek. Ascending the rocky slopes of Blue Canyon, the trail alternates between steady and steep climbing through a moderate forest cover that includes white fir and Jeffrey pine, with manzanita and deerbrush underneath. Some cottonwoods appear along the creek, and as we climb higher some aspens, junipers and lodgepole pines join the forest's ranks. Looking back down Blue Canyon, one has **V**'d views across the Middle Fork Kings River to the "turrets" surrounding the Gorge of Despair.

Flowers along this ascent include Indian paintbrush, pennyroyal, Mariposa lily, pussy paws, scarlet gilia and larkspur. Just north of the large packer site, the trail crosses to the east side of the creek via a shallow wade-across ford, and then continues its steady climb. Above this ford, Blue Canyon Creek exhibits some interesting granite-bottomed chutes. The water slides down these chutes, which are up to several hundred feet long, and are marked at either end by cascades or waterfalls. At the head of one of these series, the trail emerges at Blue Canyon meadows. Here, in contrast to the white-water maelstrom below, Blue Canyon Creek winds docilely in typical meadow-meandering fashion, and immediately on the left one can see the old notched-log sheepherder cabin across the creek. Good campsites lie near the cabin, and angling for brook and rainbow (to 10") in Blue Canyon Creek is good. These campsites make a good base camp for angling and discovery side trips to the head of Blue Canyon basin.

5th, 6th, and 7th Hiking Days: Retrace your steps, 18½ miles.

Mt. Goode over Long Lake

40　South Lake to Treasure Lakes

TRIP　From South Lake to Treasure Lakes (round trip). Topo maps *Mt. Goddard* (W.P.V.) 15′; *Mt. Thompson* 7½′. Best mid or late season; 5 miles.

Grade	Trail/layover days	Total recom- mended days
Leisurely	2/0	2
Moderate	....	....
Strenuous	day	....

HILITES　This short trip is a fine "weekender." Touching the upper reaches of a tributary of South Fork Bishop Creek, it exposes the traveler to three life zones with a very limited expenditure of energy and time. As a bonus, the Treasure Lakes don't get the high use found just over the ridge along the Bishop Pass Trail.

DESCRIPTION (Leisurely trip)

1st Hiking Day (**South Lake** to **Treasure Lake**, 2½ miles): From the roadend (9760′) the trail climbs steadily along the east side of South Lake. A moderate-to-dense forest cover of lodgepole pine lines the rocky route as it meets and turns onto the Treasure Lakes Trail. Mostly over duff and sand, the trail descends to ford a stream, ascends briefly, and then descends again to a bridge over Bishop Creek's South Fork. This stretch affords good views of Hurd Peak and the backgrounding, glacially topped peaks to the north. The trail then meanders over to the outlet from the Treasure Lakes, parallels it briefly downstream, and crosses it on a log. Beyond this ford we begin a moderate-to-steep ascent on a duff-and-sand trail. As the elevation increases, the forest cover shows increasing whitebark pine mixed with the lodge-poles, and there is an abundance of wildflowers lining the trail and clustered in the grassy patches that seam the granite. Although this trail does see some stock traffic, it is, for the most part, a hiker's trail. The ascent steepens, crosses an area of smoothed granite slabs dotted with glacial erratic boulders, and fords the outlet stream from Lake 10668 (difficult in early season). Then, in an easy ½ mile, we arrive at the good campsites on the northeast side of that lake, directly under dramatic, pointed Peak 12047. This lake, the largest in the Treasure Lakes basin (12 acres), affords fair-to-good fishing for golden (to 12″). Anglers who wish to spend a layover day here will find that, contrary to the usual rule of thumb, the fishing gets better as one tries the lakes of the upper basin.

2nd Hiking Day: Retrace your steps, 2½ miles.

Peak 12047 over Treasure Lake 10668

41

South Lake to Treasure Lakes

TRIP   From South Lake to Treasure Lakes, return via cross-country route to Long Lake (semiloop trip). Topo maps *Mt. Goddard* (W.P.V.) 15'; *Mt. Thompson* 7½'. Best mid or late season; 8 miles.

Grade	Trail/layover days	Total recom- mended days
Leisurely	....	....
Moderate	2/0	2
Strenuous	day	....

HILITES Like the previous trip, this two-day trek explores the Treasure Lakes chain, but, unlike the previous trip, it returns by a cross-country route to the Bishop Pass Trail. Views from the summit of the cross-country leg are more than worth the scramble.

DESCRIPTION (Moderate trip)

1st Hiking Day: Follow trip 40 to **Treasure Lakes**, 2½ miles.

2nd Hiking Day (**Treasure Lakes** to **South Lake** via Long Lake, 5½ miles, part cross country): Following the faint fisherman's trail that ascends from the south end of the largest of the Treasure Lakes (10,668'), one follows a ridge east of the intervening stream to the cirque-basined three upper lakes. This ascent sees the timber cover thinning until, at the upper triad, all that remains is low-lying whitebark pine. Like the lower Treasure Lakes, these three lakes contain good populations of golden trout (to 15"). Trout were originally backpacked in by A. Parcher, son of the pioneer resort owner W. C. Parcher, and the spawn of that initial plant provide good fishing for today's anglers.

From the upper lake, our route crosses the outlet and ascends 500 vertical feet up moderate slopes to the saddle east of the lake. This ascent crosses ledges and some loose rock south of the gray fractured slopes of the southern outlier of Hurd Peak. Grand views from this saddle include Mts. Gilbert, Johnson and Goode to the west, and the spectacular comb ridge of the Inconsolable Range rimming the South Fork Bishop Creek drainage to the east.

From the saddle, the best route descends gently north-northeast about 100 yards, then veers over beside the little stream here, paralleling it momentarily beside a short waterfall. From there you scramble and stroll almost directly to Margaret Lake, visible down the valley. On the northwest side of this lovely lake you'll find a use trail that leads northeast to the southernmost point of Long Lake. A few steps up the inlet of this lake are places to ford the inlet, which is the South Fork of Bishop Creek. Then walk quickly past some incredibly overused campsites to find the Bishop Pass Trail, and turn left (north) on it.

After fording the willow-infested outlet of Ruwau Lake, your trail passes a lateral trail to that lake and then closely skirts the east shore of Long Lake. At the lake's north end you ford another inlet stream and pass the Chocolate Lakes Trail as you begin the long descent to the trailhead. The trail is dusty and overused, but it passes a number of charming pocket meadows and crosses dozens of runoff rills. Not far beyond the Mary Louise Lakes Trail we cross the outlet of those lakes on a small log bridge, and then reach the start of the Treasure Lakes Trail, from where we retrace the first mile of the first hiking day.

The Inconsolable Range (Mt. Agassiz at right)

42

South Lake to Dusy Basin

TRIP   From South Lake to Dusy Basin via Bishop Pass (round trip). Topo maps *Mt. Goddard* (W.P.V.) 15′; *Mt. Thompson, North Palisade* 7½′. Best mid or late season; 14 miles.

Grade	Trail/layover days	Total recommended days
Leisurely	....	....
Moderate	2/1	3
Strenuous	day	....

HILITES   A popular route, the Bishop Pass Trail climbs the scenic course of South Fork Bishop Creek. At Bishop Pass, the trail enters King Canyon National Park, but, more significantly, it begins the adventure of the high, barren, granitoid country of Dusy Basin. Grand side-trip possibilities are sufficient reason for planning layover days on this trip.

DESCRIPTION (Moderate trip)

1st Hiking Day (**South Lake** to **Dusy Basin**, 7 miles): Starting from the roadend (9760′)—about ¼ mile above the South Lake dam—the route ascends through a moderate-to-dense forest cover of lodgepole, fir and aspen on a somewhat rocky trail. This ascent traverses the morainal slope on the east side of South Lake, bearing toward Hurd Peak, and then passes a trail to the Treasure Lakes. After turning southeast, your trail soon crosses the Mary Louise Lakes outlet on a log bridge and then passes the trail to these lakes. Frequent patches of lupine, forget-me-nots, wallflowers and swamp onions delight the traveler as he fords streamlets and crosses swampy sections.

The trail then switchbacks up to a junction with the Bull-

Chocolate Lakes Trail and levels off to reach the islet-dotted north end of Long Lake. After crossing this lake's inlet, it undulates along the east side of this popular lake (rainbow, brook and brown, to 17″). Near the lake's south end another trail goes east to Ruwau Lake, and then we cross the sparkling outlet stream from that lake to arrive in "tent city," the overused knolls above the south end of Long Lake.

The memorable vistas of the wooded and meadowed shores of Long Lake stay with the visitor as he ascends through sporadic subalpine tarn-dotted meadows. Sometimes steep, this steadily ascending trail climbs past spectacular Saddlerock Lake (rainbow to 10″), and the unmarked fisherman's spur trail to Bishop Lake (brook to 14″).

Beyond Saddlerock Lake, the trail passes timberline and begins a series of steep switchbacks at the head of a spectacular cirque basin. Excellent views of Mt. Goode appear on the right, and the incredible comb spires of the Inconsolable Range on the left accompany the panting climber, making his breather stops unforgettable occasions. Glacially smoothed ledge granite and quarried blocks on every hand line this well-maintained trail. Occasional pockets of snow sometimes blanket the approach to Bishop Pass (11,972′) late into the season, and care should be exercised in the final steep part of the ascent to the summit. Views from the pass are excellent of the Inconsolable Range to the north; Mt. Agassiz to the southeast; Dusy Basin immediately to the south, flanked by Columbine and Giraud peaks; and the Black Divide on the distant western skyline.

From the pass our route descends on a sometimes switchbacking southwestern traverse. This sandy descent contours over rock-bench systems some distance north of the basin's northernmost lake (11,350′). Where the trail comes near the lake's inlet, our route branches left, leaving the trail and crossing smooth granite and tundra to the fair campsites at the west end of this lake. Other fair campsites can be found a few yards to the southwest, along the outlet stream. Fishing for golden and brook trout on this northernmost lake is fair, but anglers should try the good-to-excellent golden and brook angling (to 22″) at Lake 11393 (on the 15′ topo) and the lake just west of it, along with the connecting stream.

Alpine scenery from the above campsites is breathtaking in its vastness. One can see the Inconsolable Range as it rises behind Bishop Pass, and the climber's Mecca, the Palisade crest, fills the eastern skyline. Also to the east towers symmetrical Isosceles Peak. A very sparse forest cover of gnarled whitebark pine dots the granite landscape on all sides, and the fractures in the granite are filled with grassy, heather-lined pockets.

2nd Hiking Day: Retrace your steps, 7 miles.

Dusy Basin

South Lake to Chocolate Lakes

43

TRIP   From South Lake to Chocolate Lakes (round trip)
Topo maps *Mt. Goddard* (W.P.V.) 15′; *Mt. Thompson* 7½′. Best mid season; 6 miles.

Grade	Trail/layover days	Total recommended days
Leisurely	2/0	2
Moderate	....	....
Strenuous	day	....

HILITES   The barren heights of the Inconsolable Range mirrored in the lakes of the Chocolate chain make this trip one to be remembered. The good fishing on the lakes is a bonus, and the package ties up as a grand "warm-up" for the hiker starting his season late.

DESCRIPTION (Leisurely trip)

1st Hiking Day (**South Lake** to **Chocolate Lakes**, 3 miles): Proceed to the Bull Lake Trail junction as described in the 1st hiking day, trip 42. Here our route turns left, away from the Bishop Pass Trail. Ascending moderately, the trail fords a tributary of South Fork Bishop Creek, and arrives at sparsely timbered, moderate-sized (10-acre) Bull Lake. Rock-encircled clumps of willows alternate with grassy sections as the trail skirts the north side of the lake. Fishermen may wish to sample this lake's fair brook-trout fishing (to 9″) before continuing up the lake's inlet stream to lower Chocolate Lake.

This ascent crosses rocky talus stretches as it fords and refords the stream. Breather stops offer sweeping views back across the South Fork Bishop Creek drainage to Mts. Goode, Johnson, Gilbert and Thompson. Dominating all views to the east are the barren, pinnacle-comb formations of the somber Inconsolable Range. The granitic Chocolate Lakes chain consists of three lakes that are progressively larger as one ascends the basin. Necklaced together, they hang like sapphire jewels around the northeast side of red-rocked Chocolate Peak. The trail passes several good campsites at lower Chocolate Lake. All these lakes have a fair fishery of brook (to 10''), and the upper, larger lake (11,100') affords good campsites.

2nd Hiking Day: Retrace your steps, 3 miles.

Chocolate Peak over Bull Lake

South Lake to Palisade Basin **44**

TRIP   From South Lake to Dusy Basin, Palisade Basin, Deer Meadow, Middle Fork Kings River, Bishop Pass (semiloop trip). Topo maps *Mt. Goddard* (W.P.V.), *Big Pine* 15′; *Mt. Thompson, North Palisade* 7½′. Best mid or late season; 37½ miles.

Grade	Trail/layover days	Total recommended days
Leisurely	....	....
Moderate	6/2	8
Strenuous	5/2	7

HILITES   Those who yearn to go "high and light" will find this rugged route to their liking. For scenery the incomparable Palisade crest dominates the route, except along the section on the John Muir Trail down Palisade Creek and up LeConte Canyon.

DESCRIPTION (Moderate trip)

1st Hiking Day: Follow trip 42 to **Dusy Basin**, 7 miles.

2nd Hiking Day (**Dusy Basin** to **Glacier Creek**, 6 miles cross country): The backpacker can contemplate crossing to Palisade Basin via any one of three foot-walkers' passes: 1) Knapsack Pass; 2) the unnamed pass between Columbine Peak and Isosceles Peak; and 3) what has come to be known as "Thunderbolt Pass," just southwest of Thunderbolt Peak. Our route uses Knapsack Pass (11,673′). Leaving our campsite at the northernmost large lake of Dusy Basin, we cross the low ridge to the east and obtain a view of Lake 11393, then wander generally southward down this upper chain of lakes. We pass one beautiful lake or pond after another, skirt pocket meadows bright with wildflowers in season, and are awed by the sheer walls of Isosceles and Columbine peaks. This route crosses the outlet of the lowest large lake in the basin and then bends south-southeast toward the lower end of a boulder avalanche on the southwestern slope of Columbine Peak. Cross-country routes to Knapsack Pass converge here at a well-beaten path through the boulder field.

The steady ascent over heavily fractured rock requires a little route-finding, and becomes steeper on the final climb to the pass. Impossible as it may seem, there are recorded visits to Palisade Basin via this pass with stock! Views from the pass include Black Giant, Mt. Powell and Mt. Thompson to the northwest, and the Palisade Basin and Crest to the east. From this vantage point, the vast expanses of Palisade Basin appear totally barren of life except for an isolated whitebark pine or a spiring snag, but a closer examination later in this hiking day will reveal much more. The continuing bracing views of the Palisade Crest, as our route descends from Knapsack Pass, stir the most blasé non-mountain climber. These peaks look, as one climber expressed it, "like mountain peaks are supposed to look." Precipitous faces composed of relatively unfractured rock, couloirs, buttresses and glaciers combine to make this crest one of the finer climbing areas in the Sierra Nevada.

Our route keeps to the left as it first ascends and then descends over a moderate-to-steep ledge system to the westernmost lake of the Barrett chain. After passing around the south end of this rockbound lake, this route crosses the easy saddle east of the lake to the largest lake of the chain, and follows a fisherman's trail around the north end. From this lake the sheer cliffs of the west face of North Palisade dominate the skyline, and our route continues east past several tiny, rockbound lakelets. In contrast to the granite of lower Dusy Basin, this granite looks "newer," since it shows much less fracturing and exfoliation, but both were formed at the same time.

After contouring around the head of the drainage at the east end of Palisade Basin, our route crosses the definite saddle between Point 12692 (12698 on the 7½' map) and the main Palisade Crest, Potluck Pass. Along with the continuing views of the Palisades, this vantage point also looks across the Palisade Creek watershed to Amphitheater Lake. To the southwest the terrain has an appearance similar to the top of a meringue pie.

The descent from Potluck Pass is a scramble over a steep, smoothed granite ledge system, keeping to the right. This downgrade continues over scree and then levels out at Lake 11672, and our route follows the west shore of the lake to the good campsites on that edge of the lake and along the outlet creek just below the lake. Fishing at this lake is poor-to-fair for golden (to 8"). Grassy sections around the sandy-bottomed lake provide a foothold for colorful alpine wildflowers, including yellow columbine, sturdy white heather, and blue sky pilot.

3rd Hiking Day (**Glacier Creek** to **Deer Meadow**, 5 miles, part cross country): After fording Glacier Creek, our route ascends the sloping basin east to a saddle overlooking the Palisade Lakes basin. Views from this saddle are good of Devils Crags and Mt. McDuffie to the west, North Palisade to the north and Middle Palisade to the east. Sometimes over snow, this route descends past several tiny glacial tarns across fractured granite as it veers westward. Part way down this moderate-to-steep grade, Palisade Lakes and the glacially smoothed bowl-like cirque surrounding the lakes come into view. Then, by route-finding down a ledge system, you will encounter sparse whitebark pine just before you meet the John Muir Trail just west of lower Palisade Lake.

Westward on the Muir Trail, the route descends by zigzagging switchbacks along the north side of Palisade Creek. The head of these switchbacks is an excellent vantage point from which to see the crest of Middle Palisade peak to the northeast, and, west beyond Deer Meadow lying immediately below, Devils Crags, Wheel Mountain and Mt. McDuffie. Slopes on both sides of this steep descent are dramatically glacially smoothed. As the trail reaches the head of the flats above Deer Meadow, it enters a moderate stand of lodgepole and silver pine. Abundant wildflowers, including western mountain aster, Douglas phlox, pennyroyal, red columbine and tiger lily, appear as the trail comes close to the creek, and red fir, juniper and aspen occasionally mingle with the predominant lodgepole forest cover. The trail then passes several good campsites before fording Glacier Creek via several step-across branchlets. There are excellent views across the Palisade Creek canyon to the cascading falls of Cataract Creek as they tumble down the steep south wall.

The trail soon reaches Deer Meadow, not really a meadow since it is overgrown with lodgepole pines. You are now two days' walk from any trailhead, and even though you are on the Muir Trail you may find considerably privacy. In June of 1976 here, we saw grass growing in the tread of the John Muir Trail! There are several good campsites (8870'), and fishing for golden and brook trout is excellent (to 12").

4th Hiking Day (**Deer Meadow** to **Grouse Meadows**, 5 miles): About 100 yards below these campsites the trail fords the unnamed multibranched outlet of Palisade Basin, and then it descends moderately through a moderate-to-dense forest cover. This descent passes a packers' campsite about 1½ miles farther on, and then more campsites a short distance beyond that. Concentrations of wildflowers include Indian paintbrush, penstemon, white cinquefoil, Mariposa lily and goldenrod. The underfooting is mostly duff and sand, through alternating forest and meadow, where camping and fishing are good. Then the trail veers away from Palisade Creek, only to return, and, keeping to the north side of the creek, descends steadily over morainal debris to the Middle Fork Kings River Trail. Our route turns right, up the Middle Fork, and proceeds for a gentle uphill mile over an easy ridge to the campsites at the east side of Grouse Meadows. If these are full, back-track about ¼ mile.

5th and 6th Hiking Days: Follow trip 56, 5th and 6th hiking days. 14½ miles.

Palisade Crest from the air (looking west)   *E. P. Pister*

South Lake to Courtright Reservoir

TRIP From South Lake to Courtright Reservoir, via Bishop Pass, Dusy Basin, Muir Pass, Evolution Valley, Goddard Canyon, Hell-for-Sure Pass, Rae Lake, Post Corral Meadows (shuttle trip). Topo maps *Mt. Goddard* (W.P.V.), *Blackcap Mountain* 15'; *Mt. Thompson, North Palisade, Mt. Goddard, Mt. Darwin, Blackcap Mtn., Courtright Reservoir* 7½'. Best mid or late season; 58½ miles.

Grade	Trail/layover days	Total recommended days
Leisurely	....	....
Moderate	8/2	10
Strenuous	6/1	7

HILITES So much laudatory prose has been written about the famous Muir Trail that it seems redundant to add to it. Suffice it to say that this trans-Sierra trail tours the essence of high country, and has the added contrast of finishing via the elegant forest stretches found west of Hell-for-Sure Pass.

DESCRIPTION (Moderate trip)

1st Hiking Day: Follow trip 42 to **Dusy Basin**, 7 miles.

2nd Hiking Day (**Dusy Basin** to **Little Pete Meadow,** 6 miles): The trail from the northernmost lake of the Dusy Basin descends over smooth granite ledges and tundra sections. Occasional clumps of the flaky-barked, five-needled whitebark pine dot the glacially scoured basin, and impressive Mts. Agassiz and Winchell and Thunderbolt Peak continue to make up the eastern skyline. To the south the heavily fractured and less well defined summits of Columbine and Giraud peaks occupy the skyline. This moderate descent swings westward above the lowest lakes of the Dusy Basin, and begins a series of steady switchbacks along the north side of Dusy Branch creek. Wildflowers along this descent include Indian paintbrush, pennyroyal, lupine, white cinquefoil, penstemon, shooting star and some yellow columbine. Just below a waterfall, a wooden bridge crosses to the creek's east side. Views of the U-shaped Middle Fork Kings River canyon are seen constantly during the zigzagging downgrade, and on the far side of the valley one can see the major peaks of the Black Divide, foregrounded by The Citadel and Langille Peak.

As the trail descends, the very sparse forest cover of stunted whitebark seen in most of Dusy Basin gives way to the trees of lower altitudes, including silver pine, juniper, lodgepole, aspen and some red fir near the foot of the switchbacks. The trail recrosses Dusy Branch creek at the head of a stepladdering bench, and then makes the final 1½-mile switchbacking descent to a junction with the John Muir Trail in LeConte Canyon. Emergency services are usually available from the ranger station just a few yards northwest of the junction.

Our route turns right, onto the famous Muir Trail, and ascends moderately over a duff trail through moderate-to-dense stands of lodgepole. Langille Peak dominates the views to the left, and its striking white, fractured granite face is a constant reminder of the massive forces expended by the river of ice that once filled this canyon. Abundant fields of wildflowers color the trailside, including corn lily, tiger lily, buckwheat, fireweed, larkspur, red heather, shooting star, cinquefoil, monkey flower, pennyroyal, penstemon, goldenrod and wallflower. As the trail approaches the south end of Little Pete Meadow, occasional hemlock will be found mixed with the lodgepole, and the view north at the edge of the meadow includes Mts. Powell and Thompson. There are good but heavily used campsites at Little Pete Meadow, and fishing for rainbow, golden and brook is good (to 13").

3rd Hiking Day (**Little Pete Meadow** to **Wanda Lake**, 9½ miles): The trail from Little Pete to Big Pete Meadow makes a moderate ascent on rock and sand through a sparse-to-moderate forest cover of lodgepole and occasional hemlock. Looking back over one's shoulder rewards one with fine views of LeConte Canyon, while ahead the granite walls where the canyon veers west show glacially smoothed, unfractured faces. Some quaking aspen can be seen as the trail ascends through Big Pete Meadow and passes the large area of campsites. As the trail turns westward, one has his first, excellent views of the darker rock of Black Giant, and a few yards beyond the turn the trail fords the stream draining the slopes of Mts. Johnson and Gilbert. Passing more campsites, the trail continues west on an easy-to-moderate ascent through grassy extensions of Big Pete Meadow. Most of the rock underfooting encountered to this point has been of the rounded morainal variety, but as soon as the trail leaves the westernmost fringes of Big Pete Meadow, the rock exhibits sharp, fractured edges. Over this talus, the trail ascends more steeply through a moderate forest cover of silver, lodgepole and whitebark pine and some hemlock. The meadowed flat where the trail jogs north toward the tiny, unnamed lake east of Helen Lake supports a sparse forest fringe of lodgepole, silver and some whitebark pine.

The ascent to Muir Pass starts with a steady climb over sand and rock through a sparse timber cover of whitebark pine. That timber cover soon disappears, giving way to low-lying heather. At the talus-bound, round, unnamed lake east of Helen Lake, the trail veers west, crossing and recrossing the trickling head-waters of Middle Fork Kings River. Excellent views to the south-east of the Palisades and Langille, Giraud and Columbine peaks make the breather stops welcome occasions. The trail becomes rocky and the slope more moderate as it passes the next unnamed lake and winds up the terminal shoulder of the Black Divide to Helen Lake. Rocks in colorful reds, yellows, blacks and whites that characterize this metamorphic divide are on every hand. The trail rounds the loose-rocked south end of this barren lake, and ascends steadily over a rocky slope that is often covered with snow throughout the summer. Looking back, one can see the striking meeting of the black metamorphic rock of the Black Divide and the white granite just east of Helen Lake.

Muir Pass (11,955′) is marked by a sign and a unique stone shelter. This hut, erected by the Sierra Club in memoriam to John Muir, the Sierra's best-known and most-loved mountaineer, stands as a shelter for stormbound travelers. In a sense, it is a wilderness monument, and should be treated as such—leave nothing but your boottracks. (Even human waste has become a problem in the vicinity.) From this pass the views are magnificent. In the morning light, the somber crags to the north and south relieve the intense whites of the lighter granite to the east. Situated in a gigantic rock bowl to the west, Wanda Lake's emerald blue waters contrast sharply with its lower white edges, which, on the south side, merge into the darker rock of the Goddard Divide. The descent from the pass is moderate and then gentle over fragmented rock, and then it levels out, passing the southeast end of Lake McDermand. Skirting the east side of Wanda Lake, the trail affords excellent views of snow-and-ice necklaced Mt. Goddard, and then arrives at the fair if barren campsites near the lake's outlet. The expansive views from these campsites include Mt. Goddard and the Goddard Divide to the south, and Mts. Huxley, Spencer, Darwin and Mendel to the north.

4th Hiking Day (**Wanda Lake** to **Colby Meadow**, 6½ miles): Soon occasional wildflowers, including heather, wallflower and penstemon, can be seen as the trail descends over rock and sand. Below Wanda Lake the trail crosses Evolution Creek and stays on the west bank on a moderate descent that becomes switchbacks above Sapphire Lake. Fine views of the Sierra crest to the east make watching one's footing a difficult task. Sapphire Lake is indeed a high-country gem, fringed with green, marshy grass, and situated on a large glacial step, with some very large trout. Our route traverses its steeper west side, and, after a steady descent, refords Evolution Creek just above Evolution Lake (difficult ford in early or mid season). The trail crosses a meadowy section before winding the length of the lake's east shore. Glacial smoothing and some polish can be seen in the granite surrounding the lake, and on the abrupt walls on either side of the lake. After passing several campsites at the lower end of the lake, the trail makes a brief northward swing before switchbacking down to Evolution Valley. This northward swing passes the unsigned, ducked trail ascending to Darwin Canyon, and the route to the Darwin Glacier. The zigzagging downgrade over morainal debris re-enters forest cover and passes clumps of wildflowers that include penstemon, paintbrush, swamp onion, lupine, forget-me-not, cinquefoil, buckwheat and tiger lily. At the foot of the grade, where the trail fords the stream emptying Darwin Canyon, our route passes more campsites, and then continues for some distance on a relatively level course through moderate stands of lodgepole to the good campsites at Colby Meadow. Fishing for golden is fair (to 9″) in nearby Evolution Creek.

5th Hiking Day (**Colby Meadow** to **Lower Goddard Canyon**, 5½ miles): From Colby Meadow the trail continues westward, passing McClure and Evolution meadows. The trail joining these meadows is a pathway that winds through moderate and dense stands of lodgepole, and, midway down McClure Meadow, passes a ranger station (emergency services usually available here). The friendly intimacy of the meadows has, over the past seventy years, made this valley a favorite camping site for back-country travelers, and one which, with the subsequent establishment of the John Muir Trail, has subjected these delicate wild pastures to serious overuse. As our route winds past the campsites in McClure Meadow, the largest of the Evolution group, the traveler can see for himself the toll taken by the heavy traffic, both human and stock. Before controls were exerted upon grazing stock of large pack-train parties, the foraging animals trampled tender, young spring shoots of grass in such quantities as to change the meadow almost to a patchwork of barren hillocks. In the absence of grasses to hold back the water, serious erosion became a matter of concern, and today, to preserve these meadows, stock forage is necessarily limited, and the trail has been rerouted to skirt the meadows on the north side.

Our duff trail passes the drift fence below McClure Meadow on a moderate-to-steady descent that fords several tributaries draining the Glacier Divide. These fords are usually accomplished via footlogs or easy rock-hopping. Below Evolution Meadow the trail crosses Evolution Creek (on a log—difficult at high water) for the last time, and then continues west to the head of the switchbacks that drop down to South Fork San Joaquin River. Views before the dropoff are excellent of the cascades of the stream draining Emerald Peak, the falls and cascades of Evolution Creek below the ford, and the South Fork San Joaquin River drainage. Midway down the switchbacks, one has impressive views of Goddard Canyon, part of the route for the 6th hiking day. The forest cover along the zigzags is sparse-to-moderate lodgepole, juniper and some aspen, and flowers seen along the trail include pennyroyal, larkspur, penstemon, cinquefoil, currant, monkey flower, buckwheat and paintbrush. The switchbacking trail crosses glacial polish exhibiting some striations, and, at the bottom, passes a packer campsite and several good primitive sites as it passes through a heavy stand of lodgepole. Just beyond these campsites, our trail crosses the footbridge, meets the Goddard Canyon/Hell-for-Sure Pass Trail, and branches left. The forest cover of lodgepole, with large concentrations of quaking aspen, continues as the trail ascends moderately past a drift fence. About ½ mile above the drift fence, near a small meadow, the trail reaches several good-to-excellent campsites. Fishing on nearby South Fork San Joaquin is fair for rainbow, some golden and brook (to 10″).

6th, 7th and 8th Hiking Days: Reverse the 3rd hiking day, trip 32, the 2nd hiking day, trip 27, and the 1st hiking day, trip 25, 24 miles.

Mt. Goddard over Wanda Lake

TRIP   From South Lake to North Lake via Dusy Basin, LeConte Canyon, Muir Pass, Evolution Valley, Blayney Hot Springs, Piute Canyon and Piute Pass (shuttle trip). Topo maps *Mt. Goddard* (W.P.V.), *Mt. Tom, Mt. Abbot, Blackcap Mountain* 15'; *Mt. Thompson, North Palisade, Mt. Goddard, Mt. Darwin, Mt. Hilgard, Mt. Tom* 7½'. Best mid or late season; 60 miles.

Grade	Trail/layover days	Total recommended days
Leisurely	....	....
Moderate	8/1	9
Strenuous	6/0	6

HILITES   The authors' policy is to have no trips consisting entirely of hiking days borrowed from other trips. This trip has been made the exception because it is a quintessential High Sierra hike. In between two crossings of the Sierra backbone, it visits beautiful and famous Evolution Valley, and spends a night at a campground by a hot-spring pool which beats any hot tub. As a bonus, the nearness of the two trailheads to each other makes the shuttle almost short enough to walk.

DESCRIPTION (Moderate trip)

1st 5 Hiking Days: Follow trip 45 to **Lower Goddard Canyon**, 34½ miles.

6th Hiking Day: Follow part of the 4th hiking day, trip 32, to **Blaney Hot Springs** ("a natural hot-spring pool" in that day's description), 7 miles.

7th Hiking Day: Reverse part of the 3rd hiking day, trip 18, to **Hutchinson Meadow,** 8 miles.

8th Hiking Day: Reverse trip 17 to **North Lake,** 11 miles.

Taboose Creek Roadend to Bench Lake **47**

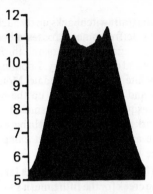

TRIP From Taboose Creek Roadend to Bench Lake (round trip). Topo maps *Big Pine, Mt. Pinchot* 15′; *Fish Spring, Mt. Pinchot,* 7½′. Best mid or late season; 25 miles.

Grade	Trail/layover days	Total recommended days
Leisurely	....	....
Moderate	....	....
Strenuous	4/0	4

HILITES The expansive views, the delightful flower-bedecked basin just over the pass, and the direct access via this route to the sparkling gem of Bench Lake make the great effort worthwhile *if* you are in top shape.

DESCRIPTION (Strenuous trip)

1st Hiking Day (**Taboose Creek Roadend** to **Upper Taboose Creek,** 6½ miles): From the trailhead we cross a low lateral moraine and ascend gently westward over a sandy, sage-covered desert plain, with the awesome rampart of the Sierra just ahead. As we enter the broad portal of Taboose Creek canyon, the path veers left and rises steeply, staying above the rushing creek. After a while we drop momentarily alongside the willow-and-birch-lined creek, before climbing steeply up-canyon on footing alternately gravel and rock. The trail zigzags up a steep slope, then contours over to the creek, which we cross by boulders and logs, taking care not to slip.

From the ford, the trail switchbacks up through a mini forest of white fir and a few Jeffrey pines, crosses a bench, and climbs steadily west, once again in the open, through thickets of chinquapin, willow and other greenery. Looming high on the left are the red and white spurs of Goodale Mountain. The trail crosses the creek and climbs steeply up the north side of the canyon to a picturesque bench valley, shaded around the edges by gnarled whitebark pines and hemmed in between rust-colored cliffs, where there are several excellent campsites on the left (south) side of the bench.

2nd Hiking Day (**Upper Taboose Creek** to **Bench Lake,** 6 miles): After the trail crosses the creek for the fifth time, it switchbacks steeply up through very rocky terrain to a last bench just east of Taboose Pass. Though well above timberline, lush grasses and colorful wildflowers make the scene delightful. We wind up between granite outcroppings, passing several limpid tarns, and finally reach Taboose Pass, marked by a large sign announcing one's entry into Kings Canyon National Park. The scene that abruptly unfolds is breathtaking. Directly ahead is the deep crease of the Kings River's South Fork. Slightly to the left is beautiful Bench Lake, with the symmetrical spire of Arrow Peak as a backdrop. To the right is the ragged citadel of Mt. Ruskin.

From the pass, the trail drops southwest down a gradual slope, passing through sky gardens of buttercup, shooting star and senecio, carpeted with velvet green. In these gardens we ford a rivulet, pass just north of a rockbound tarn, and reach a hard-to-spot junction. After turning left here, we climb and then contour along a rocky slope, staying above the U-shaped bowl of the South Fork, to a junction with the John Muir Trail. Just 100 yards south on the Muir Trail is the lateral trail to Bench Lake, and we turn west onto this high, easy trail. Hikers will appreciate the short side trip to this sublime mountain lake, less than an hour's walk off the Muir Trail. The pathway leads west across a flower-bedecked meadow, descends a short distance, and then contours southwest along a granite bench under a canopy of lodgepole pines. We ford a shallow stream, pass two limpid tarns, and in 1½ miles from the John Muir Trail reach the northeast shore of Bench Lake. In the clarity of its waters and in its splendid setting amid granite peaks and spurs, this sparkling jewel has few peers in the High Sierra. The whitish pyramid of Arrow Peak, reflected in the lake's mirrorlike waters, is one of the classic views in the Sierra. Many fine campsites are among the lodgepoles along the north shore.

3rd and 4th Hiking Days: Retrace your steps, 12½ miles.

Sierra Crest near Independence

48 Taboose Creek Roadend to Twin Lakes

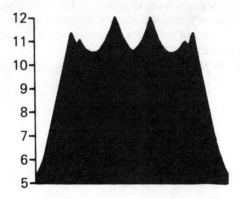

TRIP   From Taboose Creek Roadend to Twin Lakes (round trip). Topo maps *Big Pine, Mt. Pinchot* 15'; *Fish Spring, Mt. Pinchot* 7½'. Best mid or late season; 40 miles.

Grade	Trail/layover days	Total recommended days
Leisurely	....	....
Moderate	....	....
Strenuous	5/1	6

HILITES   In addition to the attraction of the previous trip, this route offers the alpine beauties of Lake Marjorie, which has one of the most colorful settings in the High Sierra. Off-the-beaten-path camping at Twin Lakes is ample reward for the long hike to them.

DESCRIPTION (Strenuous trip)

1st and 2nd Hiking Days: Follow trip 47 to **Bench Lake**, 12½ miles.

3rd Hiking Day (**Bench Lake** to **Twin Lakes**, 9 miles): After retracing the path to the John Muir Trail, this day's route turns south and climbs through rocky meadows and clumps of lodgepole and whitebark pine, passing above a shimmering lakelet on the left, then another one on the right. Gnarled whitebark pines, harbingers of approaching timberline, begin to replace the lodge-

poles as the forest thins to scattered groves. After skirting
another rock-bound lake, the granite-paved trail climbs to the
north shore of magnificent Lake Marjorie. The setting here is as
richly colorful as any in the Sierra: to the right, ramparts of steel-
gray granite rise abruptly from the lake. South, above the lake's
head, are slopes of black and ruddy brown. Just visible on the
southeastern skyline is the dark notch of Pinchot Pass. To the
left, rising above all, are the broken, multihued cliffs of Mt.
Pinchot.

Amid this grandeur we pass above the east shore of Lake
Marjorie and climb above the last, stunted whitebarks into a
world of snow and bare rock. We ascend steadily over granite
benches and through boulder fields, passing above two stark
lakelets. After fording an icy rivulet, the path traverses upward
and then switchbacks steeply up over rocky terrain to 12,110-
foot Pinchot Pass, on the divide that separates the waters of the
Kings' South Fork from its tributary, Woods Creek. The views in
both directions are inspiring. Far to the north, over Mather Pass,
loom the black sentinels of the Palisades. South, beyond the
serrated face of Mt. Cedric Wright, ridge after ridge fades into
the distance.

From Pinchot Pass the pathway descends a steep talus slope,
crosses a slight rise and drops into a high, open basin lush with
grass and wildflowers. Particularly abundant are clusters of red
heather and shooting star. Here we veer east, passing several
placid tarns and fording the twin headwaters of Woods Creek,
then turn south again and parallel the vibrant stream through
alpine meadow country. As the trail descends toward 11,000
feet, clumps of whitebark pine welcome us back to timberline.
The dominating round bulk of Mt. Cedric Wright looms up close
by in the south, and the knifelike peak on the southern skyline is
Mt. Clarence King, monarch of the Sixty Lake Basin. The trail
drops steadily southward, passing a marshy lakelet on the right.
Occasionally visible down to the left are Twin Lakes, nestled
close under the spines of Mt. Cedric Wright. A quarter mile
below the lower lake we meet the Twin Lakes Trail and turn
northeast into it for ⅓ mile to the good campsites along the west
shore of the lower lake.

4th and 5th Hiking Days: Retrace your steps, omitting Bench
Lake, 18½ miles.

49   Sawmill Creek Roadend to Sawmill Lake

TRIP   From Sawmill Creek Roadend to Sawmill Lake
                 (round trip). Topo map *Mt. Pinchot* 15'; *Aberdeen*
                 7½'. Best early season; 16 miles.

	Grade	Trail/layover days	Total recommended days
Leisurely		....	....
Moderate		....	....
Strenuous		2/0	2

HILITES   This strenuous trip up from hot Owens Valley to a
                lovely, cool lake at 10,000 feet gives one the satis-
                faction of getting high on his own sweat, and the
                thrill of strolling back down with next to no effort.

DESCRIPTION (Strenuous trip)

1st Hiking Day (**Sawmill Creek Roadend to Sawmill Lake**, 8 miles): The
route up from the trailhead climbs the hot, dry, sage-covered
slope. In early summer, this desert slope is splashed with
flowering shrubs and blossoms of bright blue woolly gilia and
yellow and white buckwheat. From the trail you look down on
the Big Pine volcanic field, spotted with reddish cinder cones and
black lava flows that erupted from the west side of Owens Valley.
After meeting a lateral trail, the trail rounds the ridge of Sawmill
Point high above the waters of Sawmill Creek, visible as a white
ribbon far below. The pathway descends slightly, then contours,

and finally climbs along the precipitous north wall of Sawmill Creek canyon. As we near the sloping ridge known, appropriately, as The Hogsback, Jeffrey pines and white firs make a most welcome appearance. If one looks carefully at the lower end of The Hogsback, one can spot the remains of the Blackrock sawmill and flume, dating from the 1860s, after which Sawmill Creek and Sawmill Pass are named. For some distance above The Hogsback, one can occasionally see stumps, felled trees, and logs used as "gliders" in this century-old operation to supply Owens Valley miners with lumber.

The trail climbs to meet a tributary stream north of The Hogsback, the first water on this hot climb. The trail fords this creek three times before crossing The Hogsback. Once over the top of this long, rounded ridge, the path veers south, contouring and climbing on a moderate grade, back into the main canyon, and reaches Sawmill Meadow, boggy and lush green in early summer, but drying considerably as the summer months progress. Beyond, the trail follows the creek, then zigzags steeply upward through Jeffrey pine and red fir to Mule Lake, perched on a small bench high up the canyon. After fording the creek, we climb through a jumbled mass of metamorphic rocks that are home for a large colony of grass-harvesting conies. After recrossing the creek, we finally arrive at the northeast shore of beautiful Sawmill Lake. Good campsites under clumps of foxtail pine are located here, and fishing for rainbow trout is fair to good.

2nd Hiking Day: Retrace your steps, 8 miles.

50 Sawmill Creek Roadend to Twin Lakes

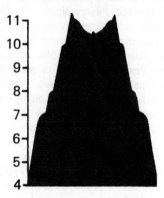

TRIP From Sawmill Creek Roadend to Twin Lakes (round trip). Topo maps *Mt. Pinchot* 15′; *Aberdeen, Mt. Pinchot* 7½′. Best mid or late season; 28 miles.

Grade	Trail/layover days	Total recommended days
Leisurely	....	....
Moderate	....	....
Strenuous	4/0	4

HILITES This trip proceeds by way of a horrendous ascent to Sawmill Pass and then takes you through the headwaters of Woods Creek, in a high basin clothed with whitebark pine, verdant meadows and multihued alpine flowers.

DESCRIPTION (Strenuous trip)

1st Hiking Day: Follow trip 49 to **Sawmill Lake**, 8 miles.

2nd Hiking Day (**Sawmill Lake** to **Twin Lakes**, 6 miles). Above Sawmill Lake the trail winds up through a thinning forest of foxtail and whitebark pine, passes a lakelet, crosses a small timberline basin, and climbs steeply upward to Sawmill Pass (11,347′), on the border of Kings Canyon National Park. From the pass you walk northwest across nearly level talus and sand, then drop into a resplendent lake-dotted alpine basin, the headwaters of Woods Creek. The trail winds westward, gradually descending as it passes just north of two small, nameless lakes. The largest body of water in the basin—Woods Lake—is a short cross-country jaunt south of the trail. Our route descends to the lower end of the basin, then turns abruptly north to climb and contour along the lower slopes of Mt. Cedric Wright. Finally, the trail drops to North Fork Woods Creek, goes north along its east bank a short distance, and then fords the creek to a junction with the John Muir Trail. A short half mile up this arterial route the Twin Lakes Trail turns off and leads northeast to the good campsites on the west shore of Lower Twin Lake.

3rd and 4th Hiking Days: Retrace your steps, 14 miles.

Lake 11599, Upper Basin

51 Sawmill Creek Roadend to Oak Creek

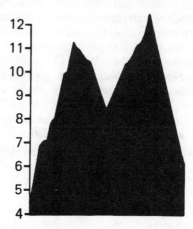

TRIP   From Sawmill Creek Roadend to Oak Creek Roadend (shuttle trip). Topo map *Mt. Pinchot* 15′; *Aberdeen, Mt. Pinchot, Kearsarge Peak* 7½′. Best mid season; 33½ miles.

Grade	Trail/layover days	Total recommended days
Leisurely	....	....
Moderate	....	....
Strenuous	4/1	5

HILITES   Another trip for those in top condition, this strenuous jaunt uses a small piece of the John Muir Trail to permit passage between two out of the way, lake-dotted alpine basins—the headwaters of Woods Creek and the Baxter Lakes basin.

DESCRIPTION (Strenuous trip)

1st Hiking Day: Follow trip 49 to **Sawmill Lake**, 8 miles.

2nd Hiking Day (**Sawmill Lake** to **Woods Creek Crossing**, 8½ miles): Follow the 2nd hiking day, trip 50, to the John Muir Trail and turn left (south) on it.

Your path veers southwest, ever dropping, following the U-shaped canyon of the glacier that flowed down Woods Creek.

You pass another fine campsite on the left, and when you abruptly emerge from the forest, the great trough of Woods Creek opens in full grandeur ahead. For the next 3 miles, the trail descends through the gorge, sometimes alongside the joyous creek but more often well above it, through tangled thickets of dwarf aspen, willow and other greenery. Wildflowers add an abundant splash of color, and you may see paintbrush, larkspur, purple aster, mountain violet, Bigelow sneezeweed, Labrador tea and yarrow. A ribbon of white water plunges from the dark cliffs high on the left. We cross several benches shaded by isolated clusters of lodgepoles, then ford the White Fork of Woods Creek (sometimes difficult in early season when the water runs high). Ahead is the great bend of Woods Creek, with the stupendous ramparts of King Spur as a backdrop. A descent over rocky terrain brings us back into the forest, now consisting of Jeffrey pine and gnarled junipers. The trail fords another side stream and drops alongside Woods Creek, its white froth spilling wildly over huge, inclined granite slabs. On the final descent to the canyon floor, manzanita provides a thick and thorny ground cover, with scattered Jeffrey pines for shade. At a major trail junction, the fork to the right is the Woods Creek Trail down to Paradise Valley; the Muir Trail goes left, and so do we. Where we re-reach Woods Creek, it is swollen to river proportions by the addition of its South Fork's waters, but a bridge is there. There are fair campsites, shaded by tall aspens and verdant white alders, on both sides of the creek. Fishing for brook and rainbow trout to 10 inches is fair to good.

3rd Hiking Day (**Woods Creek Crossing** to **Baxter Lakes**, 7 miles): After crossing the creek (difficult in early season), we turn southeast and begin the long climb up the South Fork. Juniper and red fir provide forest cover as we pass several adequate campsites on the left, along the creek. Also to the left, half-hidden by foliage, is one of Shorty Lovelace's pigmy log cabins. Shorty ran a trap line through this country during the years before Kings Canyon National Park was established. Remains of his other miniature cabins are located in Gardiner Basin and along Bubbs Creek.

Presently the trail rounds the base of King Spur and climbs well above the stream, through alternating stretches of lush greenery and patches of wildflowers, and sparse forest of aspen, red fir and lodgepole pine. We jump the rivulet that hurries down from Lake 10296 and enter an open, rocky area. Beyond, a wooden span provides an easy crossing of a boggy meadow.

From the meadow, the trail climbs over a rocky ridge and fords the major creek descending from Sixty Lake Basin, passing through a gate in a drift fence. There are several small campsites here, under scattered pines. Across the canyon, Baxter Creek stitches a ribbon of white down the rock-ribbed slope. The trail climbs through rocky terrain, then approaches the main creek, passing a lodgepole-sheltered campsite on the left before again breaking into the open and ascending bouldery terrain. Ahead looms the peaked monolith of Fin Dome, heralding your approach to the beautiful Rae Lakes. To your right are the impressive steel-gray ramparts of King Spur. In contrast, the massive, sloping Sierra crest in the east is made up of dark metamorphic rocks. The long black striations that cross the face of Diamond Peak and the ridge north of it are metamorphosed lava, visual evidence of ancient volcanic activity.

Finally this long ascent climbs over a low, rounded spur and abruptly reaches the northernmost of the Rae Lakes chain, jewel-like Dollar Lake. The setting here is magnificent; lodgepoles crowd the shore amid granite outcroppings, and Fin Dome, along with some blackish spires beyond, provides a jagged backdrop for the mirroring blue waters of the lake. (It is illegal to camp at Dollar Lake.) The unmarked Baxter Pass Trail takes off northeast from the north side of Dollar Lake. From this junction follow most of the 4th hiking day, trip 62.

4th Hiking Day: Follow the 5th hiking day, trip 62, 10 miles.

Fin Dome over Dollar Lake

Cedar Grove to Kennedy Lakes   **52**

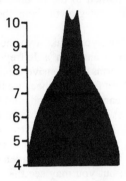

TRIP   From Cedar Grove to Kennedy Lakes (round trip). Topo map *Marion Peak* 15′; *Cedar Grove, Slide Bluffs* 7½′. Best mid or late season; 23 miles.

Grade	Trail/layover days	Total recommended days
Leisurely	....	....
Moderate	4/1	5
Strenuous	4/0	4

HILITES   By going north instead of east out of Cedar Grove, this trip avoids the hordes of hikers bound for the John Muir Trail and instead brings the traveler to secluded little ponds in the meadows just over Kennedy Pass, which lie in a private cirque virtually on top of the Monarch Divide.

DESCRIPTION (Strenuous trip)

1st Hiking Day (**Cedar Grove** to **Frypan Meadow**, 6 miles): Heading north from the parking area you make a few short switchbacks under shady incense-cedar, ponderosa pine and black oak. Once beyond the mouth of Lewis Creek canyon, the cover diminishes, for much of this drainage was burned, at different times, between 1979 and 1984. As a result, much of this trip crosses areas that are in different stages of forest succession. By the time you reach Kennedy Pass, over 6000′ above, you will have seen how the plant communities along the way are well-adapted to periodic fires. Along many of the open slopes you can see manzanita and snowbush that was burned to the ground. These same plants have since sprouted new growth from the crowns of their roots.

Climbing moderately, you make two more sets of switch-backs before the grade eases in a Jeffrey-pine forest where fragrant kit-kit-dizze forms an extensive ground cover. Conifers, especially pines, benefit from fires because the heat helps open their cones so seeds can reach the soil, and fire also clears the ground so young trees can get enough sun. Beyond a junction with the Hotel Creek Trail you descend to cross a small stream whose channel was the path of a debris flow in 1984. The deposits of mud and tree stumps that mark a debris flow will be gone in a few years, but you may see the tell-tale signs else-where, since this phenomenon is common in the Sierra. A debris flow, like a conventional flood, indicates excess runoff, but unlike a flood a debris flow is viscous and slow-moving, being composed not only of water but also dirt, rocks, trees, snow—anything available. Beyond the creek you climb unevenly under canyon live oak, where Western fence lizards scurry along the trail as you walk. Soon you reach the ford of Comb Creek (diffi-cult in early season). Beyond the ford you leave the shade for a while as you climb through sunny stands of young Jeffrey pines, indicating that you are crossing another burned area.

Shade trees reappear near the ford of Lewis Creek (difficult in early season). Beyond the ford you climb moderately past Jeffrey pines showing signs of a ground fire: their trunks are blackened only near the ground. The route then becomes steep and dusty, but you have good views of Comb Spur to the east and the Great Western Divide in the distance. Just beyond a junction with a trail to Wildman Meadow, the grade eases and you enter Frypan Meadow. Near the upper end of the flowery glade is a well-used campsite under towering white firs. This campsite is just below the Grizzly Lakes Trail junction. Unfortunately, the last California grizzly was shot near Kings Canyon in 1926, but there are still black bears nearby, so hang your food accordingly.

2nd Hiking Day (Frypan Meadow to tarns, upper Kennedy Canyon, 5½ miles): Between Frypan Meadow and Kennedy Pass the trail climbs 3000 feet in 5 miles, and the last 1600 feet are both waterless and very steep. Initially the trail makes an undulating ascent under tall conifers, fording 2 creeks and then Lewis Creek. From here the trail makes several switchbacks and then begins a traverse around the south side of Kennedy Mountain. In ½ mile the forest diminishes and soon you are climbing on a sunny, manzanita-covered hillside. Far to the south are the Great Western Divide and the Kings-Kaweah Divide. The trail then enters an extensive grove of aspens, where many flower-lined creeks provide cool rest stops. Aspens, as well as the flowers you see here, are well-adapted to fire; this verdant hillside was quite charred after a fire in 1980.

Beyond the largest and last creek you leave aspen behind as you begin the last, steep 1600 feet to the pass. As you gain altitude, other tree species are left behind, too, and the end of the climb is through sparse whitebark pines. Upon reaching Kennedy Pass (10,800) you are greeted by an extensive view over the Middle Fork Kings River canyon into northern Kings Canyon National Park. From the pass you can see several small tarns to the north, where you can find good campsites. The descent to the first tarn is very steep and may be difficult or dangerous if there is a lot of snow.

3rd and 4th hiking days: Retrace your steps, 11½ miles.

Rae Lakes, Painted Lady   *Tom Ross*

53 ## Cedar Grove to Volcanic Lakes

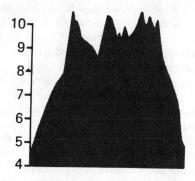

TRIP From Cedar Grove to Kennedy Pass, cross-country to Volcanic Lakes, return via Granite Pass, Granite Lakes (shuttle trip). Topo map *Marion Peak 15'*, *Cedar Grove, Slide Bluffs, Marion Peak, The Sphinx 7½'*. Best mid or late season; 25½ miles.

Grade	Trail/layover days	Total recom- mended days
Leisurely	....	....
Moderate	5/1	6
Strenuous	4/0	4

HILITES The little-traveled divide that separates the gigantic gashes of the south and middle forks of the Kings River, the Monarch Divide, is the setting for this loop trip through high, wild, dramatic country dotted with dozens of lakes, named and unnamed, on-trail and off-trail.

DESCRIPTION (Strenuous trip)

1st 2 Hiking Days: Follow trip 52 to **tarns, upper Kennedy Creek canyon,** 11½ miles.

3rd Hiking Day (**tarns, upper Kennedy Creek canyon,** to **Granite Lake,** part cross-country, 5½ miles): The cross-country route to Granite Pass is short, but one can easily spend a whole day exploring the mostly treeless upper Volcanic Lakes basin. From the tarns near Kennedy Pass follow the switchbacking trail toward Kennedy Creek until you are just above a little lake on your right. Turn right and go past the left side of the lake and straight up the hill to the northwest shore of East Kennedy Lake (poor campsites). Beginning at the outlet of East Kennedy Lake, we skirt the north shore for a few hundred feet and then head uphill. Staying on the left side of the slope, our route passes through the little forested area and arrives at the top of the ridge. A little to the left of the shallow saddle is an excellent viewpoint, Point 10979 on the 15' topo map. From it we can see Mt. Gardiner and the Kings-Kern Divide above the Monarch Divide, and also Arrow Peak, the Palisades, the Black Divide, Mt. Goddard, and the Sierra crest beyond.

From about 50 feet south of this point the route descends down a grassy gully that leads toward the head of the largest of the Volcanic Lakes. Near the lake, the slabs can be avoided by walking several dozen yards to the right. From the head of the lake, follow the inlet stream toward the highest two Volcanic Lakes, where there are rainbow and golden trout (to 16″). Walk around the rocky north side of the first lake and cross the low saddle to the northeast. It's worthwhile strolling up to the highest lake: nestled under the Monarch Divide, this lake presents a scene of alpine splendor at its finest. Just below the saddle is a fishless lake. Descend to its south shore and walk around the east side to where two points of rock jut into the lake. From here a grassy gully angles up, right, to the top of the ridge on the east. From this ridgetop contour east to Granite Pass (10,673′). Then from the pass, the rocky-sandy trail descends, steeply at times, to a small meadow filled with lavender shooting stars in early season, where there are several good campsites. Our trail then descends moderately through lodgepole forest to a junction with the spur trail to Granite Lake (10,100′). Here we turn right (west) and skirt the north side of a meadow to the fair campsites on that lake, where fishing is fair-to-good for brook trout (to 10″).

4th Hiking Day (**Granite Lake** to **Cedar Grove Roadend**, 10 miles): Reverse the steps of the 1st hiking day, trip 54.

Cedar Grove to Granite Lake

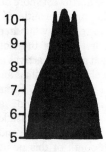

TRIP   From Cedar Grove to Granite Lake (round trip).
Topo maps *Marion Peak*, 15'; *The Sphinx, Marion
Peak* 7½'. Best early or late season; 20 miles.

	Grade	Trail/layover days	Total recom- mended days
	Leisurely	....	....
	Moderate	3/1	4
	Strenuous	2/0	2

HILITES   This trip is tough, for it involves a 5000-foot climb
out of one of the deepest canyons in the country. As
such it should be undertaken only after some condi-
tioning. However, the fine views and good alpine
campsite at Granite Lake are well worth the effort.

DESCRIPTION (Moderate trip)

1st Hiking Day (**Cedar Grove Roadend** to **Lower Tent Meadow**, 4½
miles): The Copper Creek Trail begins on the north side of the
parking loop (5035') under tall pines, but soon you are climbing
the hot, dry north wall of Kings Canyon. Canyon live oaks
provide intermittent shade for most of the 1¾ miles to the first
stream. The canyon walls reflect much sunlight, and on a summer's day the trail can be like a glaring furnace. Even so, this
route has been well-used for centuries.

The first set of switchbacks gains 1400 feet, and then you
swing into Copper Creek canyon. The trail is now partly shaded
under Jeffrey pine, sugar pine, incense-cedar and white fir.
Beyond a small creek the forest cover increases. Along the dusty

trail you might see dismantled white-fir cones, chewed apart by chickarees. These small, squirrel-like rodents emit a rapid-then-slowing series of high-pitched squeaks, and are more often heard than seen. Where the trail descends to cross a flower-lined creek, you encounter the first aspens. Soon you pass a large campsite by a seasonal stream, and ¼ mile beyond, you come to the dashing creek in Lower Tent Meadow. Campsites are on the east side of the creek, but bears can find you anywhere, so hang your food accordingly.

2nd Hiking Day (**Lower Tent Meadow** to **Granite Lake**, 5½ miles): Climbing moderately, the trail crosses an area burned in 1980. After two long switchbacks you near the creek in a wide avalanche path where only low-lying bushes and a multitude of wildflowers grow. The trail switchbacks again and nears the creek for the last time—fill your bottle here. Now the trail enters shady red-fir forest and begins a long series of switchbacks that climb 1300 feet up a moraine to the divide between Copper Creek and Granite Creek. Enroute, you cross the belt of silver pines, and then the ridgetop is shaded by lodgepole pines. From here you can see two prominent peaks to the east, Mt. Clarence King, on the left, and Mt. Gardiner.

As the trail descends into aptly named Granite Basin, it is at first steep and rocky. After many switchbacks it turns north to make a winding, rolling ascent under lodgepole pines, passing several small ponds and meadows. A mile or so up the basin you top a low ridge, and from it you can see the bowl to the northwest that holds Granite Lake. Skirting a large meadow, you soon arrive at the signed lateral to Granite Lake. Here you turn left, cross a creek, and then wind up an easy slope to the north side of beautiful Granite Lake (10,100'). Good campsites can be found above the lake here. Fishing for brook trout is fair (to 8"). Since the environment around this heavily used lake is delicate, please use your best environmental ethics in order to minimize your impact.

3rd Hiking Day: Retrace your steps, 10 miles.

Cedar Grove to State Lakes

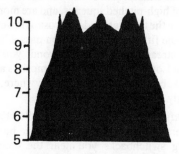

TRIP   From Cedar Grove Roadend to State Lakes via Granite Basin, Granite Pass (round trip). Topo map *Marion Peak, 15'; The Sphinx, Marion Peak 7½'*. Best mid or late season; 34 miles.

Grade	Trail/layover days	Total recom- mended days
Leisurely	....	....
Moderate	5/2	7
Strenuous	4/2	6

HILITES   Once past the initial 5000-foot climb, the route to State Lakes stays high and elevation change is small. Beneath the Monarch Divide, this trip visits the lowest State Lake, where there is good fishing. Side trips to Glacier and Horseshoe lakes offer more fine angling potential.

DESCRIPTION (Moderate trip)

1st and 2nd Hiking Days: Follow trip 54 to Granite Lake, 10 miles.

3rd Hiking Day (**Granite Lake** to **lower State Lake**, 7 miles): You begin this hiking day by retracing your steps to the Granite Pass Trail, where you turn left to climb moderately under lodgepole pines. Beyond a meadow you leave the creek and the forest cover, and then the trail switchbacks steeply up a narrow, rocky gully. The last ¼ mile to the pass is easy, and the good views southward soon give way to the extensive panorama at Granite Pass (10,673'). From the pass the oversize trail descends moderately, and then skirts a meadow where it has been rerouted to allow the turf to recover. You then head down a small canyon, where the stream's straight course is determined by fractures in the bedrock. The grade eases at a second glacial-lake-turned-meadow. Just beyond, you pass a drift fence and descend rocky switchbacks to the forested environs along Middle Fork Dougherty Creek. After a gentle ¾-mile descent and three creek fords, you meet the signed trail to Kennedy Pass, but you continue north, soon fording a small creek at 9493'. In another ½ mile the trail climbs over a ridge, where you pass another drift fence and get a good view of the Dougherty Creek drainage.

Turning east, the trail makes a short descent, passes a seasonal pond and then meets a junction with a trail to Simpson Meadow. The lodgepole-pine-shaded trail then climbs around a low ridge before crossing the small creek in Glacier Valley (wet in early season). Turning north, you cross the cascading outlet from lower State Lake (difficult in early season) and switchback steeply up before leveling off in the meadowy environs near lower State Lake (10,300'). Wildflowers adorn these wet meadows, and one may see shooting star and cinquefoil near the good campsite on the north side of the lake. Fishing is good for golden trout (to 12"). The easy, shaded trail to the next State Lake (fishless) passes many currants and gooseberries (ripe in late summer), and the shores of the middle lake are a lovely place to see State Peak reflected in still waters on a quiet evening.

4th and 5th Hiking Days: Retrace your steps, 17 miles.

The Sphinx from the Paradise Valley Trail

56   **Cedar Grove to South Lake**

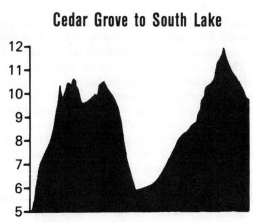

TRIP   From Cedar Grove Roadend to South Lake via
             Granite Basin, Granite Pass, State Lakes, Simpson
             Meadow, Middle Fork Kings River, Dusy Basin,
             Bishop Pass (shuttle trip). Topo maps *Marion Peak,
             Mt. Goddard* (W.P.V.) 15′; *The Sphinx, Marion
             Peak, North Palisade, Mt. Thompson* 7½′. Best
             mid or late season; 49½ miles.

Grade	Trail/layover days	Total recommended days
Leisurely	....	....
Moderate	7/3	10
Strenuous	6/3	9

HILITES This trans-Sierra route is relatively little used
             between Granite Lake and the Muir Trail. Fine
             angling and magnificent vistas are expectations to
             be realized. The sweeping variety of flora and fauna
             encountered gives one the feeling of having crossed
             a large mountain range—as indeed one has.

DESCRIPTION (Strenuous trip)

1st and 2nd Hiking Days: Follow trip 55 to **State Lakes,** 17 miles.

3rd Hiking Day (**Lower State Lake** to **Simpson Meadow,** 8 miles): This
hiking day entails a descent of 4400 feet in 7 miles, and can put a
tremendous strain on your legs. The first mile, however, is an
easy ascent past the grassy fringes of middle State Lake to a

junction with the trail to Horseshoe Lakes. From this junction your trail gently descends a forested ridge for 1¼ miles to a junction with a trail (left) back to Dougherty Creek. Here you turn right, and soon begin the big drop into the Middle Fork Kings River canyon. The long descent today will reflect elevation loss by the appearance of 11 different tree species along the way. At first you saw whitebark and lodgepole pine. As you descend, you leave those trees behind and pass silver pine and Sierra juniper. Tall red fir is plentiful by the time you reach another trail coming in on the left from Dougherty Creek. (There is a year-round stream ⅓ mile along this trail.)

The dusty trail then descends steeply through an area burned in 1985. Much of your route from here to the east side of Simpson Meadow was burned in varying degrees during a lightning fire that burned slowly for weeks. Sequoia-Kings Canyon National Park policy now recognizes fire as a normal part of forestry ecology, and allows natural fires to run their course in the backcountry. Indeed, many trees, such as the giant sequoia, require fire for reproduction. Cones of various trees, especially some pines, release their seeds if heated, and young trees usually grow better after a fire because fire clears the soil and opens the ground to sunlight. Fire also releases nutrients from dead plant matter back into the soil. Even if most of the trees are killed in a fire, enough usually survive to quickly reseed an area. Hardwood plants such as manzanita, aspen and black oak, even if burned to the ground, can quickly sprout new foliage from the crown of their roots. Sometimes, large trees literally explode when water in their trunks is superheated by fire. Depressions you see along the trail mark the sites of large trees whose roots were burned below ground level. Trees with thick bark, such as Jeffrey pine and incense-cedar, usually won't burn unless fire gets under the bark and starts burning the trunk.

The downward grade eases temporarily on a moraine at 8000 feet—2000 feet to go. The next few hundred feet are extremely steep and rocky. Soon you meet the first white fir, and then aspen and incense-cedar. The grade eases again on an open slope where there are sugar pines, and you can see Windy Peak to the northeast, now high above. By the time the trail levels off on the canyon floor, you can feel the warm, oxygen-rich air here at 6000′. After you cross an open area, you come to a junction with the trail to Tehipite Valley. The bridge ½ mile downstream washed out in 1982, and those who don't mind rattlesnakes and wish to visit Tehipite Valley may have to find a wet ford near this junction or else upstream. Around Simpson Meadow, you can find unburned campsites near the trail on this side of Horseshoe Creek, ¼ mile up-canyon, or farther up, near the river. Anywhere you camp, a hungry bear can find your food, so hang it accordingly. Fishing in Middle Fork Kings River is good for rainbow trout (to 12″).

4th Hiking Day (**Simpson Meadow** to **Grouse Meadows**, 10 miles): Starting at the junction with the trail to Tehipite Valley, you head east, soon ford Horseshoe Creek, and cross more burned area. The trail skirts a meadow and then contours around the base of Windy Peak. The Middle Fork Kings River flows nearby, tucked against the base of Windy Peak, opposite Goddard Creek Canyon. The river channel here has been pushed to this side of the canyon by the sediments deposited by Goddard Creek as it debouches from its canyon. This process is widespread; farther upstream Middle Fork Kings River flows on the north side of the canyon floor opposite the alluvial fan at the base of Windy Canyon. As you gently ascend this shadeless alluvial fan there are many black oaks, indicating a high water table, and there are more of these trees as you approach Windy Canyon Creek, where the water table is at the surface. Beyond this creek the main canyon turns north, becoming steep and narrow. Your trail steepens, too, as it winds up through thickets of black oak where you follow a 20-foot-wide swath cut by a trail crew in 1985. Soon you pass a drift fence and then cross Cartridge Creek on a wood bridge.

From here to Palisade Creek the rocky canyon is very steep and narrow, and your trail climbs steeply, usually high above falls and pools in the river below. Flowers seen along this stretch are generally of the dry-country variety, including paintbrush, penstemon, Collinsia, forget-me-not, lupine and fleabane.

The trail climbs steeply to the flats just below Devils Washbowl. To the right, the east canyon walls provide a fascinating study in convoluted glacial polish, and the views to the west and northwest of the Great Cliffs and the heavily fractured rock of Devils Crags portend later, equally exciting views of the Black Divide. The trail touches the river briefly near some sandy campsites, and then switchbacks up to awesome Devils Washbowl, a wild, spectacular falls and cataract in a granite gorge setting. Leaving the tumult of the water behind, the trail continues to ascend over rock to the innocuous-looking but treacherous ford of the unnamed creek draining Windy Cliff to the southeast. The flora around these tributary fords deserves the traveler's attention because of both its lushness and the presence of the water birch, rare in westside Sierra canyons though common on the east side. Among the wildflowers one is sure to find at stream crossings are white Mariposa, cinquefoil, tiger lily, lupine, columbine and elderberry.

Ascending and descending steeply, the vacillating trail is sometimes at river's edge, and other times 200 feet above. The underfooting is very rocky and treacherous until we near the Palisade Creek crossing. This crossing is preceded by a reacquaintance with a timber cover of Jeffrey, lodgepole and silver pine and white fir. Just after the steel bridge crossing of Palisade Creek, our route meets and turns left onto the John Muir Trail and passes several excellent campsites. Continuing north, the trail crosses an easy ridge, fords the unnamed tributary draining the west slopes of Giraud Peak, and arrives at the excellent campsites at the east side of Grouse Meadows. The intimate views are excellent of the lush meadows and the quiet waters of the meandering river. Fishing is good for golden trout (to 11″).

5th Hiking Day (**Grouse Meadows** to **Dusy Basin**, 7½ miles): Leaving the pleasant grasslands of Grouse Meadows behind, the trail continues its gentle but steady ascent. On the left, the river foregoes the placid temperament of its winding meadow course and resumes its mad, white-water plunge. Beyond the river to the west, The Citadel's granite face stands guard over the south side of an obvious hanging valley, and the early-morning traveler is often treated to a burst of reflected sunlight from glacially polished surfaces high on the canyon's west wall north of that valley. The trail undulates up and down the east wall, sometimes 80 to 100 feet above the river, sometimes right alongside it. The thin lodgepole forest cover occurs mostly in stands, with intermittent stretches of grassy pockets, and the underfooting is mostly rocky. Ahead, the canyon narrows, and the trail crosses Dusy Branch via a substantial steel footbridge to meet the Bishop Pass Trail. A few yards north of this junction is the LeConte Ranger Station (emergency services usually available).

Our route turns right (east) and begins the steep, switchbacking ascent of the east canyon wall. This ascent is broken into two distinct steps that gain 2000 feet in about 2 miles, but the steepness of the slope is tamed by the well-graded switchbacks. Touching the creek at strategic intervals (a cold drink on this climb is always welcome), the trail offers magnificent views of the monolithic granite structures on the far side of the canyon. Near the creek, the wildflower lover will find lush shooting star, fireweed, penstemon, pennyroyal and some yellow columbine nestling next to damp, moss-covered rocky grottos. Along the switchbacks, occasional lodgepole and juniper break the monotony of the slab granite, and one particular juniper stands out with a near record girth. Like a beetle-browed sentinel this ancient specimen guards one of the switchbacks near the top of the first climb. Views of the chutes and cascades of Dusy Branch reward the dusty trail-pounder as he finishes the first climb and enters a cooling bower of a mixed stand of lodgepole and aspen. The trail crosses the creek on a bridge and then returns over another as it continues the switchbacking up through a sparse cover of aspen. This ascent levels out near the lowest of the Dusy Basin lake chain, and emerges to open, breathtaking views of Mt. Winchell, Mt. Agassiz, Thunderbolt Peak, and Columbine Peak. Rounding the north side of the lower Dusy Basin lake chain, the trail turns north and climbs a series of grass-topped ledges. A short, well-worn spur trail branches right, leading to campsites situated both alongside Dusy Branch and on the middle lakes of the Dusy Basin chain.

Our route veers away from the creek, climbing above it, and where it rejoins the creek while on an eastward jog, our route turns right a short cross-country distance and descends through an alpine fell field to the fair campsites near the west side of the northernmost large lake in the basin. Fishing for golden and golden hybrids is good (to 8"). This campsite offers the camper a fine base for further explorations of Dusy and Palisades basins, and a granite outcropping just east of the lake provides the finest panoramic viewpoint in the entire basin.

6th Hiking Day (**Dusy Basin** to **South Lake**, 7 miles): Reverse the 1st hiking day, trip 42.

Cedar Grove to Vidette Meadow

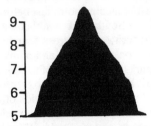

57

TRIP   From Cedar Grove Roadend to Vidette Meadow (round trip). Topo maps *Marion Peak, Mt. Pinchot* 15'; *The Sphinx, Mt. Clarence King* 7½'. Best early-to-mid season; 26 miles.

Grade	Trail/layover days	Total recom- mended days
Leisurely	4/1	5
Moderate	3/0	3
Strenuous	2/0	2

HILITES   Climbing 4000 feet, this trip follows an old Indian trade route paralleling Bubbs Creek. Beyond the realm of the Park's dayhiker, the trail climbs the path of an old glacier to beautiful Vidette Meadow, a "high country crossroads." Here in the shadow of the spectacular Kearsarge Pinnacles this route meets the famous John Muir Trail.

DESCRIPTION (Moderate trip)

1st Hiking Day (**Cedar Grove Roadend** to **Charlotte Creek**, 7½ miles): From the paved roadend loop (5035') the wide, sandy trail heads east through a mixed forest of ponderosa pine, incense-cedar, black oak, sugar pine and white fir. But soon the shade is left behind, and there is only a sparse cover of ponderosas. The balmy climate usually characteristic of the gently sloping canyon floor made this area a favorite of the Indians, who had their summer hunting camps here. Foraging parties of Yokuts Indians made their "spur" camps along Bubbs Creek at many of the same spots chosen by today's backcountry travelers.

Soon our trail enters a cool, dense forest of alder, white fir and ponderosa and sugar pine, and we pass the Paradise Valley/ Woods Creek Trail branching north just before crossing a large steel bridge over the South Fork. We then pass a trail heading down-canyon and turn east to cross four branches of Bubbs Creek on expertly constructed log-and-plank bridges. The last bridge crossing marks the beginning of a series of steady switchbacks. This climb is hot and dry, so try to get an early start. Along this climb we find some rare (for this side of the Sierra) piñon pines. This tree, whose fruit provides the delicious pine nut, is of the single-needle group, and may be identified by either its single needle or its distinctive spherical cone. Most noticeable about the cone is its very thick, blunt, four-sided scale. This ascent offers fine views back into the dramatic U-shaped South Fork Kings River canyon. On the south side of the Bubbs Creek canyon the dominating landmark is the pronounced granite point known as The Sphinx. To the east its namesake stream cuts a sharp-lipped defile on the peak's east shoulder.

Above the switchbacks, as we angle toward tumbling Bubbs Creek, we re-enter the cool shade of tall conifers and climb past a drift fence. Soon you enter a section of the canyon that burned in 1976. One of the few noticeable effects of the fire now is the lack of shade. Fire is part of the ecosystem in Sierran forests. The extent to which trees are killed in a fire is partly a function of how hot the fire is. Generally, fires here are relatively cool, and they burn mostly dead wood and brush near the ground. But if dead wood accumulates for a long time due to natural conditions or human fire suppression, the eventual inevitable fire is likely to be hot, and will kill even tall trees. Fire-adapted plants regrow quickly, and on the trail here you see manzanita, black oaks, young Jeffrey pines and white firs. Some of the young trees may eventually produce a mature forest like the one at Charlotte Creek. There are good campsites several hundred feet beyond this creek under tall white firs (one-night stay only; bear boxes). In nearby Bubbs Creek fishing is good for brown, brook, rainbow and golden-rainbow hybrid trout (to 10″).

2nd Hiking Day (**Charlotte Creek** to **Vidette Meadow**, 5½ miles); From Charlotte Creek the grade alternates between shady and fern-lined, and steep, rocky and dusty. The steep southern rampart of Mt. Bago is up to the left as we arrive at the campsites at the west end of long Junction Meadow, where there are two major camping areas, each with a bear box: at the west end just before a drift fence below the meadow proper, and at the east end across Bubbs Creek along the East Lake Trail. (No grazing.) At the east end of the meadow our route passes the East Lake Trail, begins a steady, rocky climb and soon emerges onto a sparsely forested hillside. Bubbs Creek, on the right, flows down through a steep, narrow gorge, and it is worthwhile to walk over a few yards at one of the right-hand switchbacks to look at the spectacular cascades and waterfalls.

The steepest part of the climb ends at the top of these switchbacks, and then the trail proceeds on a moderate ascent past the ruins of a drift fence under an old, weathered foxtail pine. Looking back, one has fine views of the avalanche-scarred north face of West Spur. The ascent is gentle now, and we soon arrive at a junction with the John Muir Trail at Lower Vidette Meadow (bear box). Here our route turns right, fords the outlet creek from Bullfrog Lake, and arrives at the good campsites (9600') above beautiful Vidette Meadow, scattered along Bubbs Creek. Fishing for brook and rainbow trout (to 8") is fair. Because of the area's heavy use, a toilet pit is located several dozen yards down-canyon from the trail junction, just uphill from the Bubbs Creek Trail.

3rd Hiking Day: Retrace your steps, 13 miles.

Southern rampart of Mt. Bago

58

Cedar Grove to Charlotte Lake

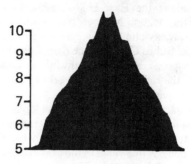

TRIP   From Cedar Grove Roadend to Charlotte Lake
            (round trip). Topo maps *Marion Peak, Mt. Pinchot*
            15'; *Mt. Clarence King* 7½'. Best mid or late
            season; 33 miles.

| | Trail/layover | Total recom- |
Grade	days	mended days
Leisurely	5/1	6
Moderate	4/1	5
Strenuous	2/1	3

HILITES   Striking right into the heart of the high country, this
            route ascends a lengthy stretch of the Bubbs Creek
            drainage to the charming meadows at the foot of the
            Kearsarge Pinnacles and Videttes. The terminus of
            this trip, Charlotte Lake, is a base camp location for
            cross-country trips to Gardiner Basin.

DESCRIPTION (Leisurely trip)

1st and 2nd Hiking Days: Follow trip 57 to **Vidette Meadow,** 13
miles.

3rd Hiking Day (**Vidette Meadow** to **Charlotte Lake,** 3½ miles): First,
retrace your steps to the junction of the John Muir Trail and the
Bubbs Creek Trail. Following the Muir Trail as it switchbacks up
the steep north side of the canyon, the traveler is treated to
breathtaking views of the Kearsarge Pinnacles to the east and of
the Videttes and snow-necklaced Deerhorn Mountain to the

south. It is easy, while viewing this spectacle, to understand the popularity of the Muir Trail, and it is with a sense of loss that one leaves the Bubbs Creek valley and crosses the lip of the Bullfrog Lake basin. Our route crosses a small creek twice, bypasses the first of several laterals to Bullfrog Lake (no camping) and continues northwest on a series of switchbacks to a junction with the Charlotte Lake Trail. This trail leaves the Muir Trail at an **X** junction in a sandy saddle (not shown on the 7½′ topo) and, after providing one last look back to the Bubbs Creek drainage and far south into Center Basin, with the Kings-Kern Divide in the background, zigzags down to Charlotte Lake. High on the left of the switchbacks tower the several summits of red-rocked Mt. Bago. Good campsites and a bear box may be found along the north side of the lake (10370′). Emergency services are usually available from a resident summer ranger. Fishing for rainbow and brook trout (to 10″) is good.

4th Hiking Day (**Charlotte Lake** to **Junction Meadow**, 5 miles): Retrace the steps of the 3rd and part of the 2nd hiking day.

5th Hiking Day (**Junction Meadow** to **Cedar Grove Roadend**, 11½ miles): Retrace the steps of part of the 2nd and all of the 1st hiking day.

Tarn on Bullfrog Lake's outlet stream

59   **Cedar Grove to Gardiner Basin**

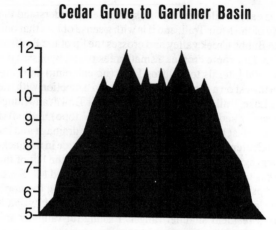

TRIP   From Cedar Grove Roadend to Sixty Lake Basin
            (round trip). Topo maps *Marion Peak, Mt. Pinchot*
            15'; *The Sphinx, Mt. Clarence King* 7½'. Best mid
            or late season; 49 miles.

Grade	Trail/layover days	Total recommended days
Leisurely	....	....
Moderate	7/1	8
Strenuous	5/0	5

HILITES   The hiker who values serenity and seclusion amid
            true alpine surroundings, and is tired of encoun-
            tering the swarms of hikers and campers who crowd
            the Muir Trail and other popular routes in the Sierra,
            will appreciate Sixty Lake Basin. This sanctuary,
            ringed by granite ridges and sharp peaks, offers a
            genuine wilderness experience and the option of an
            exciting cross-country excursion to upper Gardiner
            Basin.

DESCRIPTION (Moderate trip)

1st 3 Hiking Days: Follow trip 58 to **Charlotte Lake**, 16½ miles.

4th Hiking Day (**Charlotte Lake** to **Sixty Lake Basin**, 8 miles): First retrace your steps to the **X** junction on the sandy saddle. From there take the Muir Trail over Glen Pass to the junction with the Sixty Lake Basin Trail just before the isthmus between the upper Rae Lakes mentioned in the 3rd hiking day of Trip 60.

We leave the junction bearing northward, cross a marshy area, and begin climbing west on switchbacks offering superb views of Rae Lakes. A northwest traverse and some switchbacks bring us to the lake just below the unnamed saddle that is our "pass". We round the lake on its north, traverse to the saddle (11,200′), and take in the fine view to the west of stark, sharp-peaked Mts. Cotter and Clarence King before descending on steep, rocky switchbacks to the shore of a lake at about 11,000′ with a sandy campsite near its outlet. Beyond its outlet we round the ridge that separates upper Sixty Lake Basin into east and west sub-basins, and pause to get our bearings near a good campsite that over-looks the lake at 10,720′ north of the nose of this ridge. Fin Dome serves as our reference point from most of the basin, which is higher and less forested than adjacent Rae Lakes. This basin is convoluted, particularly at its southern, higher end, and each hollow in the granite holds a pleasant surprise for the rambler: a meadow, a small campsite, a bubbling stream, or a lake or two. Hang food away from bears, gear from marmots.

The "trail" leads northwest from here as a beaten track; look for it or for the occasional duck. Small trout inhabit the northern, lower lakes.

A cross-country trek southwest brings you to the narrow lake southeast of Mt. Cotter, which offers access to upper Gardiner Basin via the Class 2–3 col a mile south of Mt. Cotter. If you are comfortable on Class 2 terrain, you can go high around the lake's west side to avoid cliffs around the bay at its inlet. Then you can work your way up granite ledges to the col. A possible route down to magnificent, desolate Lake 3477 (metric) in upper Gardiner Basin descends talus and sand ledges from about the middle of the col. Further exploration of Gardiner Basin is pos-sible from here. (The old trail over Gardiner Pass has vanished in dense forest and is not recommended.)

5th through 7th Hiking Days: Reverse your steps, 24½ miles.

60

Cedar Grove to Rae Lakes

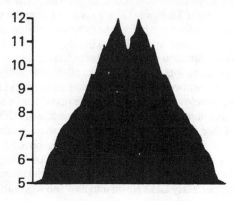

TRIP   From Cedar Grove Roadend to Rae Lakes via Vidette Meadow, Glen Pass (round trip). Topo maps *Marion Peak, Mt. Pinchot* 15′; *The Sphinx, Mt. Clarence King* 7½′. Best late season; 42 miles.

Grade	Trail/layover days	Total recom- mended days
Leisurely	6/2	8
Moderate	5/1	6
Strenuous	4/1	5

HILITES   Rae Lakes have long been a favorite of the high-country hiker and photographer—and with good cause. Situated beyond Glen Pass, and between the Sierra crest and the King Spur, these lakes are a scenic paradise. Because of this, and because of the central location, anyone contemplating this trip should plan on spending some days exploring the surrounding terrain.

DESCRIPTION (Moderate trip)

1st 2 Hiking Days: Follow trip 57 to **Vidette Meadow**, 13 miles.

3rd Hiking Day (**Vidette Meadow** to **Rae Lakes**, 8 miles): From Vidette Meadow our route follows the John Muir Trail north as it climbs out of Bubbs Creek canyon. This climb parallels and sometimes crosses a tributary stream in a series of switchbacks.

Excellent views of the Kearsarge Pinnacles to the east complement the view of the Videttes to the south. Beyond the Videttes tower the peaks of the Kings-Kern Divide, foregrounded by the barren granite of Center Basin. The peaks of the main Sierra crest appear to the northeast, and although mostly white granite, some of the higher peaks reveal more ancient sedimentary and metamorphic rocks.

Our route, on the John Muir Trail, passes a trail lateral to Bullfrog Lake (no camping) and, at the top of the climb, a lateral to Charlotte Lake and a trail to Kearsarge Pass. From the Charlotte Lake Trail, our route turns north on a long, steady ascent that rounds a granite promontory; then it descends slightly and veers east. As the headwall of Glen Pass comes into view, it is hard to see where a passable trail could go up it. And indeed the last 500 feet up to the top are steeply switchbacking—but never on the edge of a cliff. This trail section offers good views of Charlotte Lake, the Charlotte Creek canyon, Charlotte Dome and Mt. Brewer. At the pass (11,978'), one can look north down on the unnamed glacial lakes immediately to the north, and several of the Rae Lakes below.

The descent from the pass is by zigzagging, rocky switchbacks down to the granite bench holding the unnamed lakes seen from the pass. (The bad underfooting here requires care in placing one's feet.) After crossing the outlet stream of these lakes, the trail resumes its switchbacking descent, re-enters a pine forest cover and skirts the west shore of upper Rae Lake. Just before the trail crosses the narrow isthmus separating the upper lake from the rest of the chain, we pass a spur trail branching west to Sixty Lake Basin. After crossing the sparsely timbered isthmus, the route swings north, passes the unmarked, unmaintained lateral to Dragon Lake, and arrives at the many good campsites near the east shores of middle and lower Rae Lakes (10,560'). Fishing is good for brook trout and some rainbow (to 16"). (Camping is limited to one night each at the three Rae Lakes.) Views from the campsites across the beryl-green lake waters to dramatically exfoliating Fin Dome and the King Spur beyond are among the best and longest remembered of the trip, along with sun-up views of Painted Lady in the south. A summer ranger is stationed on the east shore of the middle lake. Bears are a serious problem here; you must guard your food and use the bear boxes.

4th and 5th Hiking Days: Retrace your steps, 21 miles.

61

Cedar Grove to Rae Lakes

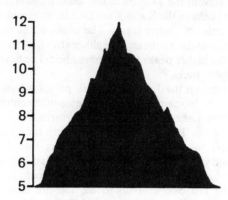

TRIP   From Cedar Grove Roadend to Rae Lakes, return via South Fork Woods Creek, Paradise Valley (loop trip). Topo maps *Marion Peak, Mt. Pinchot* 15′; *The Sphinx, Mt. Clarence King* 7½′. Best late season; 41½ miles.

Grade	Trail/layover days	Total recom- mended days
Leisurely	7/2	9
Moderate	6/1	7
Strenuous	4/1	5

HILITES   Known as the "Rae Lakes Loop," this fine trip circles the King Spur. The landscape viewed en route is dramatic enough to challenge the most accomplished photographer or artist as the route circles beneath the Videttes and the Kearsarge Pinnacles and visits the exceptionally beautiful Rae Lakes.

DESCRIPTION (Moderate trip)

1st 3 Hiking Days: Follow trip 60 to **Rae Lakes**, 21 miles.

4th Hiking Day (**Rae Lakes** to **Woods Creek Crossing**, 6½ miles): The trail covered in this hiking day is an easy downhill stretch that traces the length of South Fork Woods Creek. Beginning from the campsites on the east side of Rae Lakes, the trail continues along the east side of the lake chain and the intervening stream on a moderate descent. Fin Dome drops behind, and the outstanding landmark is then Diamond Peak to the east. The long black striations seen along the face of Diamond Peak and the continuing ridge to the north are metamorphosed lava, one of the few remaining bits of volcanic evidence to be found in this area. Just west of Diamond Peak the trail fords South Fork Woods Creek and skirts the west side of the lowest lake of the Rae Lakes chain. At the outlet our route passes the turnoff to Baxter Pass, and then descends more sharply over rocky stretches that are interrupted by pockets of alluvial sand. The valley floor is relatively open as the trail descends and crosses the stream draining Sixty Lake Basin (difficult ford in early season) and the stream draining Lake 10296.

Rounding the northernmost prominence of the King Spur, the trail veers west, and its moderate descent levels off as it approaches the Woods Creek Crossing. A few yards above this crossing the traveler should keep an eye peeled for one of this region's most interesting historic landmarks, one of Shorty Lovelace's unusual line cabins, which still stands on the west side of the creek. Those who take time out to examine this structure will soon discern its unique character. Appearing to be almost a miniature replica of the real article, it was erected to suit the needs of its builder, and it would scarcely accommodate the average person—standing or sleeping. It was from this cabin and several others in this general area that Shorty worked his trap line before it was included within the Park's boundaries. The trail crosses Woods Creek (8492') just below the confluence of the south and north forks. Fair campsites may be found near the crossing (difficult in early season). Fishing in the creek is good for brook and rainbow (to 10").

5th Hiking Day (**Woods Creek Crossing** to **Paradise Valley**, 7 miles): Leaving the John Muir Trail our route turns west, staying on the north side of Woods Creek. The underfooting is alternately sandy and rocky as the trial descends gently between the narrowing canyon walls. The forest cover, still predominantly lodgepole, shows inclusions of red fir as the altitude lessens, and clumps of the water-loving quaking aspen dot the stream banks. This smooth-barked, whispering tree is the most conspicuous member of the deciduous group found in the high country.

Always found near running water or at the edge of porous seepage areas (lava, talus, gravel), it acts as a native water locator, and its ghostly white trunk can be seen for great distances. Hikers who have camped in a grove of aspen will always remember the tree's gentle rustling sound as the leaves, responding to the slightest breeze, tremble against one another.

Soon the trail passes a burn scar and winds through Castle Domes Meadow, named for the obvious landmarks to the north. Undulating up and down the north canyon wall, the trail descends on a moderate grade, fords two unnamed right-bank tributaries, and then descends more steeply to a ford of South Fork Kings River. In late season the ford of the South Fork, which is in two channels here, is not difficult. The first channel is forded by proceeding down from where the trail meets the river for about 75 yards to a log jam, and then the next channel can be boulder-hopped. In early and mid season this is not possible. About 100 yards east of where the trail meets the river there is a trail leading up the east bank of the South Fork to an area above the divergence of the two channels. Above this there are two footlogs. Cross one of these logs and follow the west bank down to the point where the trail fords the South Fork by its confluence with Woods Creek. After the ford, the trail turns southwest and descends gently past a drift fence to the open expanses of Paradise Valley (6640'). Good campsites are near the stream, and fishing for rainbow and some brown is fair (to 8").

6th Hiking Day (**Paradise Valley** to **Cedar Grove Roadend**, 7 miles): On a gentle descent through a mixed forest cover of lodgepole, red fir, white fir, Jeffrey pine and some juniper and aspen, the trail continues southwest. At the lower end of Paradise Valley, the descent steepens, and the smooth, serpentining South Fork Kings River straightens out and dashes down the canyon. Views during this descent include the already familiar landmark, The Sphinx. Midway down this stretch the trail pauses in its descent near Mist Falls, a cascade that deserves its name only during times of high water, because by midsummer this white-water tumble becomes sedate and subdued. Beyond Mist Falls the grade eases before leveling out in the area above the confluence of South Fork Kings River and Bubbs Creek. A short distance farther on, our route meets and joins the Bubbs Creek Trail, and returns over the short 2-mile stretch described in the 1st hiking day.

Cedar Grove to Oak Creek Roadend   **62**

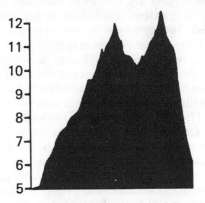

TRIP

From Cedar Grove Roadend to Oak Creek Roadend via Bubbs Creek, Glen Pass, Rae Lakes, Baxter Pass (shuttle trip). Topo maps *Marion Peak, Mt. Pinchot* 15'; *The Sphinx, Mt. Clarence King, Kearsarge Peak* 7½'. Best late season; 36½ miles.

Grade	Trail/layover days	Total recommended days
Leisurely	7/2	9
Moderate	5/2	7
Strenuous	4/1	5

HILITES

This trans-Sierra crossing makes a delightful **S**-curve as it journeys north from Bubbs Creek canyon over Glen Pass to Rae Lakes and then emerges on the east side via little-used Baxter Pass. The scenic lakes and towering, Alp-like peaks of this route make this a fine route for photography.

DESCRIPTION (Moderate trip)

1st 3 Hiking Days: Follow trip 60 to **Rae Lakes**, 21 miles.

4th Hiking Day (**Rae Lakes** to **Baxter Lakes**, 5½ miles): The first 2½ miles of this day's hike follow the gentle-to-moderate descent of South Fork Woods Creek. From Rae Lakes the trail passes through granite slab areas broken by stands of dwarfed

lodgepole as it skirts the east side of the lower lakes of the Rae
Lakes chain. Anglers will want to try their luck for the good
brook trout fishing on some of these lakes and the stream flowing
between them. The route fords the stream between the lowest
and next to lowest lakes, and circles the west side of the lowest
lake before leaving the John Muir Trail at the outlet of this lake,
sometimes called Dollar Lake. We cross the outlet on logs and
pick up a faint, unsigned, sometimes ducked trail that diagonals
up the east wall of the valley. This ascent makes a long northward
traverse, and from it we have fine views down the canyon of the
South Fork. On the far side, a very evident line is the John Muir
Trail, and most likely we will see a number of hikers on this
wilderness boulevard. After a mile of ascent, the trail descends
down into the Baxter Creek drainage, into a handsome grove of
foxtail pines that give welcome shade. Then it swings east to continue the steep ascent to the Baxter Lakes. The trail here is
ducked but sometimes hard to see as it follows the course shown
on the topo map. The sparse forest cover thins as the route fords
Baxter Creek and passes several tiny lakelets. Fair campsites
may be found in a grove of whitebark pines below the treeless
highest lake (11,150'), where fishing for brook trout (to 12") is
good.

5th Hiking Day (**Baxter Lakes** to **Oak Creek Roadend**, 10 miles): After
rounding the north side of the highest and largest lake of the
basin, the trail turns south as it ascends the steep granite slope
above the lake. Excellent views of Mt. Baxter and Acrodectes
Peak to the north accompany the climb.

Our rocky footpath ascends southwest, mostly on a moderate
grade, and then descends momentarily across a snowfield. Even
in this high, mineral world the vegetable kingdom stays alive, in
the form of small specimens of alpine sorrel, Davidson's
penstemon and Sierra primrose. Finally, the trail switchbacks up
to scree-laden Baxter Pass (12,320'), where one has fine views
of the Sierra crest, including multistriped Diamond Peak to the
southwest, the North Fork Oak Creek canyon to the south,
looking like a vertical-sided, giant gash, and even the town of
Independence, far below in Owens Valley. The trail is over loose
rock as it descends to Summit Meadow, where one can enjoy the
russet and copper colors of the nearby rocks. The trail stays
mostly well above the tumbling waters of North Fork Oak Creek,
undulating down through many fields of very colorful wild-

Sierra South Update

Page 176: Substitute the following for all of pp. 176-77:

lodgepole as it skirts the east side of the lower lakes of the Rae Lakes chain. Anglers will want to try their luck for the good brook trout fishing on some of these lakes and the stream flowing between them. The route fords the stream between the lowest and next to lowest lakes, and circles the west side of the lowest lake before leaving the John Muir Trail at the outlet of this lake, sometimes called Dollar Lake. Look north across this outlet for a little ridge that trends northeast-southwest. Cross the outlet to get to that ridge, and pick up the unsigned, faint, sometimes ducked Baxter Pass "Trail" on it. Our route crosses the valley and then diagonals north up the valley's east wall, sometimes very steeply, over scree. From it we have fine views down the canyon of the South Fork. On the far side, a very evident line is the John Muir Trail, and most likely we will see a number of hikers on this wilderness boulevard. After a mile of ascent, the trail descends down into the Baxter Creek drainage, into a handsome grove of foxtail pines that give welcome shade. Then it swings east to continue the steep ascent to Baxter Lakes. The route here is ducked but sometimes hard to see as it follows the course shown on the topo map. The sparse forest cover thins as the route fords Baxter Creek and passes several tiny lakelets. Fair campsites may be found in a grove of whitebark pines below the highest lake (11,150'), where fishing for brook trout (to 12") is good.

5th Hiking Day (**Baxter Lakes** to **Oak Creek Roadend,** 10 miles): After rounding the north side of the highest and largest lake in the basin (last reliable water until you are below timberline on the other side of the pass), the trail turns south as it ascends the steep scree slope above the lake. Excellent views of Mt. Baxter and Acrodectes Peak to the north accompany the climb, and the coloring of the scree is extraordinary. Our mostly rocky footpath ascends southwest, mostly on a steep grade, and then descends momentarily across a snowfield. Even in this high, mineral world the vegetable kingdom stays alive, in the form of small specimens of alpine sorrel, Davidson's penstemon and Sierra primrose. Finally the trail twists steeply up to scree-laden Baxter Pass (12,320'), where one has fine views of the Sierra crest, including multistriped Diamond Peak to the southwest, the North Fork Oak Creek canyon to the south, looking like a vertical-sided, giant gash, and even the town of Independence, far below in Owens Valley.

The east side of Baxter Pass involves a descent of 6300 feet in 9 miles on an irregularly maintained route through a narrow canyon of rotten rock. This descent calls for patience and care; the upper

1300 feet are scree. The route is subject to washouts and slides, so we may encounter precipitous detours over loose rock and unexpected fords. It generally stays well away from the creek, limiting our opportunities for water. Lower portions may be heavily overgrown. Expected campsites may have been buried under rubble or be filled with chaparral. Along the trail in 1990, places combining level open ground and access to water included a bench near 11,000' next to the creek and another near 8700' with a very steep trail of use 75 feet down to the creek. In spite of these difficulties, breather stops allow us to enjoy the spectacular scenery and the patches of very colorful wildflowers that include monkey flower, arnica, milfoil, cinquefoil, pennyroyal, buckwheat, spiraea, gilia and penstemon.

As we descend below the bench near 8700', the route begins to resemble a trail. We ford the creek (difficult in high water) in the middle of a mixed forest cover, and soon embark on another long set of zigzags. These are succeeded by a gentle, sandy descent to end with a few more quick switchbacks down to the last crossing of the rubble-filled main creek. As the trail drops to the creek, one encounters a good sampling of typical east-side Sierra flora including rabbit brush, bitter brush, sagebrush and mountain mahogany. Recent washouts may have erased the trail, but we can escape the creek bed by climbing north over a heap of boulders and picking up a sandy trail that soon dips under black oaks, crosses a tributary, and emerges on an exposed ridge. We descend this ridge past the wilderness boundary to the parking area under the welcome shade of oak trees.

193: There is one overnight campground at Horseshoe Meadow.

196: The described saddle is 0.6 mile west-southwest of Mt. Tyndall.

213: Whitney Creek is the last reliable water until Wallace Creek in a dry year.

223: The Shepherd Pass Trail east of the pass was considerably improved by a trail crew in 1989. No wood fires are permitted at Anvil Camp.

246: The "Guyot Flat Trail" is really the Pacific Crest Trail.

247: Total trip mileage is 21 3/4. Fourth day mileage is 4.

253: Total trip mileage is 28. First day mileage is 4.

257: We join the Pacific Crest Trail before reaching the large meadow.

259: Total trip mileage is 35 1/2;. First day mileage is 4. "1 easy mile" in first day should be 2/3 mile.   5th ed. 2nd ptg.

flowers that include monkey flower, arnica, milfoil, cinquefoil, pennyroyal, buckwheat, spiraea, gilia, penstemon, Queen Anne's Lace, shooting star, paintbrush and buttercup.

Midway down this long, flowery descent we ford the creek (difficult at high water) in the middle of a mixed forest cover, and soon embark on another long set of zigzags. These are succeeded by a gentle sandy descent to end with a few more quick switchbacks down to the last crossing of the creek. As the trail drops to the creek, one encounters a good sampling of typical east-side Sierra flora including rabbit brush, bitter brush, sagebrush, juniper, and mountain mahogany. Beyond a log over North Fork Oak Creek we leave the John Muir Wilderness, boulder-hop a side stream, and arrive at a dirt road west of Oak Creek Campground.

Mist Falls on the South Fork Kings River

63

Cedar Grove to Lake Reflection

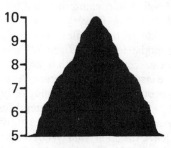

TRIP   From Cedar Grove Roadend to Lake Reflection (round trip). Topo maps *Marion Peak, Mt. Pinchot, Mt. Whitney* (W.P.V.) 15'; *The Sphinx, Mt. Clarence King, Mt. Brewer* 7½'. Best mid or late season; 30 miles.

Grade	Trail/layover days	Total recommended days
Leisurely	6/1	7
Moderate	4/1	5
Strenuous	3/1	4

HILITES Those who appreciate the serenity of high, alpine lake basins will find this trip to the upper reaches of East Creek a rewarding choice. Excellent fishing amidst spellbinding surroundings makes this a fine angling trip, and if one doesn't fish, it is time well spent just "soaking up the country."

DESCRIPTION (Moderate trip)

1st Hiking Day (**Cedar Grove Roadend** to **Charlotte Creek**, 7½ miles): Proceed to Charlotte Creek as in the 1st hiking day, trip 57.

2nd Hiking Day (**Charlotte Creek** to **Lake Reflection**, 8 miles): Proceed to Junction Meadow, as described in part of the 2nd hiking day, trip 57. At Junction Meadow our trail branches right, fords Bubbs Creek by a log, and starts to ascend East Creek canyon. This ascent is accomplished via rocky switchbacks that zigzag through a sparse-to-moderate forest cover of lodgepole, fir, silver pine and some aspen. The view back to the north is dominated by the red metamorphic rocks of Mt. Bago, with Mt. Gardiner coming into view beyond it. As one tops the first rise of the ascent, peaks of the Kings-Kern Divide come into view. Anglers trying their luck along East Creek will find rainbow and brook trout (to 8″), but the trout are somewhat larger in East Lake.

After a brief stretch of moderate uphill going the trail crosses East Creek via a log-and-plank bridge and then climbs steadily along the creek's east bank. The grade steepens and our route enters a forest of pines and firs. After the ford of an unnamed, fern-lined creek, our trail levels off near the outlet of East Lake. One's first view of these picturesque waters with their grassy fringes may be accompanied by a sighting of one of the many mule deer that frequent the canyon. The trail rounds the lake's east side to the fair-to-good campsites in dense forest at the head of the lake. The barren, unjointed granite walls that rise on either side—especially Mt. Brewer on the west—are an impressive backdrop for leisure moments spent on the shores of this mountain gem, and it is always with some reluctance that visitors move on. Beyond the head of East Lake the trail climbs steadily past a drift fence through rock-broken stands of lodgepole and foxtail pine. Just before crossing a 50-yard-wide rockpile, we pass the unmarked start of the Harrison Pass Trail. Beyond the talus slope, the easy grade traverses many wet areas along the east side of East Creek to the good campsites beside the little lake below Lake Reflection and at the northeast end of Lake Reflection (10,005′). The angler will find good fishing for golden, rainbow and hybrids (to 16″). When a breeze is not stirring the waters of this lake, the tableau of peaks reflected in their depths is a memorable scene of a scope seldom matched in the Sierra. At the head of the cirque basin, all side excursions are up, but the expenditure of sweat and effort required to explore the surrounding lakes and lakelets is repaid by great views and a sense of achievement that has been shared by many mountaineers since the Brewer Party first ascended these heights.

3rd and 4th Hiking Days: Retrace your steps, 15 miles.

64

Cedar Grove to Upper Kern River

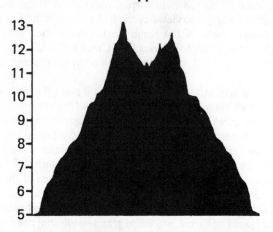

TRIP

From Cedar Grove Roadend to Upper Kern River via Bubbs Creek, Forester Pass, return by Harrison Pass, East Lake (semiloop trip). Topo maps *Marion Peak, Mt. Pinchot, Mt. Whitney* (W.P.V.) 15'; *The Sphinx, Mt. Clarence King, Mt. Brewer* 7½'. Best late season; 49 miles.

Grade	Trail/layover days	Total recommended days
Leisurely	....	....
Moderate	7/3	10
Strenuous	6/2	8

HILITES

Crossing two high passes, this trip explores the glaciated upper reaches of the Kern Trench and circumnavigates a good piece of the Kings-Kern and Great Western divides. This is a long and rugged route that is recommended for the hearty backcountry traveler possessed of a sense of adventure and a liking for high, barren surroundings.

DESCRIPTION (Strenuous trip)

1st Hiking Day: (**Cedar Grove Roadend** to **Junction Meadow,** 10 miles): Proceed to Junction Meadow as described in the 1st and part of the 2nd hiking day, trip 57.

2nd Hiking Day (**Junction Meadow** to **Upper Bubbs Creek**, 6½ miles):
Follow the 2nd hiking day, trip 57, to Vidette Meadow, where our
route joins the John Muir Trail and turns southeast, ascending
beside Bubbs Creek. About ½ mile above Vidette Meadow our
route passes an old trapper's cabin. Shorty Lovelace trapped this
country until it was made into a national park, and a network of
his cabins remains to remind today's travelers of an era of the
not-too-distant past. After the initial steep ascent above Vidette
Meadow, the trail levels out to a moderate but steady ascent
along the east bank of the creek through a moderate forest cover
of lodgepole and occasional hemlock. Several campsites line
Bubbs Creek, and those at 10,200 feet offer fine views of University
Peak to the east, Center Peak to the southeast, and East
Vidette and East Spur to the west. However, to be nearer
Forester Pass, we continue to the good campsites near the junction
with the Center Basin/Junction Pass Trail. Fishing for brook
trout (to 7") is good. Side excursions for golden-trout fishing or
mere pleasure can be made via the old Muir Trail route to Center
Basin.

3rd Hiking Day (**Upper Bubbs Creek** to **Outlet Stream of Lake 11440**, 9
miles): From these campsites the trail ascends more steeply over
the barren granite west of Center Peak. This climb takes one
above timberline as it winds back and forth over the tributary
that drains Lake 12248, and over one's shoulder the peaks of the
Sierra crest march away on the northern horizon. After fording
the outlet of Lake 12248, the trail climbs the west wall of the
canyon and then switchbacks steeply up to the narrow notch in
the Kings-Kern Divide that is Forester Pass (13180'). Views
from the pass to the northeast include Mt. Pinchot, University
Peak, Mt. Bradley and Mt. Keith. To the south are Mt. Kaweah,
the Kaweah Peaks Ridge, the Red Spur, Kern Point and Black
Kaweah. Close by, Caltech Peak is to the west and Junction Peak
to the east.

Leaving this windy orientation point behind, the trail descends
steeply by numerous, short switchbacks, some of which are mere
shelves carved into the steep face of the Junction Peak ridge. A
few hardy polemonium and some yellow hulsea share the high
slope with scurrying conies, and the traveler who lifts his eyes is
sometimes treated to a sighting of a golden eagle soaring high
above the granite steeples. After the trail levels off somewhat,
the rocky route winds among a number of unnamed lakes that

make up the headwaters of this branch of Tyndall Creek. To the east the unusual formation called Diamond Mesa appears as a sheer-walled, flat-topped ridge dangling from the jumbled heights of Junction Peak. Here, the trail passes through "marmot land," and the traveling human intruder is looked upon indulgently as a seasonal part of the scenery—accepted, at a respectful distance. Near timberline, our route intersects the signed Lake South America/Milestone Creek Trail and turns right onto it. This trail soon turns west, and then ascends gently at timberline for ½ mile to another signed junction, where the Lake South America Trail turns north and our route veers southwest. At the outlet stream of Lake 11440, the hiker should turn left and descend cross country to the good campsite (11,220′) in foxtail pines at the edge of the meadow ¼ mile south.

4th Hiking Day (**Outlet Stream of Lake 11440** to **East Lake**, 10 miles, part cross country): Retrace the steps of the previous hiking day to the Lake South America/Milestone Creek Trail junction, where this day's route turns north and ascends gently up the east side of a long, boulder-strewn meadow. At the head of this ascent, the trail becomes steeper and switchbacks up 500 feet of barren, broken granite to a saddle which give access to the large cirque basin at the head of the Kern River. Beside a charming little lake that feeds the Kern River our route meets a trail coming up from the river and turns right, toward Lake South America (so called from its shape), where the angler may wish to try the good fishing for golden (to 12″).

From here the trail is ducked as it climbs toward Harrison Pass. Ahead, locating the pass by visual sighting is difficult, as the lowest point on the headwall of the canyon is nearer Mt. Ericsson than the actual pass is. Our ducked route veers eastward, toward Mt. Stanford, where the best descent on the north side may be had. This descent is often snow-choked until late summer. Views from Harrison Pass to the south include Mt. Kaweah, Kaweah Peaks Ridge, Milestone Mountain and Mt. Guyot. Looking north, Deerhorn Mountain with its avalanche chutes and talus fans stands athwart the view, but Mt. Goddard can be seen far in the distance to the left of it, and Middle Palisade in the distance to its right. From the pass, the route leads north down the talus (sometimes over snow).

We carefully pick our way downward, toward the first lake visible on the cirque floor. Then we cross its outlet and veer west to ford the stream connecting the second and third lakes in the cirque. From here the ducked route ascends somewhat and then drops to the outlet of the third lake, passing close under the buff and tan granite cliffs of soaring Ericsson Crags. In the canyon below the third lake we encounter timber, and also achieve our first view of Mt. Brewer, due west across the canyon of East Creek. The route then levels off briefly in a meadow and fords the crystal stream to the north side. The white color of the trumpet-shaped flowers of alpine gentian in this meadow tells us we are still quite high; blue gentians lie below. After passing several lovely tarns not shown on the topo map, the ducked and some-times blazed trail easily crosses a little divide on a southbound course and traverses down to Golden Lake, where there is one excellent campsite. From the lake we have a direct view of Lucys Foot Pass, on the Kings-Kern Divide. This pass is Class 3 in places and it is not advised for ordinary backpacking or for inexperienced mountaineers. Due to all the loose "garbage" on the north side, the best passage is south-to-north.

From Golden Lake the route has a short level segment and then it descends steeply on a rocky-dusty, ill-maintained trail down poorly built switchbacks to the East Creek Trail, meeting it at an unsigned junction a few yards north of a rockslide. Here we turn right (north) and descend gently, sometimes moderately, for 1 mile to the good campsites at the north and south ends of East Lake, described in the 2nd hiking day, trip 63.

5th Hiking Day (**East Lake** to **Charlotte Creek**, 6½ miles): Descend to Junction Meadow, reversing part of the 2nd hiking day, trip 63, then retrace your steps to Charlotte Creek.

6th Hiking Day (**Charlotte Creek** to **Cedar Grove Roadend**, 7½ miles): Reverse the 1st hiking day, trip 57.

65   **Cedar Grove to East Lake**

TRIP   From Cedar Grove Roadend to Upper Kern River
and East Lake via Colby Pass and Harrison Pass
(semiloop trip). Topo maps *Marion Peak, Mt.
Pinchot, Mt. Whitney* (W.P.V.), *Triple Divide Peak*
(W.P.V.) 15′; *Mt. Kaweah, Mt. Brewer, Mt.
Clarence King, The Sphinx* 7½′. Best mid to late
season; 69½ miles.

Grade	Trail/layover days	Total recom- mended days
Leisurely	....	....
Moderate	9/4	13
Strenuous	7/2	9

HILITES   Few trips that do not involve shuttling cars offer the
variety of this loop around the major portion of the
Great Western Divide. This is a trip for experienced
backpackers, whose rewards for much effort will
include almost continuous views of the highest High
Sierra and great stretches of wilderness solitude.

DESCRIPTION (Moderate trip)

1st through 4th Hiking Days: Reverse the 8th through the 5th
hiking days, trip 71, 30 miles.

5th Hiking Day (**Kern-Kaweah River** to **Upper Kern River**, 7 miles): Reverse the 4th and part of the 3rd hiking day, trip 76 to the junction of the Kern River Trail and the High Sierra Trail. One half mile up the canyon from the junction is a roofless cabin that was a powder magazine used by crews constructing trails in this region. Beginning here are several good campsites along the river, where fishing is good for rainbow and golden trout (to 10″).

6th Hiking Day (**Upper Kern River** to **Outlet Stream of Lake 11440**, 9 miles): Reverse most of the 3rd hiking day, trip 70. At Lake 10650 our route turns right up a short, steep ascent through a cover of moderate lodgepole and foxtail. After half a mile the trail passes a picturebook lake which is fast (geologically speaking) becoming a meadow. The trail continues eastward up a moderate ascent through alternating rocky and meadowy sections, where the Oregon junco is likely to be seen flitting among the willows. Careful study of the ground as one walks along may discover a junco nest under the overhang of a boulder, a fallen log or a tree bole. This route climbs above timberline and crosses the ridge coming down from Point 12223, where there are good views back to the west of Mt. Jordan, Thunder Mountain, Milestone Mountain, Midway Mountain, Kern Ridge and the Red Spur. Beyond this point the trail descends slightly and skirts the north side of a small, unnamed lake. Just beyond this lake the trail meets the outlet stream of Lake 11440. Here the hiker should turn right and descend cross country to the good campsite at the edge of the meadow ¼ mile south.

7th, 8th and 9th Hiking Days: Follow the 4th through the 6th hiking days, trip 64, 23½ miles.

Onion Valley to Flower Lake

10 ⌐
9 ⌐

TRIP   From Onion Valley to Flower Lake (round trip).
Topo map *Mt. Pinchot* 15'; *Kearsarge Peak* 7½'.
Best early or mid season; 5 miles.

| | Trail/layover
days | Total recom-
mended days |
Grade	days	mended days
Leisurely	2/0	2
Moderate	....	....
Strenuous	day	....

HILITES   Employing one of the "easiest" east-side entries,
this trip climbs to the friendly lakes making up the
headwaters of Independence Creek. The ample
opportunities for good angling and the exciting
alpine scenery occupy one's weekend time in grand
style.

DESCRIPTION (Leisurely trip)

1st Hiking Day (**Onion Valley** to **Flower Lake**, 2½ miles): The trail
leaves the road a few yards north of the Onion Valley campground and switchbacks up a dry, manzanita-covered slope.
Switchbacks always seem to come in bunches, and this ascent is
no exception. The first set of switchbacks is relatively open and
exposed, offering fine views back on Onion Valley and south to
the heavily diked summit of Independence Peak. After about ⅓
mile there is a short level stretch where one may study the
distinctive shapes of the large foxtail pines nearby. Then the trail
enters the John Muir Wilderness and switchbacks steadily again,
until after a mile it comes close enough to tumbling Independence Creek that only a few steps are needed to reach the wild-
flower-lined stream bank and slake one's thirst.

After this draught, on a more gradual slope, our path crosses
many runoff rills in early and mid season, where a neophyte
botanist may identify specimens of Queen Anne's lace, paintbrush, wallflower, tiger lily, columbine, shooting star and
whorled penstemon. At the top of this gentle grade is Little

Pothole Lake, not much for camping, but boasting two beautiful, willow-lined cascades pouring into its south and west bays.
After another set of rocky switchbacks, the trail levels off in a
slightly ascending groove across glacial moraine and then
reaches small, round Gilbert Lake (10,417'). Poor-from-over-
use campsites dot the shores of this fine swimming lake, and
fishing for rainbow and brook trout is good in early season (bear
pole near outlet). This small lake absorbs much of the day-hiking
impact from people camping at Onion Valley, as does Flower
Lake, at the top of the next set of switchbacks. Less used and
more scenic are Matlock and Bench lakes, the first reached by an
unmarked trail that leads south from the east side of Flower
Lake, and the second, cross country west from the first. There
are a bear pole and many highly used campsites along the north
and east sides of this shallow lake (10,531'). Fishing for rainbow and some brook trout is fair on this small lake, but serious
anglers will hike to the more distant lakes in the timbered cirque
basin to the south.

2nd Hiking Day: Retrace your steps, 2½ miles.

Kearsarge Lakes and pinnacles

67

Onion Valley to Cedar Grove

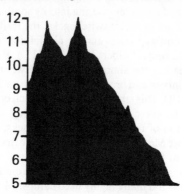

TRIP
From Onion Valley to Cedar Grove Roadend via Kearsarge Pass, Charlotte Lake, Glen Pass, Rae Lakes, South Fork Woods Creek, Paradise Valley (shuttle trip). Topo maps *Mt. Pinchot, Marion Peak 15'; Kearsarge Peak, Mt. Clarence King, The Sphinx 7½'*. Best mid or late season; 34 miles.

Grade	Trail/layover days	Total recommended days
Leisurely	6/2	8
Moderate	5/2	7
Strenuous	4/2	6

HILITES
Kearsarge Pass, because of its relatively low elevation and its proximity to an east-side roadend, is a popular way to reach the John Muir Trail. Because of this popularity, many of the lakes and meadows en route have been overrun, and Park officials have felt it necessary to close these "impacted" areas to grazing and camping. Despite these restrictions, the country retains its popularity, and anyone planning to tramp the Muir Trail in the vicinity of this pass should expect company.

DESCRIPTION (Leisurely trip)

1st Hiking Day: Follow trip 66 to **Flower Lake**, 2½ miles.

2nd Hiking Day (**Flower Lake** to **Charlotte Lake**, 5½ miles): At Flower Lake the Kearsarge Pass Trail turns north and ascends steeply to a viewpoint overlooking Heart Lake. From this point the trail switchbacks up to another overlook—this time the lake is the nearly perfect blue oval of Big Pothole Lake. From the trail high above the water, the lake, with its backgrounding granite finger, is particularly photogenic. From the switchbacks on, the trail rises above timber, except for a few hardy whitebark specimens, and then makes two long-legged traverses across an exposed shaley slope to the low saddle of Kearsarge Pass (11,823'). To the west, the view is impressive, as it includes the Kearsarge Lakes, Bullfrog Lake and the serrated spires of the Kearsarge Pinnacles.

On the west side of the pass our route descends easily on a traverse high above the basin holding the Kearsarge and Bullfrog lakes. After passing a spur trail branching left to the Kearsarge Lakes (one-night stay limit; bear boxes) and Bullfrog Lake (no camping), the route continues westward on a gentle descent into sparse timber. Crossing several small runoff streams in early season, the rocky-sandy trail contours high on the viewful slopes above Bullfrog Lake.

Now descending steadily through sparse-to-moderate white-bark and foxtail pine, the trail offers fine views south to Center Peak and Junction Peak. On this viewful slope we reach a fork whose branches both go to the John Muir Trail. We take the left fork southwest. Our route descends gently onto a sandy flat in a broad saddle overlooking Charlotte Lake, where at an **X** junction (not shown on the 7½' topo) we take a signed trail that switchbacks down moderately-to-steeply for a short mile to Charlotte Lake (10,370'). Good campsites line the north shore (bear box), and fishing for rainbow and brook trout (to 10") is fair. Emergency services are usually available from the resident summer ranger on the north shore.

3rd Hiking Day (**Charlotte Lake** to **Rae Lakes**, 5½ miles): Retrace your steps to the John Muir Trail and then proceed as in the 3rd hiking day, trip 60.

4th, 5th and 6th Hiking Days: Follow the 4th, 5th and 6th hiking days, trip 61, 20½ miles.

Bubbs Creek to Lower Kern

This stretch of country composes the least visited, least known, and least trampled region in the southern Sierra. It owes its integrity not to its lack of scenic or recreational potential, but rather to the presence of a fortuitously placed series of natural barriers—the Great Western Divide, the Kings-Kern Divide, and the Sierra crest. Joined together in a U, they protect the first 24 miles of the Kern River watershed with a wall of mountains crossed only by 1) people who have business here (rangers, packers, etc.), 2) people who have a love for the high country, and 3) people who fly over. There's no need to take aircraft over this region, and low-flying supersonic jets especially detract from one's wilderness experience. Within the mountainous U shape, the Kern River flows through a 30-mile section of straight, glacier-scoured canyon. This deep, spectacular canyon is very unusual for the Sierra in that it runs north-south instead of east-west.

The one area described in this region that sits outside this protective cup of divides and ranges is the Roaring River Country. Remoteness from roads and a convoluted terrain guarantee its sanctuary. And sanctuary it is, for in the remote headwaters of Roaring River a hiker can walk for one, two, or even three days without seeing a soul.

This high region has a delicate balance between plant and animal life, which is nowhere more manifest than in the alpine fell fields over Cottonwood Pass just west of Horseshoe Meadow, or around the subalpine meadows just south of Little Claire Lake over the crest from Mineral King. Here, in an incredibly brief 6–7-week span, some 40 varieties of hardy-yet-vulnerable grasses, sedges and flowering plants grow, bud, blossom, seed, and are harvested, running their appointed course under the daily threat of killing frost, and before the juggernaut deadline of the first winter snows. Caught in the complex "web of life," year-round resident animals like the cony, the marmot and the pocket gopher stake their very existence on the plants' explosively short summer tenure. Inexorably linked in the ecological chain, the migrating and hibernating carnivores, such as the coyote, mountain lion, black bear, red fox, marten, weasel and wolverine, would perish without their dependable rodent and squirrel food supply. So fragile and tenuous is this balance that the trampling by man and his livestock of a high, grassy meadow—particularly during the early, wet days of spring—can have and has had catastrophic effects upon the food chain.

This is not to argue that man does not have a place in this setting. His trails, within strict practical and esthetic limitations, are as legitimate as those of the deer. He has the right to share the fish of the streams and the berries of the hillside with the bear. Like the marmot, he has his place in the sun—preferably a big flat rock where he too can laze away a warm afternoon. Man's propensity for mountaintops and places of quiet solitude is as valid as the bighorn sheep's. And, like the Hermit thrush at nesting time, or the Brewer blackbird at sundown, he has the right to sing of his exultation at being alive and here.

But, because he knows the devastation wrought by large, concentrated numbers of his species upon this country, he owes it to his co-habiters, and to himself, to expand rather than constrict the size of primitive country, and to disperse his impact upon the country. Implicit within both of these obligations should be a profound respect for the ecological chain, of which man is a part, for this respect will give birth to a deeper knowledge and appreciation of the re-creating benefits of a region such as this. The authors hope that, beyond sharing their appreciation of and passion for this grand part of the Sierra, they might, with this modest guide, call the attention of the prospective traveler to the less traveled byways and thereby contribute, in small measure, to the distribution of human impact. Because many of the routes described here are the lesser traveled, they are therefore sometimes faint, but that is as it should be. The passes are sometimes steeper than those used on the more traveled routes, but the rewards of scenery and solitude are commensurate.

As the quality of the wilderness experience is important, so is the quantity. For it is only through public support that requisite public legislation and administrative decisions will reflect man's desire and need for wild areas. The more people that are introduced to basic wilderness values, perhaps through guides like this, the greater will be the demand for more and better wilderness areas and national parks. If pieces of untrammeled country like that between the Kings-Kern Divide and the lower Kern River remain bastions of peace and solitude, it will be not so much because government officials discourage and restrict wilderness travel as because more wilderness alternatives are created for people to use. The sooner people recognize this fact, the sooner the trend to wilderness attrition will be reversed.

Wood fires are *prohibited* in the following places: Kings Canyon National Park above 10,000'; Kern River drainage above 11,200' and in Nine Lake Basin; Kaweah River drainage above 9000' and at Hamilton Lakes; Cottonwood, Cirque, South Fork, and Rocky Basin lakes; anywhere within ¼ mile of Chicken Spring Lake. *Use a gas stove.*

There are seven trailheads cited in the text that give access to this region—three on the west side, and four on the east. You will need to pay a national park entrance fee or have an equivalent pass to get to the Lodgepole Campground, Crescent Meadow, and Mineral King trailheads.

Lodgepole Campground (6800'). From the north, go 50 miles east from Fresno on State Highway 180 to a junction with State Highway 198, then 26 miles southeast on 198 to Lodgepole Village; turn east and go to a parking area near the Lodgepole Nature Center. From the south, take 198 east through Visalia and Three Rivers. Continue northeast on it to Lodgepole, about 63 miles.

Crescent Meadow (6800'). Go about 2 miles south and east of Giant Forest Village on a road running past Moro Rock to the road's end.

Mineral King (7830'). Go 37 miles east from Visalia on State Highway 198, turn east, and go 23 miles on a mostly paved road. This narrow, winding 23 miles takes more than an hour to drive. Marmots were reported to have eaten parts of parked cars here a few years ago. Check with the ranger station for the current situation.

Symmes Creek Trailhead. Go 4½ miles west from Independence on the Onion Valley Road, turn left on Foothill Road and go 1.3 miles to a fork. Take the right-hand fork and go past an old corral on the left, then immediately cross Symmes Creek. In ½ mile take the right fork, and take the right fork again at the next two forks. Then proceed ½ mile to the trailhead near Symmes Creek. Some of these forks may have small signs.

Whitney Portal (8360′). Go 13 miles west from Lone Pine on the Whitney Portal road. A special permit situation exists for the Mt. Whitney Trail. For details, write Reservations, P.O. Box 8, Lone Pine, CA 93545 or phone them at 619-876-5542.

Cottonwood Lakes/Creek Trailhead (10,040′). From the center of Lone Pine on US 395 drive 3.5 miles west on the Whitney Portal Road, turn left, and go south 20 miles on Horseshoe Meadow Road past the old Cottonwood Lakes trailhead. Turn right at the sign for Cottonwood Lakes and drive about 1 more mile to the parking lot. There are restrooms, potable water, and a one-overnight campground here.

Horseshoe Meadow (9920′. Labeled "Kern Plateau" on 1986 USDA *Golden Trout Wilderness and South Sierra Wilderness* map.) Follow the directions for the Cottonwood Lakes Trailhead above, but don't turn right for Cottonwood Lakes. Instead, follow the road about ½ mile more to its end at a large parking lot where there are restrooms and potable water but no campground—the USDA map is wrong about that.

In the pool at Blayney Hot Springs

68   Symmes Creek Trailhead to Wright Lakes

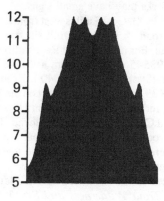

TRIP   From Symmes Creek Trailhead to Wright Lakes via Anvil Camp and Shepherd Pass (round trip). Topo map *Mt. Whitney* 15′ (W.P.V.); *Mt. Williamson* 7½′. Best mid or late season; 28 miles.

Grade	Trail/layover days	Total recom- mended days
Leisurely	....	....
Moderate	....	....
Strenuous	3/1	4

HILITES   This trip provides the great satisfaction of reaching the high, remote backcountry via a tough climb up the canyon of Shepherd Creek, one of the immense gashes that typify the eastern Sierra escarpment. The great elevation gain makes it a trip only for those in excellent physical condition. Indeed, Shepherd Pass is *the* most difficult trail pass in the Sierra Nevada.

DESCRIPTION (Strenuous trip)

1st Hiking Day (**Symmes Creek Trailhead** to **Anvil Camp,** 7½ miles): The trail begins at the mouth of the Symmes Creek canyon and gently ascends on the south side of the creek through piñon pine, sagebrush and, at streamside, alders, willows and cottonwoods.

The trail fords the creek four times (fill your water bottle at the fourth), passing clumps of early and mid-season columbine. From the fourth crossing the trail begins a long, gruelling series of rocky switchbacks that climb a whopping 2300 feet to a saddle between Shepherd and Symmes creeks. Above 8000 feet red fir and then silver pine form a moderate forest cover, and the entire hot slope supports sagebrush, mountain mahogany and creamberry. From the saddle at the head of this slope, one may take a rest while inspecting the great peak to the south, Mt. Williamson, second highest in California—though surprisingly, it is not on the Sierra crest. The deep, steep gash that contains Shepherd Creek falls away at one's feet, and it is an impressive introduction to the immense canyons of the eastern escarpment.

From the saddle, the sandy trail descends moderately over two small ridges high above Shepherd Creek before dropping 500 feet down to a dry creek bed. From here the trail rounds a ridge through a burned forest of piñon pines to arrive at the only year-round creek between Symmes Creek and Anvil Camp. Beyond this creek the trail switchbacks up to Mahogany Flat, where there are several campsites and water. At the upper end of this flat the trail begins a set of long brushy switchbacks to gain the elevation of the cascade visible to the southwest on Shepherd Creek. As the route crosses a large talus slope, the entire surroundings change dramatically within a few hundred feet. The trail has been largely on decomposed granite, and the vegetation generally sparse and desertlike. But as the trail reaches Anvil Camp (10,000') the experienced Sierra traveler suddenly recognizes that he is in the *High* Sierra: there is duff, a burbling stream, campsites, willows, grass, and young foxtail pines.

2nd Hiking Day (**Anvil Camp** to **Wright Lakes**, 6½ miles, part cross country): At Anvil Camp we ford Shepherd Creek and ascend moderately over rocky slopes on the south side of the creek. Our rough, rocky route crosses the area labeled "The Pothole" on the topo map, and then passes the ill-defined trail to Junction Pass on the right. (Until Forester Pass was opened in 1931 the John Muir Trail, in passing from the Kings River to the Kern River drainage, detoured to the east side of the Sierra crest over Junction Pass, descended to this trail junction, and recrossed westward over Shepherd Pass.) Now we ascend past great boulders to the giant declivity, below the pass, for which the name "The

Pothole" should have been reserved. Here is a gargantuan jumble of great jagged rocks that have been weathered out of the headwall of the cirque. The last 500 feet up to Shepherd Pass (12,050') are on a slope where the snow is thick in early season and may last all summer.

At the pass, the route enters Sequoia National Park. Views of the Great Western Divide are excellent, and they get even better as the trail descends down a broad, boulder-strewn field to alpine meadows and stands of foxtail pine. Immediately to the south is the northern flank of Mt. Tyndall (14,018'), which the famous mountaineer Clarence King climbed in 1864 believing it to be the highest Sierra peak. He did not realize his error until he reached the summit.

At the 11,600-foot level the hiker should leave the trail and traverse southwest cross-country to the saddle between Peak 13540 and Peak 12345. The panoramic view from this saddle includes the noble series of summits of the Great Western Divide, Junction Peak, Mts. Keith, Brewer, Kaweah, Guyot and Young, and the top of Mt. Whitney, as well as the Kern River trench. Even in this high rocky saddle there are flowers, including prostrate purple-flowered pussypaws. Our route traverses down the east wall of the cirque that lies south of the saddle, to the fair campsites in a grove of foxtails where the outlet stream of Lake 11952 meets the other two draining the upper basin. Fishing is good for golden (to 8").

3rd Hiking Day: Retrace your steps, 14 miles.

Rock glacier below Shepherd Pass

Symmes Creek Trailhead to Milestone Basin   69

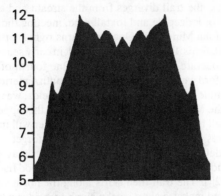

TRIP   From Symmes Creek Trailhead to Milestone Basin via Anvil Camp and Shepherd Pass (round trip). Topo map *Mt. Whitney* 15′ (W.P.V.); *Mt. Williamson, Mt. Brewer* 7½′. Best mid or late season; 38 miles.

Grade	Trail/layover days	Total recommended days
Leisurely	....	....
Moderate	....	....
Strenuous	4/1	5

HILITES   Milestone Basin is a fine choice for the lover of high country who wants to be alone. Many fish-filled lakes lie under the prepossessing heights of the Great Western Divide, where the delicate quality of the light and the air work their magic on all who come.

DESCRIPTION (Strenuous trip)

1st Hiking Day: Follow trip 68 to **Anvil Camp**, 7½ miles.

2nd Hiking Day (**Anvil Camp** to **Milestone Basin**, 11½ miles): Follow the 2nd hiking day, trip 68, from Anvil Camp to where that day's route leaves the Shepherd Pass Trail. Our route continues down the trail beside Tyndall Creek, through a huge, boulder-strewn, sloping meadow, with the 13,000-foot peaks of the Great

Western Divide filling the western horizon. After fording Tyndall Creek, the trail diverges from the stream and enters a sparse cover of lodgepole and foxtail pine, meeting the stream again at the John Muir Trail. Our route turns right (north) onto the Muir Trail, fords Tyndall Creek (difficult in early season) and ascends a moderate slope to timberline. One fourth of a mile from the last ford we turn left onto the Lake South America Trail. Then, a half mile farther on across alpine fell fields, we turn left again, onto the Milestone Basin Trail. Views in this upper Kern basin are at all times panoramic, and the traveler will mentally record pictures of the skyline he will not soon forget.

At the outlet stream of Lake 11440 the angler may wish to veer north and sample that lake's waters for the good fishing for golden (to 12"). The trail then skirts along the north side of a small lake, and makes a short, rocky climb to a ridge where the descent to the Kern River begins. From the ridge the traveler has closer views of Thunder Mountain, Milestone Mountain, Midway Mountain—all on the Great Western Divide—and Kern Ridge and Red Spur in the south. Past this viewpoint the trail descends moderately through rocky and meadowy sections with a moderate cover of foxtail, lodgepole and some whitebark pine, and arrives at a picturebook lake that is fast (geologically speaking) turning to meadow. One may regret that all these high lakes are doomed, but one may enjoy the blend of meadows and lakes existing in the time to which he was born.

After climbing slightly, our route begins the last, steep descent to the Kern River, where it emerges at an unnamed lake at 10,650 feet elevation (good fishing for golden and rainbow-golden hybrids to 10"). Our route turns left at the east side of this lake and descends gently beside the infant Kern River for about 200 yards to the trail turning west to Milestone Basin (look for ducks). If the ford here is too hard, there may be a log to cross on back at the outlet of the unnamed lake. After fording the river, the trail contours to meet Milestone Creek and then veers west up a rocky slope away from the creek. After another ½ mile it rejoins the creek at a bench where, beside a waterfall, there is a good campsite (11,110'). Fishing in Milestone Creek is good for rainbow (to 10"). Those who wish to camp as high as possible may climb to the high lake (11,900') just to the right of the words *Midway Mtn* on the topo map. Follow the ducked route that turns right up the north fork, passes through a defile, skirts a small lake barren of fish, and traverses up to the high lake, where fishing is good for golden (to 12"). There are fair campsites below this lake on the outlet stream.

3rd and 4th Hiking Days: Retrace your steps, 19 miles.

Lake Reflection

70 Symmes Creek Trailhead to Mineral King

TRIP   From Symmes Creek Trailhead to Mineral King via Anvil Camp, Shepherd Pass, Upper Kern River, Rattlesnake Creek and Franklin Pass (shuttle trip). Topo maps *Mt. Whitney* (W.P.V.), *Kern Peak, Mineral King* (W.P.V.) 15'; *Mt. Williamson, Mt. Brewer, Mt. Kaweah* 7½'. Best mid-to-late season; 53 miles.

Grade	Trail/layover days	Total recom- mended days
Leisurely	....	....
Moderate	....	....
Strenuous	6/1	7

HILITES   This long trans-Sierra trip provides a grand sample of everything the High Sierra has to offer: sweeping vistas, intimate groves, barren granite, streamside meadows, rainbow, golden, brook and brown trout, pages of geological history, access to the highest Sierra peaks, the marks of great glaciers, thick pine forests, alpine fell fields—and that feeling of grandeur which calls the backpacker to the Sierra again and again.

DESCRIPTION (Strenuous trip)

1st Hiking Day: Follow trip 68 to **Anvil Camp,** 7½ miles.

2nd Hiking Day (**Anvil Camp** to **Lake on Upper Kern River**, 10 miles): Follow the 2nd hiking day, trip 69, to the lake on the Kern River at 10,650 feet elevation, where the Milestone Basin Trail meets the Kern River Trail. There are good campsites at the lake inlet, and fishing is good for golden and hybrids (to 10″).

3rd Hiking Day (**Lake on Upper Kern River** to **Junction Meadow**, 6 miles): Your trail proceeds south along the east shore of the lake, where red penstemon, or mountain pride, is especially abundant in the broken granite slopes. After 200 yards the the Milestone Basin Trail branches right, and soon you begin the steep 600-foot descent of a granite-slabbed slope down which the young river cascades and falls. In the shade of lodgepole pines, one sees yarrow milfoil, paintbrush, penstemon, fleabane, and red mountain heather. As the descent begins to level off, the trail passes through a bank of shield fern among which grows the delicate, white-headed Queen Anne's lace. At the foot of the descent our route enters a thick stand. Yellow groundsel flowers dominate the ground cover under these pines, complemented by the hues of orange tiger lily, purple swamp onion and red columbine.

After fording the outlet stream of Lake 11440, the trail begins a dusty section where the sagebrush is spottily shaded by a few lodgepole and foxtail pines. Shortly before the unmarked junction with the Tyndall Creek Trail there is a good packer campsite beside the river and here one begins to see red fir and aspen, indicating arrival in the Canadian life zone. The sandy, exposed trail continues its gentle descent to the Tyndall Creek ford (difficult in early season). Beyond this ford, the canyon becomes steeper, and the trail becomes more dufflike and tree-shaded. The first Jeffrey pines of this trip appear, along with a few mountain junipers. One-half mile beyond a roofless, decaying cabin our route meets the High Sierra Trail coming down from Wallace Creek, and from here down almost to Upper Funston Meadow the Kern River Trail and the High Sierra Trail are "superimposed."

From this junction it is a steep descent of 1 mile to Junction Meadow. Views on this descent are good down the Kern canyon, an immense U-trough which was given that shape by the main Kern glacier, which left the tributary valleys hanging. The forest cover on this descent is sparse lodgepole and Jeffrey, along with clumps of aspen, on a slope dominated by manzanita and currant. As the trail levels off, it enters a parklike grove of stalwart Jeffrey pines that provide a noble setting for the over-used campsites near the Kern River. Fishing is good for rainbow, golden and brook trout (to 10"). (Food storage locker and bear cable here.)

4th Hiking Day (**Junction Meadow** to **Rattlesnake Creek/Kern River,** 11½ miles): This day's hike is entirely beside the young Kern River, but it is not lacking in contrasts and discoveries. After fording Wallace Creek (high water in early season) the trail descends gently down the U-trough of the Kern River. This trough is remarkably straight for about 25 miles, as it parallels the Kern Canyon fault. The fault, a zone of structural weakness in the Sierra batholith, is more susceptible to erosion than the surrounding rock. This deep canyon has been carved by both glacial and stream action: many times the glacier advanced down the canyon, shearing off spurs created by stream erosion and leaving some tributary valleys hanging above the main valley. The glacier also scooped and plucked at the granite bedrock, creating basins (like the lake at the start of the 3rd hiking day) which became lakes when the glacier melted and retreated. It is interesting to speculate that our trail probably passes over some of these ancient lake beds, now buried beneath river sediments.

The descending trail becomes a little steeper as it fords Whitney Creek, where a thirsty hiker can sample water that coursed down from the highest point in the contiguous United States. Tributaries cascading down the east face of Red Spur provide excellent views as the trail steepens again and fords the stream that drains Guyot Flat. Rounding the most salient part of Red Spur, the trail turns slightly west as it skirts the steep bluffs on the east canyon wall. The gravelly, flat canyon floor widens as the trail approaches the fords of the branchlets of Rock Creek. Just beyond the first of these is the delightful mountain spa of Kern Hot Spring—a treat for the tired, dusty hiker. To the traveler, the crude cement bathtub here becomes a regal, heated (115°) pool. Only a few feet away, the great Kern River rushes past, and its cold waters can by dipped into to cool the hot-spring water as desired. Camping here is restricted to the overused campground just north and east of the spring. There are food storage lockers, bear cables, and a toilet here. Beyond Kern Hot

Spring, you cross the Kern on a wooden bridge to its west side. The valley floor widens and the river bifurcates as it flows past Chagoopa Falls. Chagoopa Creek descends 1700 feet from its hanging valley on Chagoopa Plateau, but the actual waterfall drops only 150 feet.

Our route continues its gentle descent past the Big Arroyo turnoff—thereby leaving the High Sierra Trail—to a ford of Funston Creek. Then, keeping away from the willow-infested banks of the Kern, the trail continues south past Upper Funston Meadow through a moderate-to-heavy forest cover of white fir, Jeffrey and sugar pine and some black oak, birch and aspen. Heavy patches of bracken fern inhibit the going in the wetter stretches, and the trail crosses through the site of an old burn before passing a drift fence and crossing the steel cantilever bridge spanning Big Arroyo Creek. From the bridge it is but a mile of level going to the good packer campsite at the confluence of Rattlesnake Creek and the Kern River. Fishing on the Kern is excellent for rainbow and brown (to 8″). Emergency services, should they be required, are usually available at the Kern Canyon Ranger Station 6 miles down-canyon. A cautionary note is warranted here: Rattlesnake Creek came by its name honestly, and one should exercise some care in hiking and climbing in the vicinity.

5th Hiking Day (**Rattlesnake Creek/Kern River** to **Upper Rattlesnake Creek**, 8 miles): Reverse the 2nd hiking day, trip 100.

6th Hiking Day (**Upper Rattlesnake Creek** to **Mineral King**, 10 miles): Reverse the 1st hiking day, trip 96.

Mt. Whitney from the northwest

71 Symmes Creek Trailhead to Cedar Grove

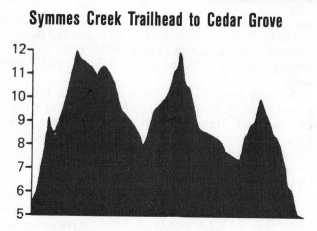

TRIP From Symmes Creek Trailhead to Cedar Grove Roadend via Shepherd Pass, Upper Kern River, Junction Meadow, Colby Pass, Scaffold Meadows and Avalanche Pass (shuttle trip). Topo maps *Mt. Whitney* (W.P.V.), *Triple Divide Peak* (W.P.V.), *Marion Peak* 15'; *Mt. Williamson, Mt. Brewer, Mt. Kaweah* 7½'. Best mid-to-late season, 59½ miles.

Grade	Trail/layover days	Total recom-mended days
Leisurely	....	....
Moderate	....	....
Strenuous	8/1	9

HILITES Staying entirely on trails sometimes limits one's experiences, but this route is diversified enough for any taste. Visiting four life zones, the trip offers a complete sampling of High Sierra ecosystems, and affords grand views of deep canyons and serrated skylines.

DESCRIPTION (Strenuous trip)

1st 3 Hiking Days: Follow trip 70 to **Junction Meadow**, 23½ miles.

4th Hiking Day (**Junction Meadow** to **Kern-Kaweah River**, 6 miles): Follow the 4th hiking day, trip 76.

5th Hiking Day (**Kern-Kaweah River** to **Big Wet Meadow**, 7 miles):
Today's 1600' ascent, 3300' descent, and great views demand an
early start. Leaving the Kern-Kaweah drainage behind, the trail
ascends steeply, beyond the sparse cover of lodgepole pine. This
steep climb offers magnificent views back into the headwaters of
the Kern-Kaweah drainage and Kaweah Peaks Ridge. Just to the
north of these distinctive summits rise the pyramidal heights of
aptly named Triple Divide Peak—this landmark peak divides the
drainages of the Kern, Kings and Kaweah rivers. The steep
ascent levels briefly as it crosses the tributaries draining Milestone Bowl, and then, by an unreliably ducked trail, resumes its
steep, steady climb to Colby Pass (12,000'). Here one has grand
views down Cloud Canyon, and of Glacier Ridge and the
cockscomblike sentinels atop the Whaleback. This pass is often
snow-covered until late in the season, but the route down to
Cloud Canyon is plain as it drops past foxtail and whitebark trees
and then around the northeast side of Colby Lake (campsites).

The well-beaten trail follows the outlet stream from the
wooded area at its source, crossing the stream in the descent and
passing the Colby Lake drift fence. Dwarfed and twisted
whitebark pines dot the slopes on either side as the route dips
steeply down over the unjointed granite shoulder of the
Whaleback to the Cloud Canyon floor, where it passes a drift
fence and soon fords to the west side of the infant Roaring River.
Our trail turns right, and proceeds downstream through aspens
and lodgepoles for about ⅔ mile to another ford, beyond which
we reach poor campsites on a rocky outcrop just south of Big Wet
Meadow (8700').

6th Hiking Day (**Big Wet Meadow** to **Scaffold Meadows**, 7 miles):
North of Big Wet Meadow the trail passes the "Big Wet Meadow
Drift Fence" and a nearby packer campsite. The descent is
moderate on a duff surface as it passes Cement Table Meadow
and a nearby campsite. The gradual loss of altitude is reflected in
the changing forest cover, which now shows red fir, juniper, and
white fir mixed with the lodgepoles. The duff-and-sand trail
takes you down past the beginning of the cross-country route to
Brewer Lakes and Brewer Creek. After passing two more drift
fences, you reach the Avalanche Pass Trail junction, turn west,
cross the footbridge, and arrive at the pleasant campsites
between the river and Roaring River Ranger Station (bear box;

toilet). Fishing in Roaring River is fair for rainbow and some golden (to 10"), and a summer ranger is stationed here. Signed "Scaffold Meadows Tourist Pasture" on the east side of the river and topo-labeled "Scaffold Meadows" on the west side are reserved for grazing stock (no camping).

7th Hiking Day (**Scaffold Meadows** to **Campsites, Sphinx Creek Ford**, 9 miles): Return to the Avalanche Pass Trail junction and take that trail northward on a steady ascent over sandy footing, through a heavy forest cover of Jeffrey pine, red and white fir, and juniper. At the Scaffold Meadows drift fence the ascent becomes moderate to steep as the trail switchbacks up a lateral moraine— identified by its rounded boulders and granite sand. Views are good up Deadman Canyon to the head of the cirque near Elizabeth Pass. Here our route begins a short, steady descent in burnt forest (lightning-caused, 1975 and 1977) to the easy ford of Moraine Creek. Look for shooting star, sneezeweed, cinquefoil, aster, groundsel and milfoil here.

The trail ascends, rounds a ridge, meets Moraine Creek again, and begins a rolling ascent toward the creek that drains the Avalanche Pass area. The forest cover of lodgepole, red fir and a few junipers is sparse, and some aspen thrive along the creek. Our trail remains on the east side of the creek, and it has a few switchbacks as it climbs from 8800 feet to 9200 feet. The faint trail becomes less steep as it nears Avalanche Pass (10,050'), which is east of the low point on this saddle. Views from the pass are inhibited by the forest cover. Along the moderate descent north of the pass, foxtail pines disappear and red fir and silver pine join the lodgepole to make a heavy cover over the sandy trail. After fording the westernmost tributary of Sphinx Creek, our trail descends moderately to ford a second tributary, and then drops again on a moderate descent to Sphinx Creek and a packer campsite. An unmaintained, unmapped trail to the Sphinx Lakes leads south from here.

8th Hiking Day (**Sphinx Creek Ford** to **Cedar Grove Roadend**, 7 miles): Leaving Sphinx Creek via a short, steady descent, the trail makes a long, level traverse high above the creek on the east canyon wall. Part of the Sphinx Crest is visible to the south through the trees, and at the ford of a tributary stream one can pause to enjoy not only a drink but a mountain garden of wildflowers and ferns. The traverse ends as the trail begins a series of long, well-built switchbacks that descend to the banks of Sphinx

Creek in its deep, **V**-shaped gorge. Both the creek and the trail follow along granite slabs for much of the way from the beginning of the switchbacks to the foot of the descent, and some of the trail has been blasted across these slabs (very poor footing). As the trail leads out onto the north side of a granite nose, there are very good views up the Bubbs Creek drainage, down the canyon to the flats around the roadend, and northwest to the peaks of the Monarch Divide, which separates the South and Middle Forks of the Kings River. The last part of the descent to Bubbs Creek is moderate, via many more switchbacks than are shown on the topo map. Then the forest cover thickens and our route crosses a bridge and meets the Bubbs Creek Trail, near a campsite (one-night limit, bear box), where we turn left to retrace part of the 1st hiking day, trip 57.

Bullfrog Lake

72

Whitney Portal to Outpost Camp

TRIP

From Whitney Portal to Outpost Camp (round trip). Topo maps *Mt. Whitney* (W.P.V.) 15′; *Mt. Langley, Mt. Whitney* 7½′. Best mid or late season; 7 miles.

Grade	Trail/layover days	Total recommended days
Leisurely	2/0	2
Moderate	....	....
Strenuous	day	....

HILITES

This overnight trip offers an experience of the high country in the shadow of Mt. Whitney. Outpost Camp can be used as a base camp for climbing Mt. Whitney or for exploring the spectacular surrounding country.

DESCRIPTION (Leisurely trip)

1st Hiking Day (**Whitney Portal** to **Outpost Camp**, 3½ miles): From just east of the small store at road's end, our route follows the old stock trail from the defunct pack station as it steadily climbs through a moderate forest cover of Jeffrey pine and red fir. After ½ mile the trail crosses North Fork Lone Pine Creek and shortly enters the John Muir Wilderness. Soon the forest cover thins, and the slope is covered with a chaparral that includes mountain mahogany, Sierra chinquapin and sagebrush. This steep slope can get very hot in mid-morning, and the trip is best begun as early as possible. (Carry water.) Breather stops on this trail section provide a view down the canyon framing the Alabama Hills. Then the trail levels off somewhat through several willow-covered pockets having a moderate forest cover of lodgepole and foxtail pines, and passes fields of corn lilies, delphinium, tall lupine and swamp whiteheads as, in 1½ miles, it approaches the ford of Lone Pine Creek.

Beyond this log ford is a junction with an unmarked lateral that leads east to Lone Pine Lake, visible from the junction. The route leads up a barren, rocky wash, then switchbacks up another slope through a moderate lodgepole tree cover to Outpost Camp (toilets) (10,365')—called "Bighorn Park" on the Government topo map), a willow-covered meadow that was once a lake. A very large abandoned stove near the upper end of this park is evidence of the days when a packer's wife ran a little camp here, renting tents and selling meals. The camp had to be removed when the area was made wilderness by Congress. There are many fair campsites here in Outpost Camp, but wood fires are forbidden, as they are on all of the Mt. Whitney Trail. Those bound for the summit of Whitney or for Crabtree Meadows and beyond may have enough steam left to climb on to overused Trail Camp (toilet), 3 miles ahead, the last legal camping place on the trail, which is above timberline.

2nd Hiking Day: Retrace your steps, 3½ miles.

Mt. Whitney over Lone Pine

73   Whitney Portal to Crabtree Ranger Station

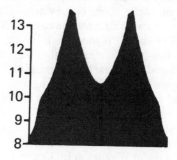

TRIP   From Whitney Portal to Crabtree Ranger Station
             (round trip). Topo maps *Mt. Whitney* (W.P.V.) 15′;
             Mt. Langley, Mt. Whitney 7½′. Best mid-to-late
             season; 30 miles.

Grade	Trail/layover days	Total recommended days
Leisurely	....	....
Moderate	5/1	6
Strenuous	4/0	4

HILITES Despite the elevation at Trail Crest, where this route
             crosses the Sierra crest, it is actually one of the
             easier routes into the Upper Kern Basin. This route
             follows the Mt. Whitney Trail and passes within 2
             trail miles of the highest point in the contiguous US.

DESCRIPTION (Strenuous trip)

1st Hiking Day: Follow trip 72 to **Outpost Camp**, 3½ miles.

2nd Hiking Day: (**Outpost Camp** to **Crabtree Ranger Station**, 11½
miles): (This hiking day is a long one, since we do not camp short
of Crabtree Ranger Station, and it involves an ascent of 3400
feet. The prudent hiker will start early.) Our trail veers away
from the waterfall that tumbles down into Outpost Camp from
the southwest, fords Lone Pine Creek and begins a short series of
switchbacks beside the cascading creek past blossoming
creambush, Indian paintbrush, Sierra chinquapin, mountain
pride, currant, pennyroyal, fireweed and groundsel. Just after

the trail crosses an outlet stream on rocks, it arrives at Mirror Lake (10,640'), cradled in its cirque beneath the south face of Thor Peak. This cold lake has fair fishing for rainbow and brook trout, but camping is no longer allowed here. The Forest Service closed the lake to camping in 1972 after severe overuse had created a montane slum. Since then, the lakeshore has begun to recover, and after a great many years it may look something like it did when first discovered.

Leaving Mirror Lake, the trail ascends the south wall of the cirque via switchbacks. Ascending steeply under the north flanks of Mt. Irvine, the rocky trail crosses the south fork of Middle Fork Lone Pine Creek and winds up past giant blocks and granite outcroppings. In the cracks in the boulders the hiker will find ivesia, cinquefoil, creambush, currant and much gooseberry, and looking across the canyon he will see the cascading outlet of Consultation Lake. Beside a rock bridge that crosses the stream are specimens of the moisture-loving shooting star. After ascending again, the trail arrives at the last campsites before the crest, Trail Camp (12,000') (toilet). Here beneath Wotan's Throne is also the last reliable water in late season. There are numerous level campsites.

As the trail begins exactly 100 switchbacks to Trail Crest Pass, Mt. Whitney disappears behind its needles. The steep, rocky slope up to the crest is not entirely barren, for in season one may see a dozen species of flowering plants, climaxed by the multiflowered, blue "sky pilot." The building of this trail involved much blasting with dynamite, and the natural fracture planes of the granite are evident in the blasted slabs. Finally the 1800-foot ascent from Trail Camp ends at Trail Crest (13,780'), and the hiker suddenly has vistas of a great part of Sequoia National Park to the west, including the entire Great Western Divide. To the east, far below, are several small, unnamed lakes, lying close under the steep faces of Mts. Whitney and Muir. These lakes may be ice-covered well into summer.

From Trail Crest the route descends for a short 100 yards to a junction with the 2-mile lateral to Mt. Whitney (14,495'). The highest mountain in the United States until Alaska was admitted as a state, this peak was first climbed on August 18, 1873, by three fishermen, who made the ascent up the southwest slope. The present trail between this junction and the summit lies close to the crest on the west side of it, and is an easy hike if one doesn't try to fight bad weather and takes proper clothing.

As our switchbacking descent on the west side of the Sierra crest begins, one can make out the Hitchcock Lakes below in a cirque basin that has been changed but little since its glacier melted. The parallel avalanche chutes on the northeast wall of Mt. Hitchcock all terminate at the upper limit of glacial erosion. Along the switchbacks, the most prominent flower is the yellow, daisylike hulsea, or alpine gold. After the long switchbacks end, the trail follows a moderate descent on a traverse of the "back" side of Mt. Whitney, leveling off at the first possible campsites, overlooking Guitar Lake. From these campsites our route crosses the outlet of Arctic Lake, descends on a moderately steep, rocky trail into a sparse cover of lodgepole, and arrives at Timberline Lake (no camping or grazing, but fair fishing for golden to 7"). After skirting the shore of this lake (viewpoints for focusing the camera on Mt. Whitney and its reflection), the trail passes a lovely meadow, and then descends the valley of Whitney Creek to a junction with the trail to Crabtree Ranger Station and the fair campsites nearby. Emergency services are usually available at the ranger station. (There is a "bear barrel" for food storage where the trail to the ranger station crosses the creek.) Fishing in Whitney Creek is fair for golden (to 7"). (During times of heavy trail traffic, the hiker who wants more solitude may choose to camp at Upper Crabtree Meadow, ½ mile southwest of the ranger station, or Lower Crabtree Meadow, 1 mile southwest. These sites are reached by taking the Rock Creek Trail at the junction west of the ranger station.)

3rd and 4th Hiking Days: Retrace your steps, 15 miles.

Trailside Meadow on Mt. Whitney Trail

Whitney Portal to Wallace Lake

74

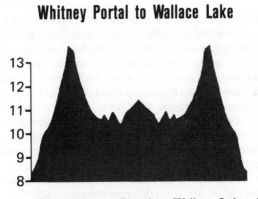

TRIP From Whitney Portal to Wallace Lake via Trail
Crest, Crabtree Ranger Station and Wallace Creek
(round trip). Topo maps *Mt. Whitney* (W.P.V.) 15′;
Mt. Langley, Mt. Whitney, Mt. Kaweah 7½′. Best
late season; 47 miles.

Grade	Trail/layover days	Total recommended days
Leisurely	....	....
Moderate	8/1	9
Strenuous	6/0	7

HILITES Wallace Lake, lying in the heart of the Mt. Whitney
region, is thought by many to be the finest fishing
lake in the region. Well off the "beaten track" it is
also a base from which to climb Mts. Barnard and
Russell.

DESCRIPTION (Strenuous trip)

1st and 2nd Hiking Days: Follow trip 73 to **Crabtree Ranger Station**,
15 miles.

3rd Hiking Day (**Crabtree Ranger Station** to **Wallace Lake**, 8½ miles):
From Crabtree Ranger Station our route branches right (north),
fords Whitney Creek and climbs the north slope of Whitney
Creek canyon into a foxtail-pine forest. On an overcast day, this
foxtail forest, with its dead snags, fallen trees, and lack of ground
cover, has an eerie, gloomy, otherworldly quality. The trail then

switchbacks up to a junction with the justly famous Pacific Crest Trail. These switchbacks offer the hard-breathing hiker views of Mts. Hitchcock, Pickering and Chamberlain, and the flanks of Mt. Whitney, whose summit is over the horizon. From the ridge, the route descends gently on a sandy trail through a moderate cover of lodgepole and foxtail to a ford (10,636') of an unnamed creek. Beginning here the trail skirts what is called "Sandy Meadow" on the topo map. Small meadowy sections of trail lie beside several little streams not shown on the topo map, and in season they are graced with the yellow blossoms of groundsel and monkey flower.

After these crossings the trail ascends a moderate slope with a lodgepole canopy and a heavy lupine ground cover to the saddle marked 10,964 on the topo map. From this saddle the route descends gently on a sandy trail around the west shoulder of Mt. Young. Leveling off, the trail winds among some massive boulders that make up a lateral moraine, and then leads down a rocky hillside from which the traveler has fine views of Mt. Ericsson, Tawny Point, Junction Peak, the flank of Mt. Tyndall, Mt. Versteeg, Mt. Williamson, and, farthest right, Mt. Barnard. After the ford of a tributary of Wallace Creek the descent becomes gentle again, through a moderate cover of lodgepole, foxtail and whitebark pines. Beyond the next tributary ford the descent steepens, and the trail switchbacks ¼ mile down to Wallace Creek. Just past the ford (very difficult in early season) the High Sierra Trail and the John Muir Trail, which have been "superimposed" from the top of Mt. Whitney to here, diverge, the High Sierra Trail turning left (west) toward Giant Forest and the Muir Trail continuing north toward Yosemite.

Our route turns right (east) up Wallace Creek canyon. Under a forest cover of sparse-to-moderate lodgepole the trail ascends gently amid sprinklings of western wallflower, penstemon, groundsel, yarrow milfoil and Labrador tea. At the meadow where the outlet of Wales Lake joins Wallace Creek, the trail fords the creek and then fords the tributary, staying on the south side of Wallace Creek. Here the ascent becomes moderate for a short distance, and then reverts to a gentler grade. This route up Wallace Creek canyon is sometimes indistinct and sometimes confused by multiple trail sections and inadequate ducking. Careful negotiation of the indistinct sections will bring one to the fair campsites at timberline (11,400') about ½ mile below

Wallace Lake. Wallace Lake lies beneath the ridge that connects Mt. Barnard with Tunnebora Peak. Fishing in Wallace Lake is good for golden (to 14″), and the same is true of Wales Lake, reached by cross country southwest from the inlet of Wallace Lake.

4th, 5th and 6th Hiking Days: Retrace your steps, 23½ miles.

Kern River Canyon *USGS*

75

Whitney Portal to Milestone Basin

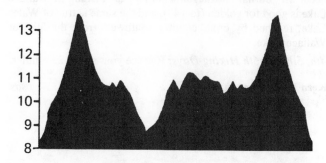

TRIP   From Whitney Portal to Milestone Basin via Trail
Crest, Crabtree Ranger Station, Wallace Creek,
Junction Meadow, Upper Kern River and Tyndall
Creek (semiloop trip). Topo maps *Mt. Whitney*
(W.P.V.) 15′; *Mt. Langley, Mt. Whitney, Mt.
Kaweah, Mt. Brewer,* 7½′. Best mid-to-late season;
59½ miles.

Grade	Trail/layover days	Total recommended days
Leisurely	....	....
Moderate	10/2	12
Strenuous	8/1	9

HILITES   This trip samples both well-traveled trails and little-
used trails, country above timberline and deep,
dense forests. Milestone Basin, set under the giant
finger of Milestone Mountain, is remote enough to
suit the solitude-seeking hiker, and the lakes
piscatorial enough to suit the most avid angler.

DESCRIPTION (Strenuous trip)

1st 2 Hiking Days: Follow trip 73 to **Crabtree Ranger Station,** 15
miles.

3rd Hiking Day (**Crabtree Ranger Station** to **Upper Kern River,** 8½
miles): Follow the 3rd hiking day, trip 74, to the junction of the
John Muir Trail and the High Sierra Trail at Wallace Creek.
Taking the High Sierra Trail from this junction, our route

proceeds down Wallace Creek canyon on sandy underfooting, with views ahead of Mt. Kaweah and the Kaweah Peaks Ridge. The trail veers away from Wallace Creek and then meets it again after a short, moderate descent on an exposed slope. Our trail passes campsites lining both sides as it winds among sparse-to-moderate lodgepole and a great variety of wildflowers (in midsummer), including fireweed, paintbrush, arnica, sulfur flower, wild buckwheat, pennyroyal, mountain pride and creamberry. After fording Wright Creek (difficult in early season), the trail descends more steeply through sparse lodgepole mixed with some foxtail pines.

As the canyon widens and the trail veers more westward, the timber cover diminishes almost to nothing, and the slope (hot in afternoon) is covered with manzanita, creambush, hollyleaf redberry, mountain mahogany and Sierra chinquapin. The main splash of color in this chaparral is the red penstemon, or mountain pride. This exposed slope offers views down the great trough of the Kern River, south to Mt. Guyot and west to Kaweah Peaks Ridge. The descent now reaches the Canadian life zone as Jeffrey pines are seen, along with mountain juniper. Here our route turns northward and traverses down the Kern Canyon wall to meet the Kern River Trail, onto which it turns right (north), leaving the High Sierra Trail. One mile up the canyon our route passes a decaying roofless cabin. Beginning here there are several good campsites along the river, where fishing is good for rainbow (to 10″). These are the Kern River rainbow, *Salmo gairdneri,* found only in the upper Kern River.

4th Hiking Day (**Upper Kern River** to **Milestone Basin,** 6 miles): Once past the cabin, the trail ascends less steeply, and soon it reaches a ford of Tyndall Creek (difficult in early season). Beyond the ford, the trail becomes sandier and drier, and the red fir and aspen gradually disappear, leaving a forest cover of lodgepole and some foxtail that is sparse on the hillsides and moderate on the river terraces. There are numerous campsites along this stretch of trail, including a packer campsite ½ mile beyond the unsigned junction with Tyndall Creek Trail. Beyond this trail, our route becomes more exposed, with considerable sagebrush. After the trail fords the outlet stream of Lake 11440, we soon come to a dell thick with lodgepole trunks. The excellent wildflower display in this large dell is dominated by groundsel, but also includes tiger lilies, swamp onions and red columbine. Then the trail ascends above the dell and passes through a bank of shield fern, Queen Anne's lace and bush chinquapin, staying on the east side of the river. Here our route ascends steeply through a sparse lodgepole cover on a rocky trail over granite slabs that rise 600 feet to the upper Kern plateau. After the trail levels off, it soon reaches a junction with the Milestone Basin Trail, where our route turns left (west) (look for ducks). From this junction, continue as in the last part of the 2nd hiking day, trip 69.

5th Hiking Day (**Milestone Basin** to **Tyndall Creek Tributary**, 6 miles): Reverse the steps of tne 2nd hiking day, trip 69, from Milestone Basin to the ford at the John Muir Trail/Shepherd Pass Trail junction, where our route turns right (south) on the John Muir Trail. The rocky trail ascends gently along the east flank of Tawny Point through a sparse-to-moderate cover of lodgepole and foxtail pines past many poor campsites, and then arrives at the good campsites on a tributary of Tyndall Creek (11,000'), near a small lake where swimming is good in late season.

6th Hiking Day (**Tyndall Creek Tributary** to **Crabtree Ranger Station**, 9 miles): Reverse the 3rd hiking day, trip 77.

7th and 8th Hiking Days: Retrace the 2nd and 1st hiking days, 15 miles.

Williamson Basin   *E.P. Pister*

Whitney Portal to Kern-Kaweah River   **76**

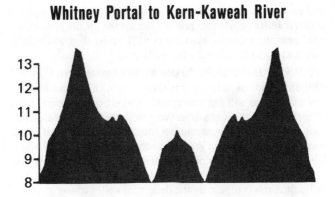

TRIP From Whitney Portal to Kern-Kaweah River via Trail Crest, Crabtree Meadow, Wallace Creek, Junction Meadow (round trip). Topo maps *Mt. Whitney* (W.P.V.) 15′; *Mt. Langley, Mt. Whitney, Mt. Kaweah* 7½′. Best mid-to-late season; 61 miles.

Grade	Trail/layover days	Total recommended days
Leisurely	....	....
Moderate	10/2	12
Strenuous	8/1	9

HILITES This route combines the high, rocky country along the Whitney crest with the alluvial meadows on the Kern River and the intimate camping in the little-visited Kern-Kaweah River canyon.

DESCRIPTION (Strenuous trip)

1st and 2nd Hiking Days: Follow trip 73 to **Crabtree Ranger Station**, 15 miles.

3rd Hiking Day (**Crabtree Ranger Station** to **Junction Meadow**, 9½ miles): Follow the 3rd hiking day, trip 75, to the junction of the High Sierra Trail and the Kern River Trail, and turn left (south). From here the rocky trail descends steeply to Junction Meadow through stands of aspen and past occasional Jeffrey and lodgepole pines, winding through a ground cover of manzanita and currant. As the trail levels off, it enters a parklike grove of stalwart Jeffrey pines that provide the setting for the poor camp-sites near the Kern River (bear box). Fishing is good for rain-bow and some brook trout (to 10″).

4th Hiking Day (**Junction Meadow** to **Kern-Kaweah River**, 6 miles): This day's route is irregularly maintained, but a backpacker with any experience will have no trouble staying on the route. Soon after the ford of the Kern River (very difficult in early season) the trail begins the steep ascent up the Kern canyon wall to the hanging valley above. Veering away from the Kern-Kaweah River, it ascends to the north side of a granite knob, or spine, and passes through what has been called "Kern-Kaweah Pass." This difficult climb is repaid by the delightful valley above it, one of the finest in the Sierra. From the "pass" the trail makes a very steep, loose and rocky—but mercifully short—decent, a moder-ate ascent and finally a slight descent to what is left of Rockslide Lake—two wide pools of crystal-clear, emerald-green water in the river.

Beyond the lake, the canyon widens into a kind of granite amphitheater, where two tributary streams, meeting, dash into the main canyon over a rocky ledge, to meet the main river below the fall by which the river arrives at the bowl. From here the ascent through a sparse-to-moderate lodgepole cover is mod-erate as the ducked route threads the deep canyon lying between Kern Point and Picket Guard Peak. One more steep ascent is required to reach the bowl that contains what is left of Gallats Lake, a lovely oxbow in a large, wet meadow (fishing is good for golden to 8″). Fair campsites are here, but the traveler will prefer those about 1 mile ahead where the trail turns away from the river toward Colby Pass, where fishing is excellent for golden (to 7″). These campsites are a good explorer's base for excursions into the lightly visited headwaters of the Kern-Kaweah River and into Milestone Bowl.

5th, 6th, 7th and 8th Hiking Days: Retrace your steps, 30½ miles.

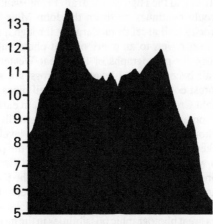

TRIP From Whitney Portal to Symmes Creek Trailhead via Trail Crest, Crabtree Meadow, Tyndall Creek, Shepherd Pass (shuttle trip). Topo maps *Mt. Whitney* (W.P.V.) 15'; *Mt. Langley, Mt. Whitney, Mt. Williamson* 7½'. Best mid-to-late season; 39 miles.

Grade	Trail/layover days	Total recommended days
Leisurely	....	....
Moderate	6/2	8
Strenuous	5/0	5

HILITES This high trip loops around "the Whitney group," the culmination of the Sierra spine, with five peaks standing over 14,000 feet. A spur trail will take the hiker to the highest point in the contiguous 48 states, 14,495 feet above sea level. The vast panoramas of the upper Kern basin along this route are unequaled in the Sierra.

DESCRIPTION (Strenuous trip)

1st and 2nd Hiking Days: Follow trip 73 to **Crabtree Ranger Station**, 15 miles.

3rd Hiking Day (**Crabtree Ranger Station** to **Tyndall Creek Tributary,** 9 miles): Follow the 3rd hiking day, trip 74, to the junction of the John Muir Trail and the High Sierra Trail. From Wallace Creek, this day's route continues north on the John Muir Trail. The sandy and rocky trail ascends moderately through a sparse-to-moderate forest cover, to an overlook that photographers will want to utilize for photographs of the Great Western Divide. Here the trail becomes quite level as it crosses a sandy flat bearing a forest cover of lodgepole and foxtail pines. The trail crosses Wright Creek via a rocky ford (difficult in early season) and passes some campsites located east of the trail.

Several short but taxing ascents separated by level stretches bring the hiker out onto Bighorn Plateau, where the panoramic view begins with Red Spur in the southwest and sweeps north along the Great Western Divide and east along the Kings-Kern Divide to Junction Peak. In addition, one can see, to the southeast, Mts. Whitney, Young and Russell. A small lake west of the trail presents great photographic possibilities in the morning, and any time of day is good for photographing the lateral moraine of the Tyndall Creek glacier, which follows a contour along the west side of the plateau. Color is provided by a large field of lupine sweeping up the slope to the east. From here a gentle descent on a rocky trail through a sparse foxtail cover leads to the good campsites (11,100′) where the trail crosses the outlet of a small lake (no fish) which offers good swimming in mid and late season.

4th Hiking Day (**Tyndall Creek Tributary** to **Anvil Camp,** 7½ miles): As this hiking day begins, the John Muir Trail descends gently on a rocky course through a forest cover of mixed lodgepole and foxtail pines to a junction with the Shepherd Pass Trail. Our route turns right (east) off the Muir Trail and begins a long, steady ascent up the meadowy, boulder-strewn upper basin of Tyndall Creek. Views improve constantly as the traveler gains elevation, and the peaks of the Great Western Divide take on new aspects as they are seen from new angles. To the north, the southern escarpment of Diamond Mesa hides an upper surface that is one of the most level areas in this region. The traveler who has read the incredible first chapter of Clarence King's *Mountaineering in the Sierra Nevada* may speculate on where King and Richard Cotter crossed the Kings-Kern Divide and traversed this basin on their way to ascending Mt. Tyndall—

which, in naming, they believed to be the highest Sierra peak until they were on top of it and saw other, higher ones nearby.

The appearance of Lake 12002 heralds the approach to Shepherd Pass (12,050'), which from this side of the crest is merely the end of a long, gentle ascent. The east side of the pass is a total contrast, with its steep scree and talus slopes which are often not passable to stock until August. From the pass, the trail switchbacks down a 500-foot scree slope into a gigantic, barren bowl scooped out by the plucking action of the Shepherd Creek glacier. After winding among boulders and topping a slight rise, the trail begins a moderate descent to timberline and a poor campsite near a junction with the Junction Pass Trail. Our rocky trail continues to descend moderately through a cover of sparse lodgepole to a ford of Shepherd Creek and the good campsites at Anvil Camp (10,000'), where fishing for rainbow (to 9") is fair.

5th Hiking Day (**Anvil Camp** to **Symmes Creek Trailhead**, 7½ miles): Reverse the 1st hiking day, trip 68.

Mt. Whitney from Timberline Lake

78
Lodgepole Campground to Ranger Lakes

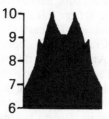

TRIP   From Lodgepole Campground to Ranger Lake via
             Silliman Pass (round trip). Topo map *Triple Divide
             Peak* (W.P.V.) 15′; *Lodgepole, Mt. Silliman* 7½′.
             Best mid-to-late season; 20 miles.

Grade	Trail/layover days	Total recommended days
Leisurely	....	....
Moderate	2/1	3
Strenuous	2/0	2

HILITES Crossing the Silliman Crest on the boundary
             between Sequoia and Kings Canyon parks, this trip
             terminates at picturesque Ranger Lake. En route,
             the trail passes through sedate fir forests, traces
             rambling brooks, and circles crystal-clear lakes.

DESCRIPTION (Moderate trip)

1st Hiking Day (**Lodgepole Campground** to **Ranger Lake**, 10 miles): The
trail begins north of a bridge over Marble Fork Kaweah River
(6800′), and curves west to skirt the campground on a moderate
ascent through a dense forest cover of fir, pine and cedar, under-
storied by abundant stickweed, pennyroyal, lupine, gilia and
pussy paws. This ascent, over alternating rocky and sandy
stretches, crests the moraine we have been walking on, then turns
north and levels to a ford of Silliman Creek. These woods teem
with wildlife, and the traveler is very apt to see a few mule deer,
many squirrels, and a host of birds. After passing shooting-star-
fringed Cahoon Meadow, the trail continues the moderate ascent

over duff and sand underfooting through patchy, dense stands of red and white fir and some meadow sections, crossing several streamlets, to Cahoon Gap. The trail then descends moderately to a ford of the unnamed tributary just south of East Fork Clover Creek (campsite, bear box). One fourth mile beyond this ford the trail veers east as the JO Pass Trail goes north (campsite, bear box), and then we ford East Fork Clover Creek.

The sometimes gentle, sometimes moderate ascent up East Fork Clover Creek witnesses the inclusion of lodgepole and silver pine in the forest cover, and as the trail approaches Twin Lakes, open stretches between the trees are a tide of colors. In season, one will find rank, knee-high corn lily, blue and white lupine, white mariposa lily, orange wallflower, purple larkspur, lavender shooting star, white cinquefoil, violet aster and golden groundsel. The last mile to the heavily timbered flats around Twin Lakes is a steep ascent, and the traveler may well contemplate a quick swim in the largest lake, whose shallow waters quickly warm to a midsummer's sun.

Continuing toward Silliman Pass, the view of the two large boulder stands of exfoliating granite (Twin Peaks) dominates the horizon during the steep progress to the pass' saddle. This ascent sees the end of the fir, and almost exclusive domination of lodgepole pine. At the pass (10,165') one has a good view of flat-topped Mt. Silliman to the south, the heavily wooded Sugarloaf Creek drainage to the northeast, the Great Western Divide to the east, and the barren flats of the Tableland to the southeast. The descent from the pass drops steeply and then turns north to the nose of a granite ridge before switchbacking down. From the switchbacks one has fine views of Ball Dome, and much of the Kings River watershed, including Monarch Divide. At the foot of the switchbacks a level duff trail leads off to the larger of the Ranger Lakes, and to the excellent campsites on the southwest side of the lake. Anglers working their way around the shallow lake plying their art on the fair-to-good fishing for rainbow trout (8–12″) will also enjoy the carpet of shooting stars and the rose-purple blossom of the heather. A layover day spent in this pleasant environment will allow the traveler to visit the nearby scenic settings of Beville (rainbow and brook), Lost (brook) and Seville (brook) lakes.

2nd Hiking Day: Retrace your steps, 9¼ miles.

Lodgepole Campground to Scaffold Meadows

TRIP   From Lodgepole Campground to Scaffold Mead-
                ows via Silliman Pass, Ranger Lakes, Sugarloaf
                Valley (round trip). Topo map *Triple Divide Peak*
                (W.P.V.) 15′; *Lodgepole, Mt. Silliman* 7½′. Best
                mid or late season; 46 miles.

Grade	Trail/layover days	Total recom- mended days
Leisurely	7/2	9
Moderate	6/2	8
Strenuous	4/2	6

HILITES   The terminus of this long trip makes a superb loca-
                tion for a base camp. From here, one can explore the
                upper reaches of several remote drainages, and in
                the course of these explorations enjoy some of the
                finest of the Roaring River country.

DESCRIPTION (Moderate trip)

1st Hiking Day: Follow trip 78 to **Ranger Lake**, 10 miles.

2nd Hiking Day (**Ranger Lake** to **Comanche Meadow**, 5½ miles): First,
return to the marked junction with the Silliman Pass Trail and go
east, then north, toward Comanche Meadow. Our trail passes the
turnoff to Lost Lake and circles Ball Dome. Passing through a
moderate-to-heavy forest cover, the trail emerges at a
meadowed crossing of the outlet stream from Seville Lake.
Beyond this crossing, the marked junction of the Seville
Lake/Marvin Pass Trail is clear. Going east, on the northwest
side of Sugarloaf Creek, our route descends sometimes steadily
and sometimes moderately over duff-and-sand underfooting.

This descent crosses an unnamed tributary, and a short distance beyond passes another trail to Marvin Pass. About 100 yards farther on, the trail passes the Kanawyer Gap Trail, which leads north and then west to Marvin Pass, and then fords the rocky creek emptying Comanche Meadow (7680'). Good campsites will be found on Sugarloaf Creek before and after this ford, and fishing for brook trout (to 8″) is fair. There's no bear box here, but there's one at Sugarloaf Meadows 2 miles farther east.

3rd Hiking Day (**Comanche Meadow** to **Scaffold Meadows**, 7½ miles): Beginning ¼ mile after the ford, the trail drops moderately on sandy underfooting over a heavily forested slope that shows the effects of a 1974 fire. Then, as the trail levels out on the floor of Sugarloaf Valley, the dome from which the name is derived can be seen through the trees. More resistant than the surrounding rock, this granite island withstood the onslaught of the ice, and today it stands as a round, smooth 1000-foot-high reminder of the ice river that carved the valley. Following the course of this old glacier through sporadic meadows, the trail passes Sugarloaf Meadow (bear box) and parallels and then fords Sugarloaf Creek.

On the south side of this wide, shallow ford, the trail passes more campsites before crossing a series of sharp wrinkles in the terrain to reach Ferguson Creek and still more campsites. After fording this creek via logs or rocks, the trail rounds a long, dry, timbered ridge nose before dropping down a steady slope to the drift fence below the topo's named Scaffold Meadows, a pasture reserved for grazing animals. Signed "Scaffold Meadows Tourist Pasture" across the river is also reserved for grazing. Living up to its name, Roaring River can be heard a few yards to the left, and with this pleasant accompaniment the trail ascends the last, gentle mile to the good campsites near Roaring River Ranger Station (bear box, toilet), fording the Barton Peak stream on the way. Fishing for rainbow and some golden trout (to 10″) is fair to good. Emergency services are usually available from the resident summer ranger, whose cabin is nearby. These campsites make a fine base camp for further explorations of the surrounding headwaters of Deadman Canyon Creek, Roaring River and Brewer Creek.

4th, 5th and 6th Hiking Days: Retrace your steps, 23 miles.

80   Lodgepole Campground to Ranger Meadow

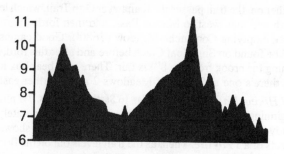

TRIP

From Lodgepole Campground to Ranger Meadow via Silliman Pass, Scaffold Meadows, Deadman Canyon, return via Elizabeth Pass, to Crescent Meadow (part cross country) (shuttle trip). Topo map *Triple Divide Peak* (W.P.V.) 15'; *Lodgepole, Mt. Silliman, Sphinx Lakes, Triple Divide Peak* 7½'. Best late season; 51¼ miles.

Grade	Trail/layover days	Total recom- mended days
Leisurely	....	....
Moderate	6/2	8
Strenuous	4/2	6

HILITES

The climax of this trip is the high, wildflower-filled meadows at the head of Deadman Canyon. Less often visited because of its remoteness, this glaciated canyon nestles against the craggy summits of Glacier Ridge in solitary splendor.

DESCRIPTION (Moderate trip)

1st 3 Hiking Days: Follow trip 79 to **Scaffold Meadows,** 22¼ miles.

4th Hiking Day (**Scaffold Meadows** to **Upper Ranger Meadow,** 7 miles): Leaving Scaffold Meadows, our trail leads south while veering away from the river on a gentle-to-moderate ascent past well-charred Jeffrey pines. Views back over one's left shoulder include a fine example of a lateral moraine in the form of Moraine Ridge, the northeast wall of the canyon. About 1½ miles above the Roaring River bridge, our route ascends past the upper drift fence and several more campsites. At the right time of summer, flowers seen during this short stretch include buckwheat, sagebrush, Indian paintbrush, Mariposa lily, pennyroyal, penstemon and shooting star. Past the drift fence, the trail fords Deadman Canyon Creek, and in 1½ miles reaches a packer campsite and then a gravesite. Located at the north end of a large, wet meadow, above 50 yards southeast of the campsite, the grave marks the derivation of the name Deadman Canyon. The citation on the grave reads: "Here reposes Alfred Moniere, sheepherder, mountain man, 18-- to 1887."

From this grave our ascent continues, offering good views up the canyon of the spectacularly smoothed, unjointed, barren walls. Soon the trail refords the creek and then climbs alongside a dramatic, green-water, granite-slab chute. At the end of this ascent, the trail levels out as it passes through a dense stand of lodgepole and fir, and, passing a campsite, emerges at the north end of the open grasslands of Ranger Meadow. The precipitous canyon walls dominate the views from the meadow, and the cirque holding Big Bird Lake is clear on the west wall. By midsummer the meadow is a colorful carpet of wildflowers, including shooting star, penstemon and red heather.

From Ranger Meadow the trail resumes its steady ascent over duff and sand through stands of lodgepole and clumps of aspen. Just before the Upper Ranger Meadow flat, the route fords the creek to the east side. Here one has awesome glimpses of the headwall of the Deadman Canyon cirque, and this view continues to rule the skyline from the good campsites just beyond the drift fence at the north end of Upper Ranger Meadow. Fishing for rainbow, brook and hybrids is good (to 10"). A cross-country route to Big Bird Lake takes off west across the creek here, becoming a well-worn tread with an occasional duck as it ascends the slope south of the lake's outlet and takes the traveler to a bench overlooking the main lake and several small ones.

5th Hiking Day (**Upper Ranger Meadow** to **Bearpaw Meadow**, 11 miles, part cross country): This day's hike is a long one, and we must get a very early start. It begins with a 2100-foot ascent, mostly cross country, to Elizabeth Pass, continues with a 3300-foot descent from the pass, and ends with a short but steep and exposed ascent and a shady descent to Bearpaw Meadow.

As we leave our campsite in Upper Ranger Meadow, our trail ascends gently through boulders, with Upper Ranger Meadow to the west. Low-lying willows line the stream, and clumps of wild-flowers dot the green expanse. The ascent steepens to a moderate grade; then, as we begin the steep ascent of the headwall, we parallel a dramatic series of cascades and falls. Near the top of the falls, we reach a bench and cross the stream above a long, dashing granite chute, and then we climb steeply by a faint, infrequently ducked route up the southwest wall of the cirque. This barren, rocky climb over light-colored granite slabs contrasts with the darker metamorphic rocks (around an old copper-mine site) seen to the east, and this contrast is even more marked from the tiny saddle of Elizabeth Pass (11,380'). Views to the southwest from the pass include parts of the Middle Fork Kaweah River watershed, Moose Lake, and the jumbled peaks of the southernmost prominences of the Tableland divide.

From the pass, the ducked trail initially descends steeply by switchbacks. Then, after a moderately descending traverse, the trail descends the steep northern wall of River Valley via a series of rocky switchbacks. At the foot of these zigzags, our route passes a spur trail to Tamarack Lake, and then, in ¼ mile, a trail that leads south to the High Sierra Trail. (Travelers ready to stop for the night may want to take the spur trail from the first junction a short way up Lone Pine Canyon, to the first wooded area near the creek.) At the second junction our route swings southwest to make a steep and mostly shadeless ascent across the sparsely timbered nose of the ridge above Bearpaw Meadow. The descent from this ridge is steep, rocky and dry as it passes through stands of lodgepole and red fir and joins the High Sierra Trail 150 yards west of a ranger station and backcountry lodge that share a magnificent view over the Middle Fork Kaweah country. The view is worth a visit! On this trail we go left a few yards and then turn right to reach a very overused campground under heavy forest cover (piped, treated water, bear boxes, toilets). Emergency services are usually available at the ranger station just east of where we left the High Sierra Trail, but open fires are not allowed around here. Meals and lodging at Bearpaw Lodge are by reservation only, but there is a tiny "store" where you can buy film, freeze-dried food and trail snacks (supplies very limited).

6th Hiking Day (**Bearpaw Meadow** to **Crescent Meadow**, 11 miles): Reverse the 1st hiking day, trip 81.

TRIP   From Crescent Meadow to Whitney Portal via
             Hamilton Lakes, Kaweah Gap, Junction Meadow,
             Wallace Creek, Crabtree Meadow and Trail Crest
             (shuttle trip). Topo maps *Triple Divide Peak*
             (W.P.V.), *Kern Peak, Mt. Whitney* (W.P.V.) 15′;
             Mt. Kaweah, Mt. Whitney, Mt. Langley 7½′. Best
             mid-to-late season; 68½ miles.

Grade	Trail/layover days	Total recommended days
Leisurely	....	....
Moderate	8/3	11
Strenuous	6/2	8

HILITES Most of this dramatic trans-Sierra route follows the
             High Sierra Trail—a trail that is, in its early stages,
             literally carved out of the rock. After crossing the
             Great Western Divide, it descends to the Kern
             Trench, and later emerges on the east side at
             Whitney Portal. The scenic terrain it visits, and the
             fine trout waters it crosses or camps near, make it a
             justly famous and popular route.

DESCRIPTION (Moderate trip)

1st Hiking Day (**Crescent Meadow** to **Bearpaw Meadow**, 11 miles): From the parking loop, we circumvent the meadow on asphalt and begin climbing steadily through a forest of giant sequoias, sugar pines and white firs. Soon after passing a trail leading to Giant Forest, we break out into the open above Middle Fork Kaweah River. In a few hundred yards, at Eagle View Overlook, the view is indeed awesome. Moro Rock pokes up in the west, far below is the river, and to the east are the heavily glaciated peaks of the Great Western Divide. Soon one is far enough from the road and its crowds to begin saying "hello" to people along the trail. One of the best things about wilderness is that many of the citified psychological barriers between a person and his fellows are fast discarded.

The trail is nearly level and mostly shady as we move up-valley in a forest of ponderosa and sugar pine, black oak, incense-cedar, and white fir, mixed with manzanita, whitethorn scrub and much kit-kit-dizze. Across the canyon, those impressive sentinels of the valley, Castle Rocks, fall slowly behind as we march on. After negotiating three switchbacks, we resume strolling and soon pass a cutoff to Wolverton Corral in the north, used mostly by stock. Innumerable spring-fed streams cross the trail in this vicinity late into the season, and even a hot afternoon start on this hike is not too bad. Yellow-throated gilia and mustang clover are abundant along the trail until rather late in the year. Beyond Sevenmile Hill, a prominent ridge jutting out in the canyon below, we pass a junction with a trail that leads up to the Alta Trail 1300 feet above.

Our trail does not follow a "natural" route, but instead stays high on the north wall of the Middle Fork Kaweah River canyon. It is not a level traverse: frequently, the trail undulates over 400-foot rises, only to drop down into a secondary tributary canyon, and then emerge to climb again. From the Alta Trail junction, the trail descends to ford an unnamed tributary and then climb steeply. Views are all to the south and southeast, where the spectacular granite-dome formations of Sugarbowl Dome and Castle Rocks rise above the timbered valley floor. At each ford of the unnamed tributaries flowing from the slopes of Alta Peak, the trail passes precariously perched campsites, and then as it rounds a hot, dry, sparsely timbered slope to the Buck Creek bridge, it passes the faint, abandoned Moose Lake Trail. From here the route ascends through dense fir forest cover to the signed turnoff to a campground 200 yards south. Here, very overused campsites (7700') have bear boxes, toilets, and piped, treated water. Emergency services are usually available from the ranger station just east of the campground turnoff, but no open fires are allowed around here.

2nd Hiking Day (**Bearpaw Meadow** to **Big Arroyo Trail Junction**, 11 miles): Returning to the High Sierra Trail, our route turns right (east), and soon passes expansive, green Bearpaw Meadow. Today, most of the meadow is devoted to the outbuildings of Bearpaw Lodge (advance reservations for bed and board are essential and should be made on January 1 of the year you plan to go). Just across the trail from the lodge is the ranger's cabin. The magnificent views from the meadow and the subsequent trail include Mt. Stewart and Eagle Scout Peak on the Great Western Divide, Black Kaweah beyond, the Yosemite-like depths of Hamilton Creek and Middle Fork Kaweah River, and the Cliff Creek drainage below. Continuing past Bearpaw Ranger Station, the trail descends moderately through mixed, sparse forest stands. As the trail rounds the slope and descends toward River Valley, it traverses a section blasted from an immense, exfoliating granite slab. Educational views of clearcut avalanche chutes on the south wall of the canyon accompany the descent to the culvert fording wild, turbulent Lone Pine Creek. This stream cascades and plunges down a narrow granite chasm below the culvert, and the force of the torrent is clear evidence of the cutting power of the water. From the creek, the trail ascends an exposed slope, passing a side trail to Tamarack Lake and Elizabeth Pass (good campsites at this junction).

Continuing the steady ascent, the traveler is overwhelmed with the gigantic scale of the rock sculpting by ice, rock and snow to the east and southeast. The trail surface, while mostly rocky, passes occasional clumps of brightly colored wildflowers, including scarlet gilia, Douglas phlox, fleabane, Indian paintbrush, penstemon, mountain bluebell, red columbine and larkspur. Overshadowing the final climb to the ford of Hamilton Creek, the sheer granite wall to the north called Angel Wings, the sharply pointed granite sentinels atop the south wall, and the wall's avalanche-chuted sides are a constant source of wonderment and awe. Under these heights the trail climbs alongside the stream and then boulder-hops across it a few hundred yards below the lowest lake of the Hamilton Lakes chain. From this ford the trail climbs steeply over shattered rock to the good campsites at the northwest end of Lake 8235. Views from the campsites, including the silver waterfall ribbon at the east end, are superlative, and fishing for brook, rainbow and golden (to 10″) is fair to good, but the lake is highly overused, and we head for Kaweah Gap. In 1987, two camping areas here were closed indefinitely for rehabilitation. There is a two-night limit on camping at the Hamilton Lakes.

The steep climb to Kaweah Gap is an engineering marvel of trail construction, which has literally blasted the way along vertical cliff sections. Beginning at the northwest end of the lake, the trail ascends steadily up the juniper-and-red-fir-dotted slope with constant views of the lake and its dramatic walls. Despite the rocky terrain, many wildflowers line this ascent and among the manzanita and chinquapin one will find lush lupine, yellow columbine, penstemon, Indian paintbrush, white cinquefoil, false Solomon's seal and Douglas phlox. After some doubling back, the trail turns south on a steep ascent to a point just above the north shore of Precipice Lake, at the foot of the near-vertical north face of Eagle Scout Peak. The jagged summits of the peaks of the Great Western Divide dominate the skyline to the east during the final, tarn-dotted ascent to U-shaped Kaweah Gap, but as one approaches the gap one can see the equally spectacular summits of the Kaweah Peaks Ridge beyond. This colorful ridge dominates the views from Kaweah Gap (10,700′), and one can see the Nine Lake Basin watershed to the north. Those with a bent for exploring barren high country, or interested in the good brook-trout fishing, may elect to detour across granite slab and ledge routes north to the Nine Lake Basin.

Our trail continues its steady-to-moderate southward descent along the west side of the headwaters of Big Arroyo Creek, fording over to the east side midway down. (In 1987, CCC crews were continuing to reroute the trail away from the vulnerable banks of the creek onto the harder soils of the sides of Big Arroyo.) This descent crosses unjointed granite broken by substantial pockets of grass and numerous runoff streams even in late season, and the open stretches afford fine views of the U-shaped, glacially wrought Big Arroyo below, and the white, red and black rocks of Black Kaweah and Red Kaweah peaks to the east. The trail then reenters timber cover and arrives at some good campsites along the stream (9600′). These campsites and an abandoned trail-crew cabin are about ¼ mile above the Little Five Lakes/Black Rock Pass Trail junction. Fishing for brook trout to 7″ is fair to good. For those anglers with extra time, the 2-mile side trip to Little Five Lakes offers fine angling for golden trout.

3rd Hiking Day (**Big Arroyo Trail Junction** to **Moraine Lake**, 8 miles): Continuing past the Little Five Lakes Trail junction, the trail begins a long moderate ascent along the north canyon wall of Big Arroyo. This route parallels the course of a trunk glacier that once filled Big Arroyo, overflowed the benches on either side, and contributed to the main glacier of Kern Canyon. Our route climbs the wall of this trough, and the timber cover of this ascent is sparse, but there is no shortage of wildflowers tucked among the sage, manzanita and chinquapin. Most colorful are yellow columbine, Indian paintbrush and lupine. The sparse forest cover thickens near the Chagoopa Plateau, and one will find lodgepole and foxtail pines, and an occasional juniper.

The trail levels off near a small, mirror-faced tarn, and, swinging away from the lip of Big Arroyo, it begins a gradual descent through alternating timber and meadow stretches. Tree-interrupted views of the jagged Great Western Divide skyline accompany the descent to a meadowed trail junction on the south side of a tributary of Chagoopa Creek. At this junction our route leaves the High Sierra Trail, and branches right (south) through meadowed clumps of shooting stars. This descent becomes steeper over coarse granite sand, through dense stands of lodgepole and foxtail pine, with superlative views down into Big Arroyo and across the Arroyo to the drainages of Soda and Lost Canyon creeks. This steadily down-winding trail brings one to the wooded shores of Moraine Lake. Good campsites on the south side of the lake (9290′) provide lake-fronted views back to the Kaweah Peaks, and gardens of wild azalea in season.

4th Hiking Day (**Moraine Lake** to **Kern Hot Spring**, 7 miles): After traversing a moraine just east of Moraine Lake, the trail descends moderately, then gently, passing an old stockman's cabin before reaching superb Sky Parlor Meadow. Views back across this flower-filled grassland to the Great Western Divide and the Kaweahs are excellent. A half mile beyond the ford of Funston Creek at the east end of the meadow, the route rejoins the High Sierra Trail and begins the moderate, then steep descent to the bottom of the Kern Trench. The initial descent sees the

lodgepole being replaced by the lower-altitude white fir and
Jeffrey pine; and still lower down, the trail descends steeply
through manzanita and snow bush that are overshadowed by an
occasional juniper and oak. Views of the unmistakably U-shaped
Kern Trench, typical of glacially carved valleys, are instruc-
tive—particularly to the south. The final climb down to the
valley floor is accomplished via a series of steep, rocky switchbacks generally paralleling the plunging drop of Funston Creek.
On the Kern Canyon floor our route turns north, upstream, on
the Kern River Trail, drops into a marshy area, and then crosses
two meadows on wooden walkways. Then the trail leads gently
up through a forest of Jeffrey pine and incense-cedar. High on
the western rim of the canyon one catches glimpses of Chagoopa
Falls, a fury of plunging white water. Past a manzanita-carpeted
open area the trail crosses the Kern on a wooden bridge and
arrives at the southern fork of Rock Creek. Then, around a point,
we arrive at the delightful mountain spa of Kern Hot Spring—a
treat for the tired, dusty hiker. To the traveler, the crude, ce-
mented bathtub here becomes a regal, heated (115°) pool. Only
a few feet away, the great Kern River rushes past, and its cold
waters can be dipped into to cool the hot-spring water as desired.
In the campground just north and east of the spring, where you
must stay if camping near the spring, there are food storage
lockers, bear cables, and a toilet. The sites are, unfortunately,
very close together and very overused, but the spring and the
setting are worth it. Fishing is good for brown, rainbow and
golden trout (to 10″).

5th Hiking Day (**Kern Hot Spring** to **Junction Meadow**, 8 miles):
Continuing north, we ford the upper fork of Rock Creek and
traverse the gravelly canyon floor below the immense granite
cliffs of the canyon's east wall. Past the confluence of Red Spur
Creek this route ascends gently, sometimes a bit stiffly, beside
the Kern River, heading almost due north. The U-shaped trough
of the Kern River, called the Kern Trench, is remarkably straight
for about 25 miles as it traces the Kern Canyon fault. The fault, a
zone of structural weakness in the Sierra batholith, is more
susceptible to erosion than the surrounding rock, and this deep
canyon has been carved by both glacial and stream action. Three
times the glacier advanced down the canyon, shearing off spurs
created by stream erosion and leaving some tributary valleys
hanging above the main valley. The glacier also scooped and

plucked at the bedrock, creating basins in the granite which became lakes when the glacier melted and retreated.

The walls of this deep canyon, from 2000 to 5000 feet high, are quite spectacular, and a number of streams cascade and fall down these walls. (The fords of the stream draining Guyot Flat, of Whitney Creek and of Wallace Creek can be difficult in early season.) Beyond the ford of Wallace Creek the trail enters a parklike grove of stalwart Jeffrey pines that provide a noble setting for the overused campsites (food storage locker and bear cable) on the Kern River, where fishing is good for rainbow and some brook trout (to 10").

6th Hiking Day (**Junction Meadow** to **Crabtree Ranger Station,** 8½ miles): Our trail leaves the parklike Jeffrey pines of Junction Meadow and ascends steeply on rocky underfooting over a slope covered by manzanita and currant. Views down the Kern Trench improve constantly, as the occasional Jeffrey, lodgepole and aspen offer frames for the photographer who would compose a "shot" of the great cleft. After one mile we arrive at the junction of the Kern River Trail and the High Sierra Trail, where our route turns right (southeast), back toward Wallace Creek canyon. From here, reverse most of the 3rd hiking day, trip 75.

7th and 8th Hiking Days: Reverse the 2nd and 1st hiking days, trip 73, 15 miles. (Alternative: If you aren't set on the Whitney route and want to be around fewer people, consider reversing the first 3 days of Trip 88 to Cottonwood Creek trailhead, 24 miles.)

Moraine Lake   *Ron Van Cleave*

82   Crescent Meadow to Mt. Whitney

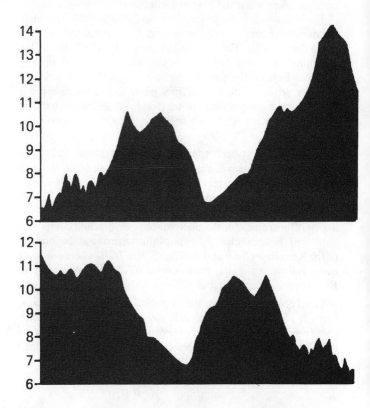

TRIP   From Crescent Meadow to Mt. Whitney via Hamilton Lake, Kaweah Gap, Big Arroyo, Junction Meadow, Wallace Creek, Crabtree Ranger Station, return via Tyndall Creek, Upper Kern River to Junction Meadow (semiloop trip). Topo maps *Giant Forest, Triple Divide Peak* (W.P.V.), *Kern Peak, Mt. Whitney* (W.P.V.) 15'; *Mt. Kaweah, Mt. Whitney, Mt. Brewer* 7½'. Best mid to late season; 136 miles.

Grade	Trail/layover days	Total recommended days
Leisurely	....	....
Moderate	13/3	16
Strenuous	10/1	11

HILITES   Many people plan for years to climb Mt. Whitney from Giant Forest, via the well-named High Sierra Trail. This trip repays the planning, and adds the dividend of getting off the main track during a looping return from the great peak. A food cache at Crabtree Ranger Station is almost a must.

DESCRIPTION (Moderate trip)

1st, 2nd, 3rd, 4th, 5th and 6th Hiking Days: Follow trip 81 to **Crabtree Ranger Station**, 53½ miles.

Layover Day, 18 miles: This "layover" day is the most strenuous of the trip. The hiker should begin as early as possible. He might camp on the Mt. Whitney Trail ½ mile above Crabtree Ranger Station in a small meadow on Whitney Creek, or hike after dinner to Guitar Lake and sleep there. Those with stoves can of course cook as high as they choose to.

From Crabtree Ranger Station our route ascends the narrow canyon of Whitney Creek. Past a small meadow we arrive at Timberline Lake (no camping, but fair fishing for golden trout). Then the trail ascends somewhat steeply past the last pine trees, crosses the outlet of Arctic Lake, and traverses above Guitar Lake to a wet meadow where the "fun" begins. Switchback is piled upon steep switchback until the panting hiker has to stop for breath, only to confront another series of switchbacks. Little windbreaks at the few flat places tell of westbound hikers who were too tired to make it down to Crabtree Meadows. Finally, after more than 1500 feet of climbing, we reach the side trail that leads to the summit. If, while on top, you should wonder how John Muir felt the first time he climbed Mt. Whitney, be it noted that he later wrote, "I reached the summit needles about 11 o'clock that night and danced most of the time until morning, as the night was bitterly cold and I was in my shirtsleeves."

7th Hiking Day (**Crabtree Ranger Station** to **Lake on Upper Kern River**, 13½ miles): Follow the 3rd hiking day, trip 77 to the Tyndall

Creek tributary. From this ford we descend gently on a rocky trail through a forest cover of mixed lodgepole and foxtail pine to a junction with the Shepherd Pass Trail. From here, our route northwest follows part of the 2nd hiking day, trip 69, to the unnamed lake with elevation 10,650 feet. This natural impoundment on the Kern River has good campsites and good fishing for golden and rainbow-golden hybrids (to 10").

8th Hiking Day (**Lake on Upper Kern River** to **Junction Meadow**, 6 miles): Follow the 3rd hiking day, trip 70.

9th–13th Hiking Days (**Junction Meadow** to **Crescent Meadow**, 45 miles): Retrace the steps of the first 5 hiking days.

Kaweah Peaks Ridge

Cottonwood Creek Trailhead to South Fork Lakes **83**

TRIP   From Cottonwood Creek Trailhead to South Fork
Lakes, return via cross country down South Fork
Cottonwood Creek (loop trip). Topo maps *Olancha*
15′; *Cirque Peak* 7½. Best mid or late season; 10¼
miles.

Grade	Trail/layover days	Total recommended days
Leisurely	2/1	3
Moderate	....	....
Strenuous	day	....

HILITES   A fine weekend loop trip, this route affords grand
scenery, and a good exposure to east-side ecology
that will benefit both beginner and old hand.

DESCRIPTION (Leisurely trip)

1st Hiking Day (**Cottonwood Creek Trailhead** to **South Fork Lakes**, 5¼
miles): From the trailhead (10040′) at the end of the right-hand
fork of Horseshoe Meadow Road, the trail leads west, then north
on a gentle and brief ascent through an open stand of lodgepole
and foxtail pine, and soon enters Golden Trout Wilderness.
Underfoot, the sandy trail soon begins to descend gently, and
then it levels out. In about 1 mile we cross the South Fork
Cottonwood Creek on a flattened log. The creek is frequently
willow-choked, but the more open stretches reveal it to be a
placid, clear-running stream—ideal for fly-rod action.

In another ½ mile we reach a junction with the old trail and
continue northward.

The trail skirts the west side of the meadows along Cottonwood Creek and ascends steadily, passing Golden Trout Camp, a
privately operated resort. Soon we enter John Muir Wilderness
and cross Cottonwood Creek. Beyond this crossing the trail
swings west, passing through meadow clearings and moderate-
to-dense stands of foxtail and lodgepole pines, with the creek and

its meadows to our southwest. The ascent levels during these stretches, and then the route comes to a trail junction, where the left fork of the trail seems to vanish into the willows. A sign near here says there are 6 Cottonwood Lakes, but there are really 5. Nevertheless, we turn left through the willows and cross Cottonwood Creek, where we pick up the trail again. Our route soon fords a fork of Cottonwood Creek not shown on the topo map and passes the South Fork Lakes Trail, branching left. Keeping to the right, we ascend a forested moraine via switchbacks to arrive at the meadowed east end of the lowest Cottonwood Lake, called Cottonwood Lake #1. Our trail skirts the south side of this lake, passing a trail leading to Old Army Pass. Cottonwood Lakes #1 through #4 are closed to fishing, but Lake #5 is open to fishing now (1989). These lakes were used at one time for research and breeding of golden trout.

Our route passes Cottonwood Lake #2 and then veers southwest through a jumbled area of near-white granite blocks. From the point where the trail turns west-northwest, a short spur trail descends a few yards to the good campsites at the west end of the westernmost South Fork Lake (11,000'). These campsites are located in a grove of sparse foxtail pines with fine views of Cirque Peak to the southwest. There are also nice campsites around the easternmost of the South Fork Lakes, reached via the lateral mentioned earlier. Anglers will fare better at this lake and at nearby Long Lake and Cirque Lake.

2nd Hiking Day (**South Fork Lakes** to **Cottonwood Creek Trailhead**, 5 miles, part cross-country): From the west side of the westernmost South Fork Lake, our route heads south and then east toward the easternmost lake, skirting the large talus area between the two lakes. We round the south side of the easternmost lake (golden to 7") and pick up a trail that leads downstream from its outlet. Keeping on the north and then the east side of the outlet stream, this route descends over heavily fractured granite past foxtail and lodgepole pines on a slope where the dashing stream cascades and falls from one rocky grotto to the next. Clumps of shooting star topped by showy yellow columbine and orange tiger lily line the stream.

The trail levels off in a meadow and then descends into a larger meadow, where the outlet of Cirque Lake joins South Fork Cottonwood Creek. Following the creek's course, we swing east and descend steeply in lodgepole forest to traverse another meadow. Beyond this meadow the trail drops steeply again, passing an old notched-log cabin where there are two cement fireplaces. The trail veers away from South Fork Cottonwood Creek and rounds the moraine between this fork and the main fork. Then our trail goes up the west side of the main fork for ⅓ mile to join the trail described in the 1st hiking day. Now our route fords Cottonwood Creek and turns south to retrace the steps of part of the 1st hiking day.

Mt. Langley from Cottonwood Basin

84 Cottonwood Creek Trailhead to Upper Rock Creek

TRIP
From Cottonwood Creek Trailhead to Upper Rock Creek via New Army Pass (round trip). Topo maps *Cirque Peak, Johnson Peak* 7½'. Best mid or late season; 23½ miles.

Grade	Trail/layover days	Total recommended days
Leisurely	4/3	7
Moderate	3/2	5
Strenuous	2/1	3

HILITES
Beautiful Rock Creek and its spectacular headwaters are the goal of this high-country trip. The tiny, unnamed lake at the end of this trip makes a fine base camp for further exploration of Miter Basin and Soldier Lakes.

DESCRIPTION (Leisurely trip)

1st Hiking Day: Follow trip 83 to **South Fork Lakes**, 5¼ miles.

2nd Hiking Day: (**South Fork Lakes** to **Upper Rock Creek Lake**, 6½ miles): From the westernmost South Fork Lake, the trail ascends west through thinning timber to Long Lake. After skirting the south shore, our route begins a long, steadily rising traverse that takes the traveler above the campsites at the west end of the lake. Views of the lake from this traverse are favorites of photographers, but it is wise to save some film for the panoramic shots farther up. This traverse brings one above timberline as the trail skirts a wet area covered with grass, willows and wildflowers. The trail touches the south edge of High Lake, and a pause at this lake's outlet will brace one for the upcoming rocky switchbacks.

The trail soon begins a series of long, gently graded zigzags which climb the cirque wall up to New Army Pass. The higher one climbs up this cirque wall, the better the views to the east of the lakes immediately below and of the Cottonwood Creek drainage.

Descending from New Army Pass into Sequoia National Park, the trail crosses a long, barren slope of coarse granite sand sprinkled with exfoliating granite boulders. A half mile north of the pass our route passes a trail that branches right to Old Army Pass. This pass, about ½ mile east, was the original pass constructed by an army troop stationed in Owens Valley in the 1890s. Beyond this junction the route swings west and descends steeply over rocky tread to level off on a more gentle descent in a barren cirque. The trail crosses to the north side of the unnamed stream in the cirque and re-enters moderate forest cover. About 2 miles from New Army Pass the trail meets a trail to Siberian Pass, and there are good campsites on the south side of the stream just south of this junction.

Our route turns to the right, continuing to descend through denser lodgepole pine, and when the forest gives way to the open spaces of a lovely meadow, our trail fords a little tributary of Rock Creek and turns left on the Rock Creek Trail. This trail descends steeply alongside a willow-infested tributary of Rock Creek until the rocky slope gives way to a meadow just above the lake on Rock Creek at 10,440'. Around these meadows one may sight the relatively rare white-tailed jackrabbit. There are fair campsites at the head of this meadow, and others are located at the lake's outlet, but more primitive ones are to be found on the south side of the lake. The campsites at the outlet are reached by fording Rock Creek and rounding the north side of the lake. Fishing for golden (to 8") in the lake and adjoining stream is good.

This marshy-meadowed lake makes a grand base camp for side trips to the rugged Miter Basin and adjoining "Soldier Lakes" (just south of the Major General, where there is good camping). Fishing for golden trout in most of the lakes below the Miter and The Major General is good. A trail of use to Miter Basin makes a hard-to-spot exit along the north side of the large, overused campsite just east of our lake's meadow. We have little trouble following it to the place where Rock Creek cascades out of the basin; from here, it's cross-country. Other fine side trips include a looping cross-country exploration of the Boreal

Plateau via Siberian Outpost, or the hardy and experienced backpacker with a yen for adventure may wish to take the Guyot Flat Trail to Crabtree Meadow and then take the scrambling cross-country route over Crabtree Pass, which rounds Mt. Chamberlin, Mt. Newcomb, Mt. Pickering and Joe Devel Peak and returns via Miter Basin.

3rd and 4th Hiking Days: Retrace your steps, 11¾ miles.

Foxtail pine

Cottonwood Creek Trailhead to Upper Rock Creek 85

TRIP
From Cottonwood Creek Trailhead to Upper Rock Creek Lake via New Army Pass, return via Cottonwood Pass (loop trip). Topo maps *Cirque Peak, Mt. Whitney, Johnson Peak* 7½'. Best mid or late season; 22¾ miles.

Grade	Trail/layover days	Total recommended days
Leisurely	4/3	7
Moderate	4/1	5
Strenuous	3/0	3

HILITES
One of the finest circuits in the Sierra, this route tours peaks of spectacle and grandeur, visits unforgettable lakes, traces streams that plummet, seep and meander, and blends them all together with a carpet of green forest and open meadows that will give all who come a sense of accomplishment and peace.

DESCRIPTION (Leisurely trip)

1st and 2nd Hiking Days: Follow trip 84 to **Upper Rock Creek,** 11¾ miles.

3rd Hiking Day (**Upper Rock Creek** to **Chicken Spring Lake,** 6 miles): You begin this hiking day by retracing your steps for 1 mile to the meadowed Siberian Pass Trail junction passed during the 2nd hiking day. Fill your canteens here; this is the last reliable water source before Chicken Spring Lake. From the junction this trail ascends southward gently over a moderate-to-densely forested slope of foxtail and lodgepole pine. Our route crosses a barren area, climbs over an easy ridge and, 1 mile south of the last junction, turns left onto the Pacific Crest Trail. We now reverse the first part of the 2nd hiking day, trip 89, to Chicken Spring Lake.

4th Hiking Day (**Chicken Spring Lake** to **Horseshoe Meadow,** 5 miles): Reverse the 1st hiking day, trip 89.

86   Cottonwood Creek Trailhead to Mineral King

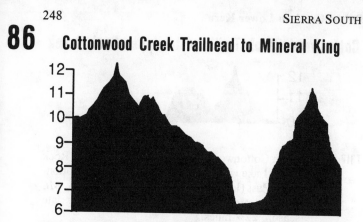

TRIP   From Cottonwood Creek Trailhead to Mineral King via Army Pass, Siberian Pass, Kern River, Rattlesnake Creek, Franklin Pass (shuttle trip). Topo maps *Mineral King* (W.P.V.) 15'; *Cirque Peak, Mt. Whitney, Johnson Peak, Kern Peak, Kern Lake, Chagoopa Falls, Mineral King* 7½'; Best mid or late season; 57¾ miles.

Grade	Trail/layover days	Total recommended days
Leisurely	....	....
Moderate	7/4	11
Strenuous	6/3	9

HILITES   This excellent trans-Sierra route visits the finest fishing lakes and streams of the lower Kern River drainage. The severe altitude changes inherent in the route, however, recommend this trip for intermediate and experienced hikers only.

DESCRIPTION (Moderate trip)

1st and 2nd Hiking Days: Follow trip 84 to **Upper Rock Creek,** 11¾ miles.

3rd Hiking Day (**Upper Rock Creek** to **Big Whitney Meadow,** 7 miles): Follow the 3rd hiking day, trip 85, for the route to Siberian Outpost. Fill your canteens at the meadowed Siberian Pass Trail junction; this is the last reliable water before Big Whitney Meadow in a dry year. From where the Pacific Crest Trail turns east, our route crosses the east end of Siberian Outpost and ascends gently past a snowmarker site to the easy rise called Siberian Pass (10,920') where we leave Sequoia National Park and enter Golden Trout Wilderness.

Our gently graded, switchbacking trail crosses the head-waters of Golden Trout Creek (may be dry) midway down the descent from the pass, and then crosses a few ridges before descending a moderate slope to the west edge of Big Whitney Meadow. The underfooting of most of this descent has been dust and some rock, but as we near the meadow it is mostly sand. The trail may seem to vanish in the sand as it descends gently to the east side of this sandy wash, but it reappears in the forest edge on the west side as we approach the north tip of the grassy area. Mats of yellow monkey flower color the forest floor, and as the trail emerges in the opener sections, one finds lupine, penstemon, cinquefoil and sagebrush. Keeping to the forest fringes on the west side of the very large grassland, our trail passes the Cottonwood Pass Trail, and a few hundred yards beyond arrives at the fair campsites at the Rocky Basin Lakes Trail junction. The meadow is a cattle-grazing allotment; expect bovine company here.

4th Hiking Day (**Big Whitney Meadow** to **Little Whitney Meadow**, 10 miles): The winding meadow trail continues south over rolling terrain. Many wildflowers line the route through the southern arm of the meadow and subsequent trail, including shooting star, monkey flower, mountain aster, scarlet gilia, and pussy paws. The sandy surface of the meadow trail continues into the moderate-to-dense forest cover of lodgepole and foxtail pine below. Shortly after re-entering forest cover, the trail fords Barigan Stringer and passes several nearby campsites. There are many good campsites along Golden Trout Creek. Now the sandy, rocky canyon walls narrow, and the stream quickens for about ½ mile, and then as the canyon opens somewhat our trail passes the Barigan Stringer Trail to Rocky Basin Lakes. This creek was the original source for golden trout used in subsequent plantings throughout the higher lakes and streams of the Sierra.

Beyond the Barigan Stringer Trail junction our trail continues a moderate sandy descent past several more campsites to the ford of Golden Trout Creek. Mounting a sandy shelf above the creek, the trail meets the Bullfrog Meadow Trail above the South Fork Kern River (flowing only 300 yards from Golden Trout

Creek) and descends gradually past Tunnel Ranger Station and one of its fenced administrative pastures (emergency services available). The final descent to the guard station affords views of Kern Peak and of the red-topped volcanic hills to the southwest. Beyond the Tunnel Ranger Station our route passes the Kern Peak/Ramshaw Meadows Trail branching east, then turns west to ford Golden Trout Creek, and passes another fenced administrative pasture. Fishing on Golden Trout Creek below Tunnel Ranger Station is restricted to artificial lures.

Across sandy, moderately forested, level terrain, the faint trail, heavily trampled by horses, mules and cattle, stays well north of the creek, and passes a trail to Volcano Meadow. Multiple tracks diverge and converge here; blazes mark the main trail. Rejoining the creek, the trail continues westward, winding along the northernmost edge of a large late Pleistocene volcanic flow (post-glacial) known as Malpais Lava. The largest single concentration of volcanic action in the upper reaches of the Kern, this basalt flow shows itself near the trail in brilliant displays of the colored rock. Predominant in the volcanic rock is a deep red, sometimes mixed with ochres and shades of tan.

These colorful displays accompany the traveler all the way down this drainage, but the interested rockhound can see extensive fields of this rock by fording the creek and exploring the mile-wide strip of old lava flow to the south. Just east of Little Whitney Meadow, the more obvious trail curves north, passes through a drift fence and, south of the cabins of still-active Little Whitney Cow Camp, fords Johnson Creek. (A less obvious fork curves south across Golden Trout Creek.) We may notice, in passing, an unsigned, unmaintained trail north to Salt Lick Meadow. There are good campsites in the forested edges of this 8420′ meadow, which is no longer a cattle-grazing allotment but attracts travelers with stock. Expect equine company here. (Cattle grazing in nearby meadows may wander back here, so bovine company is possible too.)

5th Hiking Day (**Little Whitney Meadow** to **Rattlesnake Creek/Kern River**, 11 miles): Our trip skirts the southern end of beautiful Little Whitney Meadow, climbs a rise, and passes through another drift fence. Descending steadily over a dusty granite-sand surface, the trail then refords Golden Trout Creek. Then, as the route continues its steady descent, the trail surface becomes pumice, and the forest cover of lodgepole gives way to Jeffrey and juniper.

Large concentrations of wildflowers daub the opener stretches with yellows (monkey flower), whites (Mariposa lily), mixed blues and purples (larkspur and penstemon), and reds (red dogwood). Leveling out to a moderate descent, the trail then recrosses a tributary of Golden Trout Creek via a natural bridge of basalt. Easily eroded, this pink rock shows extensive water cutting and sculpting. After Natural Bridge, the grade of the trail steepens to a steady descent over pumice and sand through a forest cover of Jeffrey, white fir and some lodgepole. At the switchbacks dropping to the Kern Canyon floor, one can see the clearly delineated volcanic overlay with its subsurface of granite where the underlying rock has been laid bare by subsequent stream cutting that has knifed through the basalt layer and exposed a rainbow of blacks, reds, tans and whites. Some columnar basalt formations, usually associated with these lava flows, may also be seen to the north. Our trail provides a good view of Volcano Falls as we twine steeply down over pumice and rock (poor footing).

With the lower altitude come sugar pine and, on the canyon floor, quaking aspen, birch, black oak and incense-cedar. It is not until the canyon floor is reached that one has views of domelike Tower Rock to the south. Through a sparse forest cover and clumps of sage, manzanita, willows and chinquapin, the trail veers south to cross the Kern River (footbridge), leaving Inyo National Forest (Golden Trout Wilderness) and entering Sequoia National Park, passes a spur trail to a natural soda spring, and meets the Kern River Trail a few hundred yards north of the Kern Canyon Ranger Station (emergency services usually available).

Our route turns right onto the Kern Canyon Trail and ascends the Kern Canyon by a series of moderate ups and downs. The forest cover is usually dense, with tiny wet sections that are made difficult of passage by dense concentrations of bracken fern. Their luxuriant growth is commonly associated with canyon bottoms, and they are frequently found in conjunction with riverside stands of alder, laurel, aspen and birch. The approach to Lower Funston Meadow (bear box) is heralded by the lower drift fence, and then the trail begins a steady climb over the alluvial fan that results from Laurel Creek's contribution of silt and rock on the canyon floor. Fording Laurel Creek is accomplished via two crossings, each marked by a campsite; during high water, the second ford is sometimes hazardous.

Fishing in the Kern River, particularly near the confluences of the many tributary streams, is excellent. Angling is sometimes made difficult by the thickets of willows lining the river, but the rewards in rainbow trout (to 20″) more than make up for the casting problems. Fishermen, or those who simply enjoy the view from streamside, should keep a sharp eye out for beavers that work this section of the river. It is not surprising that one usually makes wild animal sightings while traveling up this glacially carved trench. Animals, like men, are "channeled" down its steep-walled course, and within the canyon's relatively confined course, the hiker is apt to see bear, coyote, deer and the aforementioned beaver. From Laurel Creek the trail continues north through a moderate forest. Mostly duff, the trail surface makes pleasant walking, and the distance to the Rattlesnake Creek Trail junction is rapidly covered. At this junction, and just across the sometimes difficult ford of Rattlesnake Creek are excellent packer campsites (6600′). (Note: Yes, there are rattlesnakes in this area.)

6th Hiking Day (**Rattlesnake Creek/Kern River** to **Upper Rattlesnake Creek**, 8 miles): Reverse the 2nd hiking day, trip 100.

7th Hiking Day (**Upper Rattlesnake Creek** to **Mineral King**, 10 miles): Reverse the 1st hiking day, trip 96.

Horseshoe Meadow to Rocky Basin Lakes **87**

TRIP   From Horseshoe Meadow to Rocky Basin Lakes via Cottonwood Pass, Big Whitney Meadow (round trip). Topo maps *Cirque Peak, Johnson Peak* 7½'. Best mid season; 29 miles.

Grade	Trail/layover days	Total recommended days
Leisurely	....	....
Moderate	4/2	6
Strenuous	2/1	3

HILITES   The fine angling enjoyed at the culmination of this trip should make it a good selection for the intermediate hiker who wants good recreation as well as a challenging route.

DESCRIPTION (Moderate trip)

1st Hiking Day (**Horseshoe Meadow** to **Stokes Stringer Campsites**, 5 miles): The trail leaves the parking lot at the end of the Horseshoe Meadow Road and in a mere 150 yards enters Golden Trout Wilderness. Breaks in the lodgepole and foxtail pine forest permit views of Mulkey Pass, Trail Pass, Trail Peak and Cottonwood Pass. The rerouted trail along the forest margin is giving the overrutted meadows a chance to recover something like their pre-man condition—although ecological changes never exactly reverse themselves. On the long, gradual ascent west near the meadow, hikers who get an early start are sure to come upon a few late-grazing deer, and along with many other birds they may well see a long-eared owl, a resident of these grasslands. Usually this predatory bird is seen while swooping down on its prey— meadow mice, deer mice and other rodents, but in very early season it is sometimes seen in family groups among the willows near the stream.

At the head of the meadow, our trail makes two quick stream

crossings. A gentle incline brings one to a meadow heavy with willows, paintbrush, columbine and penstemon. Then about a dozen switchbacks suffice to mount a rocky saddle, Cottonwood Pass (11,200'). Views eastward include the Inyo and Panamint ranges, and to the west the more Sierralike Great Western Divide. A few feet west of the pass, the Pacific Crest Trail veers right toward Chicken Spring Lake, and from this junction our route descends sagebrush-covered slopes southwest for ½ mile to the several fair campsites on the right of the trail above Stokes Stringer.

2nd Hiking Day (**Stokes Stringer Campsites** to **Rocky Basin Lakes**, 9½ miles): About 20 steep switchbacks are required to get down to a ford of Stokes Stringer before the trail zigzags down a more gentle slope to the eastern precincts of Big Whitney Meadow. Most of the tiny creeks meandering through this enormous grazeland are as unhealthy as they look; purify the water, as usual. After fording Stokes Stringer again, the trail crosses a forested ridge and descends to a muddy ford or two of an unnamed creek. Then the trail tops another little rise before we arrive at a jump-across ford of upper Golden Trout Creek (last reliable water before Rocky Basin Lakes). The sandy path enters forest cover and passes the Siberian Pass Trail. Here we veer left and stroll 300 yards southwest to a junction from where the Rocky Basin Lakes Trail leads west.

Our westbound trail begins a moderate ascent through open-to-moderate stands of pine trees. This ascent makes many easy switchbacks on its southwestward traverse of the moraine just west of Big Whitney Meadow, then descends more switchbacks to a junction and turns right onto the Barigan Stringer Trail. The ascent beyond this junction is gentle, then moderate over increasingly rocky underfooting. The foxtail and lodgepole pine forest cover lining either side of this ravine ascent is a favorite habitat for a great variety of birdlife, including the long-eared owl, Steller jay, robin, chickadee, junco, calliope hummingbird, Clark nutcracker and rosy finch. The latter is often one's only contact with birdlife at the higher elevations, and is a frequently seen companion on exploratory trips around the rocky, barren expanses of Funston Lake, where fishing is good. In 1989 a sign at a crossing of Barigan Stringer indicated FOOT TRAIL northwest and HORSE TRAIL west. The indistinct foot trail offers a shorter but steeper scramble over a rocky, foxtail-clad ridge above the outlet stream of the largest Rocky Basin lake, past a wedge-shaped lakelet, to that outlet. The distinct, longer horse trail winds over a ridge and emerges at the east end of the westernmost Rocky Basin lake. The north and west walls of this cirque basin are heavily fractured granite, and are a haven for marmots. From the horse trail, the route rounds the north side of the middle lake and descends to the west side of the largest of the Rocky Basin Lakes, where fishing is good for rainbow (to 14"). The foot trail also offers access to these sites—with a little more boulder-scrambling. Three more secluded campsites are on the northeast side of the lake.

To visit nearby Johnson and Funston lakes, work up the draw that leads southwest from the southwestern end of the western-most Rocky Basin lake. Johnson Peak and lake are visible from the saddle at the top of that draw. To go directly to Funston Lake, carefully climb out of the draw over the ridge northwest of it and onto the Boreal Plateau, staying near treeline, and traverse over another gentle ridge, bearing generally northwest. Johnson Peak provides a reference point until you descend toward Funston Lake. The views of the Great Western Divide, of Kaweah Peaks Ridge, and north toward Mt. Whitney from that second ridge are worth the scramble! To reach Johnson Lake, descend to it from the saddle. To get to the Boreal Plateau and Funston Lake, work your way up the rocky slopes on Johnson Lake's north shore.

3rd and 4th Hiking Days: Retrace your steps, 14½ miles.

88

Cottonwood Creek to Whitney Portal

TRIP   From Cottonwood Creek Trailhead to Whitney Portal via New Army Pass, Rock Creek, Crabtree Meadow, John Muir Trail (shuttle trip). Topo maps *Mt. Whitney* (W.P.V.), 15'; *Cirque Peak, Johnson Peak, Mt. Whitney, Mt. Langley* 7½'. Best mid or late season; 37¾ miles.

Grade	Trail/layover days	Total recom- mended days
Leisurely	....	....
Moderate	5/1	6
Strenuous	4/0	4

HILITES   This fine shuttle trip surveys the Sierra crest from New Army Pass to Whitney Portal.

DESCRIPTION (Moderate trip)

1st Hiking Day: Follow trip 84 to **South Fork Lakes**, 5¼ miles.

2nd Hiking Day (**South Fork Lakes** to **Lower Rock Creek Ford**, 10½ miles): Follow the 1st part of the 2nd hiking day, trip 84, to Upper Rock Creek Lake. The rest of this day is an easy 4-mile stroll down lovely Rock Creek canyon. This tumbling rill slows to a murmuring brook in the meadow flats, and its fresh-from-the-source waters are crystal clear and icy cold. The dense green canopy of lodgepoles overhead allows only clumps of shade-loving gooseberry to grow along the trail, but the virile willow maintains its verdant stream-bank growth, shade or sun. Willow growth is synonymous with birdlife, and Rock Creek has its share of robins, white-crowned sparrows, chickadees, juncos, woodpeckers and olive-sided flycatchers. It is often the "*oh-see view*" call of this flycatcher that reminds the passerby of the beauty of his surroundings—surroundings that on this canyon descent, include a chain of lovely meadows. Unfortunately, this native tour guide leaves these environs in August, and the late-season traveler is left to rely on his own initiative.

Just before reaching a large meadow, the trail fords Rock Creek via logs (difficult in high water) and veers away from the stream. Interestingly enough, most anglers ignore the waters of this tiny creek and thereby miss some fine fishing for golden trout. The fish are not too large, but there are several in every hole. Past the west end of the large meadow, the trail descends to join the Pacific Crest Trail, and in 1 mile we reach the ford of lower Rock Creek (9500'), where fishing is good for golden (to 8").

3rd Hiking Day (**Lower Rock Creek Ford** to **Crabtree Ranger Station**, 7 miles): Beyond logs over the stream, the trail climbs steeply up the north wall of the canyon, then levels somewhat to the ford of Guyot Creek (last water for more than 4 miles). The jumbled, symmetrical crest of Mt. Guyot takes up the skyline to the west, and highly fractured Joe Devel Peak looms to the east as the trail begins another moderate ascent through a dense forest cover of lodgepole pine. This bouldery climb culminates at a saddle from which there are good views north across the Kern Canyon to the Kern-Kaweah drainage, Red Spur, Kern Ridge and the Great Western Divide. From the saddle, the trail descends moderately to the large, sandy basin of Guyot Flat, then traverses through the forest east of the flat. Like the Chagoopa Plateau across the canyon, this flat and the subsequent "shelf" traversed later in this hiking day were part of an immense valley floor in preglacial times. However, much of the granular sand deposits are a result of later weathering and erosion of the granite peaks to the east.

Beyond Guyot Flat the trail undulates through a moderate forest cover before dropping steeply into the Whitney Creek drainage. The descent into this drainage affords views eastward to Mt. Whitney—the long, flat-topped, avalanche-chuted mountain that towers over the nearer, granite-spired shoulder of Mt. Hitchcock. This descent concludes over a barren, rocky stretch to lower Crabtree Meadow, where, just beyond a good campsite, our route fords Whitney Creek and turns right (east) along its north bank, leaving the Pacific Crest Trail. A half mile of gentle ascents ends at Upper Crabtree Meadow, where the route passes the Crabtree Lakes Trail. (This unmaintained trail leads to the good fishing on Crabtree Lakes for golden, to 14"). Continuing northeast beside Whitney Creek, the trail ascends gently to meet the John Muir Trail beside a ford of Whitney Creek. Beyond this ford is the Crabtree Ranger Station (emergency services usually available) and fair campsites.

4th and 5th Hiking Days: Reverse the 2nd and 1st hiking days, trip 73, 15 miles.

Looking northeast from Black Rock Pass   *Ron Felzer*

Horseshoe Meadow to Whitney Portal **89**

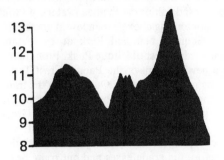

TRIP   From Horseshoe Meadow to Whitney Portal via Cottonwood Pass, Rock Creek, Crabtree Meadow (shuttle trip). Topo maps *Mt. Whitney* (W.P.V.), 15'; *Cirque Peak, Johnson Peak, Mt. Whitney, Mt. Langley* 7½'. Best mid or late season; 37 miles.

Grade	Trail/layover days	Total recommended days
Leisurely	6/2	8
Moderate	5/1	6
Strenuous	4/0	4

HILITES   Crossing three passes, this route traverses four drainages, offering a multitude of chances for angling that ranges from good to excellent. The scenery that graces most of this trail is exceeded nowhere in the Sierra, having an abundance of peaks exceeding 13,000 feet, and dozens of high, granitic cirques.

DESCRIPTION (Moderate trip)

1st Hiking Day (**Horseshoe Meadow** to **Chicken Spring Lake**, 5½ miles): Follow the 1st hiking day, trip 87 to Cottonwood Pass. At the pass we meet the Pacific Crest Trail and turn right onto it for 1 easy mile on level, dynamited footing to the good campsites east of the outlet of Chicken Spring Lake.

2nd Hiking day (**Chicken Spring Lake** to **Lower Rock Creek Ford**, 9½ miles): Except in early season there is no water until Rock

Creek, so fill your canteen. The Pacific Crest Trail switchbacks westward up the wall of the Chicken Spring Lake cirque and then levels off over sandy slopes at the headwaters of Golden Trout Creek. After contouring above a meadow in another cirque, our route enters Sequoia National Park at an unnamed point (11,350′) on a ridge west of Cirque Peak. From here our route soon joins a new segment of the Pacific Crest Trail, which is rerouted to the north of Siberian Outpost. As the trail descends through the moderate-to-dense forest of lodgepole and foxtail pine, we get good views of Mt. Kaweah and the Great Western Divide, as well as large, bleak Siberian Outpost.

The trail descends steadily past a junction with the Siberian Pass Trail before the grade eases and our route begins a long, rolling descent along the forested ridge atop the south wall of Rock Creek Canyon. Where the trail is close to the right side of the ridge, it is well worth stepping off to the right a few hundred feet to get the excellent views of the peaks surrounding Miter Basin. About 2½ miles from the junction our route makes a steep descent toward Siberian Pass Creek, but turns north before reaching it. Then it drops via rocky switchbacks through a dense forest down the north wall of Rock Creek Canyon. When the underfooting turns to duff, our route meets and turns left onto the Rock Creek Trail and descends one mile down the creek to the good campsites at the ford of lower Rock Creek (9500′), where fishing for golden trout (to 8″) is good.

3rd, 4th and 5th Hiking Days: Follow trip 88, the 3rd through the 5th hiking days, 22 miles.

Mineral King to Upper Cliff Creek

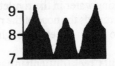

90

TRIP
From Mineral King to Upper Cliff Creek (round trip). Topo map *Mineral King* (W.P.V.). Best midseason; 17 miles.

Grade	Trail/layover days	Total recom- mended days
Leisurely	....	....
Moderate	2/1	3
Strenuous	....	....

HILITES
This is one of the easiest hikes into National Park wilderness in the western High Sierra, but still tough enough that the hiker will feel he has earned the fine alpine scenery that awaits on the banks of Cliff Creek and the pleasure of a swim in Pinto Lake.

DESCRIPTION (Moderate trip)

1st Hiking day (**Mineral King** to **Upper Cliff Creek**, 8½ miles): From the Timber Gap/Sawtooth Pass trailhead one mile beyond the Ranger Station in Mineral King Valley, our route ascends the manzanita-and-sagebrush-flanked Sawtooth Pass Trail for ¼ mile, and then diverges left at a junction. Our fork climbs relentlessly up a southwest-facing slope that is warm indeed in midsummer, but blessed by some shade from juniper and red-fir trees. After a steep series of 10 switchbacks, we traverse almost on the level across a treeless, flower-dotted hillside, and then enter a cool stand of red fir, which comes to include lodgepole and foxtail pine.

This ascent tops out at Timber Gap (9400′), where we begin to drop steeply in red-fir forest. During early summer in this forest, hikers may hear the thumping of blue grouse and the melodic flutings of hermit thrushes. As we descend above Timber Gap Creek, we find the rivulets on the slope sometimes disappearing into the loosely consolidated metamorphic rock. Soon we reach a mile-long flower garden, one of the largest and best in the whole Sierra. Although Timber Gap Creek is virtually inaccessible, there's plenty of drinking water in the rivulets that lace this high garden. Then the trail rounds the nose of the ridge on the east and switchbacks down to Cliff Creek through dense coniferous forest.

Beyond a ford of Cliff Creek (difficult in early season) are Cliff Creek Campground (bear box) and a 3-way junction with trails to Mineral King, Redwood Meadow and Black Rock Pass. After turning right, uphill through the campsites, our route climbs steadily through alternating brush and trees to reach a very verdant area watered in part by cold little streams that issue from the ground. In early summer the fine wildflower displays near the creek include Mariposa lily, rein orchid, wild strawberry, monkey flower, wallflower, corn lily, delphinium, yellow-throated gilia, yarrow and buckwheat. Beyond a grove of fir trees our route goes out onto what looks like an abandoned steam bed, and leads us toward the base of the prominent falls of Cliff Creek. Here we veer away from the falls and turn toward the cascading outlet of Pinto Lake. Now we climb the tough slope to the left through dense willow, sagebrush, whitethorn and bitter cherry. Then our trail crosses the outlet stream of Pinto Lake, tops a small rise in ½ mile, and arrives at another three-way junction. The left fork is the trail to Black Rock Pass, and the right fork is a short spur to good campsites near Cliff Creek on forested knolls (bear box). Just to the north, screened by willows, is little Pinto Lake, an excellent swimming pool much warmer that you'd expect.

2nd Hiking Day: Retrace your steps, 8½ miles.

Great Western Divide from Moro Rock   *National Park Service*

Mineral King to Little Five Lakes

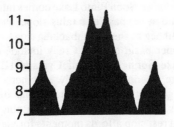

91

TRIP From Mineral King to Little Five Lakes via Cliff Creek, Black Rock Pass (round trip). Topo maps *Mineral King* (W.P.V.) 15'; *Mineral King* 7½'. Best mid or late season; 31 miles.

Grade	Trail/layover days	Total recommended days
Leisurely	5/2	7
Moderate	4/1	5
Strenuous	....	....

HILITES Next to the Sierra crest itself, the Great Western Divide is the most spectacular feature in Sequoia National Park. This trip crosses that sky-piercing divide at Black Rock Pass and leads to a large number of lakes to camp beside, all of them close under the colorful cliffs and peaks of the divide.

DESCRIPTION (Moderate trip)

1st Hiking Day (**Mineral King** to **Upper Cliff Creek**, 8½ miles): Follow the 1st hiking day, trip 90.

2nd Hiking Day (**Upper Cliff Creek** to **Little Five Lakes**, 7 miles): After crossing the meadows south of Pinto Lake, this day's route begins a gruelling 3000-foot ascent to Black Rock Pass. There's no decent campsite before Little Five Lakes, but given an early start, the hiker should be able to make it to the pass before the heat of the day reaches its maximum, and fortunately there is plenty of drinking water except in late season. Scattered foxtail pines dot the mostly open slopes, and in early summer wildflower gardens abound on the slopes above Cliff Creek, with their heather, yampa, larkspur, swamp whiteheads, Bigelow sneezeweed, paintbrush, phlox, wallflower, wild onion, groundsel and forget-me-nots. Soon Pinto Lake comes into view below, a very small pond at the base of a talus slope. Past a series of meadows the trail begins the switchbacking slog to the pass, and views of the upper basin of Cliff Creek include the cascades below Spring Lake, Spring Lake itself, Cyclamen Lake, and then Columbine Lake, icebound in early summer. The solitary traveler, moving quietly, will see numerous deer on these subalpine slopes. Finally the rocky path attains Black Rock Pass, and a good rest stop affords moments for viewing the vast scene ahead. The companion basins of Little Five Lakes and Big Five Lakes drop off into Big Arroyo, and beyond this chasm rise the multicolored, cliffbound Kaweah Peaks. In the east is the 14,000-foot Whitney Crest, backbone of the Sierra.

From the pass, the zigzagging downgrade trends southeast and then angles northeast to pass above the highest of the Little Five Lakes—actually over one dozen lakes. (When snow obscures the trail in early season, one should keep to the left so as not to get off-route too far to the right and come out onto some cliffs). There are excellent campsites on the peninsula at the north end of the first lake whose shores the trail touches, and across the bay from these is a summer ranger who could provide emergency services. The grass, sedge and dwarf-bilberry ground cover around the peninsula-tip campsite is beautiful in the early-morning and late-evening light, and an evening meal here may be raised to four-star quality by the alpenglow on the Kaweah Peaks across Big Arroyo.

3rd and 4th Hiking Days: Retrace your steps, 15½ miles.

Mineral King to Nine Lake Basin

TRIP From Mineral King to Nine Lake Basin via Timber Gap, Black Rock Pass and Big Arroyo (round trip). Topo maps *Mineral King* (W.P.V.), *Triple Divide Peak* (W.P.V.) 15′; *Mineral King, Triple Divide Peak* 7½′. Best mid or late season; 42 miles.

Grade	Trail/layover days	Total recom-mended days
Leisurely	....	....
Moderate	6/2	8
Strenuous	4/1	5

HILITES Nine Lake Basin offers the seclusion that places not reached by maintained trail always possess. Located in a south-facing amphitheater between the towering Great Western Divide and the Kaweah Peaks Ridge, this lake basin is a perfect place to explore, fish, climb, photograph and recover your sense of marvel at nature's bounty.

DESCRIPTION (Moderate trip)

1st and 2nd Hiking Days: Follow trip 91 to **Little Five Lakes**, 15½ miles.

3rd Hiking Day (**Little Five Lakes** to **Nine Lake Basin**, 6½ miles): Just below the second of the Little Five Lakes, our trail fords the outlet and passes a trail to Big Five Lakes. We continue down beside the tumbling stream past the next lake in the chain, then ford the stream back to its north side. Soon the trail crosses the outlet of the northern cluster of Little Five Lakes, and the trout in this stream promise action to the angler who is willing to sweat his way up to the lakes above.

After an easy rise out of the basin, the trail begins to descend into Big Arroyo, a large west-bank tributary of the Kern River, increasing in steepness where it turns northeast. Beyond the ford of Big Arroyo, an unsigned trail leads down Big Arroyo and we go left (northwest) on the High Sierra Trail to ascend gently up the broad glacial valley past numerous possible campsites with great views of granitic Lippincott Mountain and Eagle Scout Peak towering in the west, and metamorphic Black Kaweah and Red Kaweah piercing the eastern sky. The trail fords Big Arroyo Creek again and then climbs over grassy pockets and granite slabs toward Kaweah Gap, a distinctive low spot on the Great Western Divide in the northwest. Where this trail swings west, an unmapped trail takes off north into Nine Lake Basin, and it soon arrives at the horseshoe-shaped first lake, with numerous fair-to-good campsites and good fishing for brook trout. A base camp here makes a springboard for excursions to the increasingly secluded and dramatic lakes north and east, and for climbing expeditions to the wealth of steep faces west and east of this fine base camp.

4th, 5th and 6th Hiking Days: Retrace your steps, 21 miles.

Mineral King to Hamilton Lakes

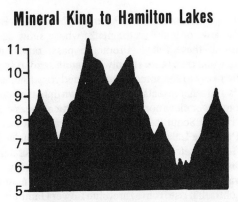

TRIP
From Mineral King to Hamilton Lakes via Timber Gap, Black Rock Pass, Big Arroyo, Kaweah Gap; return via Bearpaw Meadow, Redwood Meadow, Timber Gap (semiloop trip). Topo maps *Mineral King,* (M.P.V.), *Triple Divide Peak* (W.P.V.) 15'; *Mineral King, Triple Divide Peak, Lodgepole* 7½'. Best mid or late season; 44 miles.

Grade	Trail/layover days	Total recom- mended days
Leisurely	....	....
Moderate	6/3	9
Strenuous	4/2	6

HILITES
Backpackers who want to sample the multifold attractions of Sequoia National Park will find in this one trip high passes and barren divides, subalpine stream valleys, inviting glacial lake basins, middle-altitude meadows, deep river canyons and giant sequoia groves.

DESCRIPTION (Moderate trip)

1st, 2nd and 3rd Hiking Days: Follow trip 92 to **Nine Lake Basin**, 22 miles.

4th Hiking Day (**Nine Lake Basin** to **Little Bearpaw Meadow**, 9½ miles): After retracing the steps to the High Sierra Trail, this route turns right (west) and quickly climbs the few hundred feet to Kaweah Gap (10,640'). This pass on the Great Western Divide lies between the waters of the Kern River and the Kaweah River, and it affords views of many of the peaks whose snow-clad slopes give birth to these rivers. From the pass, our route drops moderately and then more steeply in granite sand. Early-season hikers are likely to see some gray-crowned rosy finches feeding on aphids and other insects that were blown onto the late-melting snow from lower elevations. The near-vertical faces of Mt. Stewart and Eagle Scout Peak "cradle" the trail as it passes aptly named Precipice Lake. Beyond the lake, the cirque widens and drops off. This stretch of trail is one of the most spectacular in the range: lush wildflowers and a multitude of cascades cover the valley wall and the hiker is awe-struck by the immensity of the colorful cliffs that rise from azure-blue Lower Hamilton Lake far below to the lofty crags above.

This vertical world will delight photographers, especially early in the day, and few of them will resist the spectacle of a channel for the trail that was blasted out of the canyon wall to create a "tunnel" open on one side—the cliff side. On these cliffs, white-throated swifts twinkle by, giving their mocking, laughlike cry as the trail drops and drops, 2000 feet in about 2 miles. A long switchback leg delivers the weary-kneed hiker to the west shore of Upper Hamilton Lake (8235'), where fishing is good for rainbow trout (to 16"). No open fires are allowed here.

The trail crosses Hamilton Creek just below the lake and descends in or near the riparian vegetation along the stream. Below Lower Hamilton Lake the descending trail refords the creek and then contours along an increasingly steep rock face that gives a second and equally apt meaning to the name of this trail, the *High* Sierra Trail.

Now off the cliff face, our route climbs shortly as it swings north before descending to the cement bridge crossing of Lone Pine Creek. Below, in the gorge, the collapsed old bridge lies draped over a gigantic chockstone where the old trail crossed. From this creek to Bearpaw Meadow, the trail climbs more than it drops, as we traverse the steep walls high above River Valley. Views back toward the Great Western Divide and the glacier-carved canyons of Eagle Scout, Hamilton and Granite creeks emanating from it are awesome.

As we enter the Bearpaw Meadow area (no open fires), the ranger station appears north of the trail, and south of it the tents of Bearpaw Meadow Camp, where meals, lodging (with reservations) and candy bars can be bought during the summer. We take the first trail to the left through the campground, toward Redwood Meadow. This campground gets heavy use, and it is dirty. More secluded campsites may be found at Little Bearpaw Meadow, about a mile south on a moderately-to-steeply descending trail that winds down under white fir, incense-cedar and sugar pine.

5th Hiking Day (**Little Bearpaw Meadow** to **Cliff Creek**, 6½ miles): Below Little Bearpaw Meadow we pass a marked trail on the right and continue our descent in mid-elevation mixed forest, with the spicy scent of mountain misery heavy in the air. At the bottom of this descent the trail passes a sign that points out the little used trail upstream and then fords the Middle Fork Kaweah River on logs and rocks (difficult in early season). Then our trail climbs the opposite bank and descends gently past a junction with a little-used trail down the Middle Fork, and we continue ahead, soon reaching cascading Eagle Scout Creek.

Rounding the next ridge, we come to Granite Creek, which is a roaring torrent in early season. An easy crossing by bridge and another short climb over a ridge in timber lead us to our last descent before Redwood Meadow. Even before we reach the meadow, we encounter red columnar giants standing tall among the lesser firs and pines in this forest. These are the giant sequoias, Sierra redwoods or big trees, earth's largest living things.

Our trail skirts the fenced meadow, where grazing is limited, and arrives at the Redwood Meadow Ranger Station. The building is an impressive two-story log house which in now used only by maintenance crews and park officials' guests. Camping is limited in this very peaceful place, as water is scarce. The trail climbs steadily, gradually leaving the big trees for mixed pine and fir, with patches of manzanita. Coralroot, a root parasite, grows here along the trail, commonly under firs and pines, where it feeds on living tree roots. Our route undulates through heavy forest for several miles, toward Cliff Creek and then away from it, and finally arrives at poor campsites near the junction by Cliff Creek.

6th Hiking Day (**Cliff Creek** to **Mineral King**, 6 miles): Retrace the steps of part of the 1st hiking day.

Mineral King to Spring Lake

TRIP   From Mineral King to Spring Lake via Glacier Pass, part cross-country (round trip). Topo maps *Mineral King* (W.P.V.) 15'; *Mineral King* 7½'. Best mid-season; 10 miles.

Grade	Trail/layover days	Total recom-mended days
Leisurely	....	....
Moderate	....	....
Strenuous	2/0	2

HILITES   This "weekender" makes a fine exercise for the experienced backpacker in good condition. This route crosses the Empire Mountain ridge by a little-used pass to beautiful Spring Lake. Rugged peaks, mirror-like tarns, possibilities for exploring old "prospects" and cascading streams are the rewards for a difficult climb. This trip is only for the hardier breed of hiker with experience in and a liking for the hazards of cross-country travel.

DESCRIPTION (Strenuous trip)

1st Hiking Day (**Mineral King** to **Spring Lake**, 5 miles, part cross country): Beginning from the dirt parking lot on the north side of the road, at the point where the road bends south ("Harry's Bend") our trail jogs north and then turns east on ascending switchbacks. This dusty, eroded trail winds up a dry, brushy slope, offering some views up the Mineral King valley to Farewell Gap. In ¼ mile, our trail passes the Timber Gap Trail branching north, and then continues east up the Monarch Creek drainage. Few trees screen this trail section from the sun. Sometimes but not always visible from the trail, Monarch Creek splashes down to the valley in a series of granite-bottomed falls from the "false cirque" just above. This bowl does, at first glance, appear to be a true cirque—the womb of a glacial *mer de glace*—but as the traveler continues, he will see that it is merely where the river of ice midway down the slope discovered a schistic weakness in the underlying rock, and ground down on its heel, carving, scraping and sculpting the resulting amphitheater. Early white residents brought their eastern terminology to this country and, in honor of the many marmots that inhabit the rocky fringe of the grassy-bottomed bowl, named it Groundhog Meadow.

At Groundhog Meadow we take the right trail fork across Monarch Creek. The left fork climbs directly up the canyon toward Sawtooth Pass and Glacier Pass. However, this trail is on unstable talus and it is no longer maintained.

We pass a fair campsite and begin several miles of long switchbacks which take us through open stands of red fir and silver pine with an understory of chinquapin, currant, gooseberry and lupine. Finally the trail crosses a ridge in timber that now includes some handsome foxtail pines, and just beyond the next hairpin bend is a nice lunch stop, where you can get drinking water by going 100 yards across the hillside. A short way up the trail from this lunch spot, a trail takes off to Crystal Lake.

Our trail, the new Monarch Lakes Trail, then rounds a shoulder, and now we can see the old trail across the canyon below, as well as Timber Gap, the Great Western Divide and Sawtooth Pass. We cross two forks of Monarch Creek and arrive at Lower Monarch Lake (10,380'), where camping is fair (toilet). A jumbled trail climbs around the north side of the lake through willows to upper Monarch Lake (10,640'), which is dammed and which lacks any decent campsites.

At the north end of Lower Monarch Lake we turn north and soon come to an unsigned trail junction going left. Keeping to the right, in ¼ mile we meet another unsigned junction, and take the right fork. (Many people coming down from Sawtooth Pass take the westbound fork here because it looks to be the more used trail. It connects with the old Sawtooth Pass Trail further down the canyon.) Soon the trail peters out and we follow ducks up a sandy hillside. Alternatively, we could pick our way up the sandy "staircase" formed by a vegetated slot in the white granite outcrop north of the second unsigned junction. After nearly a mile of cross-country work, we arrive at a west-trending ridge lined with a few foxtail pines. From the top of this ridge we can see many sets of footprints leading north in the granite sand nearly horizontally over to the notch that is Glacier Pass.

Glacier Pass (11,000′) is not named on the topo map, but is the first significant notch west of the sandy-backed, unnamed peak above us. The exposure at the very top on the north side of Glacier Pass is high class 2 or even Class 3. Views of the Cliff Creek drainage and barren Mt. Eisen are impressive, and they attend the hiker as he scrambles down the north side of the pass.

This side of the pass is frequently covered with late-melting snow, and care should be taken to keep to the tundra-topped granite ledges east of and above the tarn that is the beginning of the west tributary of Spring Lake. Here the track (sometimes ducked, sometimes worn into the grass) descends steeply to ford the tributary just above its final plunge into Spring Lake. The trail then traverses the sparsely timbered west slope of the Spring Lake cirque to the overused campsites (no campfires). Fishing for brook (to 8″) is good. Views from the campsites of the sheer, smoothed granite headwall at the south end of the lake fill the viewer with a sense of awe and respect for the glacier's power.

2nd Hiking Day: Retrace your steps, 5 miles.

Mineral King Valley from near Timber Gap

Mineral King to Lost Canyon

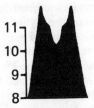

TRIP   From Mineral King to Lost Canyon via Sawtooth Pass, Columbine Lake (round trip). Topo maps *Mineral King* (W.P.V.) 15'; *Mineral King* 7½'. Best midseason; 15 miles.

Grade	Trail/layover days	Total recommended days
Leisurely	....	....
Moderate	....	....
Strenuous	2/1	3

HILITES   Strictly a backpacker's route, this trail traces the Monarch Creek drainage to cross the Great Western Divide at Sawtooth Pass. High alpine scenery climaxed by the cold, often ice-filled waters of Columbine Lake make this a fine route for all who love the High Sierra. The excellent fishing in the upper Lost Canyon drainage will reward the angler who is willing to "walk for his supper."

DESCRIPTION (Strenuous trip)

1st Hiking Day (**Mineral King** to **Upper Lost Canyon**, 7½ miles): Follow the 1st hiking day, trip 94, to the ridge from where many tracks lead north toward Glacier Pass. From here we go north nearly to the notch, where we find many ducks doubling back southeast just below the ridgecrest. Stay high—all lower routes to Sawtooth Pass are difficult, especially with a full pack.

Sawtooth Pass is signed—and you may need the sign to tell you which notch is the pass, for it is not the low point on the ridge. From the summit of this high-ridged pass there are vistas of the surrounding country exceeded only by those from the tops of nearby Sawtooth Peak and Needham Mountain. One can see the length of the Monarch Creek drainage to the west, and on down into the wooded drainage of East Fork Kaweah River. Empire Mountain and the ridge to its southeast dominate the view to the north, Sawtooth Peak is on the skyline to the south, and to the east one looks across Columbine Lake, Lost Canyon and Big Arroyo to the timbered reaches of the Chagoopa Plateau. Far on the eastern horizon, one can see the Mt. Whitney complex of peaks, south as far as Mt. Langley and Cirque Peak.

The descent on the east side of Sawtooth Pass, like the western ascent, is a steep, sandy, zigzagging affair that gives the backpacker little chance to look at the spectacular scenery. This route continues down, dropping steeply to the north side of Columbine Lake. Here glacially scoured granite slabs tilt into the lake's usually mirrorlike surface. The reflections of the nearby mineralized, rust-colored rocks blend with the chalkier whites of the lakeside granites to leave an indelible impression—despite the basin's harsh, treeless condition.

After rounding the north side of the lake, our route drops steeply down to the head of Lost Canyon on a rocky surface that does not give way to grass and trees until one is almost due north of the westernmost spire of Needham Mountain. Here good campsites will be found in an open, grassy setting (10,200′) amid a sparse forest cover of stunted lodgepole pines. Fishing for brook trout farther downstream is excellent.

2nd Hiking Day: Retrace your steps, 7½ miles.

Mineral King to Upper Rattlesnake Creek 96

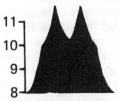

TRIP   From Mineral King to Campsites, Upper Rattlesnake Creek via Franklin Pass (round trip). Topo maps *Mineral King* (W.P.V.) 15'; *Mineral King* 7½'. Best mid or late season; 20 miles.

Grade	Trail/layover days	Total recommended days
Leisurely	....	....
Moderate	....	....
Strenuous	2/1	3

HILITES   To call this trip a colorful one is an understatement. The peaks cupping the Franklin Lakes cirque are an artist's canvas of grays, shades of red, and various tones of green. Across Franklin Pass the fine fishing and beautifully intimate scenery of Rattlesnake Creek beckon to anglers and appreciative naturalists.

DESCRIPTION (Strenuous trip)

1st Hiking Day (**Mineral King** to **Upper Rattlesnake Creek**, 10 miles): For this trip you may be able to park at the Sawtooth Pass/Timber Gap trailhead or you may have to park at the lot about halfway from the ranger station to that lot. You then walk up the road past the Mineral King Pack Station and go by a locked gate. A rough jeep road continues from this gate for about 1 mile, to an unimproved campground near the junction of Crystal Creek and East Fork Kaweah River. Looking up-canyon from this point, one can readily make out Farewell Gap at the top of **V**-shaped upper Farewell Canyon. Just west of the trail-road, the hurrying waters of the Kaweah River are hidden by a screen of willows, and the early-morning hiker is very apt to see a marmot surveying his territory. Scattered clumps of juniper and red fir contrast with the ghostly white of cottonwood trunks just below the point where the route fords Crystal Creek and, veering left where the road continues straight, begins an unrelenting ascent of several miles. Along the shaley trail, the savory odor of sagebrush assails the nostrils, and between the sagebrush and the gooseberry of these lower slopes, spots of wildflower color are provided by purple Indian paintbrush, lavender fleabane, cream cow parsnip and red ipomopsis. Soon the trail fords dashing Franklin Creek just below a lovely fall (difficult in early season) and begins a steep, flowery, switchbacking ascent above a section of the Kaweah River that flows through a deep, eroded gash.

About 1¼ miles north of Farewell Gap, our route doubles back north, passes a junction with the trail to Farewell Gap, and begins a long, stuttering traverse around the northwest slopes of Tulare Peak. This traverse provides excellent views back down the Kaweah River canyon to Mineral King and beyond to Timber Gap. The contrast between the green hillside and the red of Vandever Mountain is the south is especially pleasant in the morning light. Then your traverse enters a sparse forest cover of mature foxtail pines and crosses red-hued rocky slopes dotted with spring flowers and laced with little snowmelt rills as you turn northeast into Franklin Creek's upper canyon.

After descending briefly to ford the creek, the trail rises steeply to the rock-and-concrete-dammed outlet of lower Franklin Lake. The colors in this dramatically walled cirque basin are a bizarre conglomeration. To the northeast, the slopes of Rainbow Mountain are a study of gray-white marble whorls set in a sea of pink, red and black metamorphic rocks. To the south, the slate ridge joining Tulare Peak and Florence Peak is a hue of chocolate red that sends color photographers scrambling for viewpoints from which to foreground the contrasting blue of lower Franklin Lake against this colorful headwall. Anglers will find the fishing for brook trout (to 10″) good on the lower lake, and better at the upper lake. Some small, sandy ledges with a few trees well above the northeast shore of the lower lake make pleasant campsites with good lake views. Two of them have bear boxes, to be shared by all. Other campsites, treeless, are near the trail beside the east inlet about 400 feet higher than the lake.

From this lake the trail rises steadily and then steeply on switchbacks. Views of the Franklin Lakes cirque improve with altitude, and it isn't long before both the upper and lower lakes are in view. This ascent leaves the forest cover behind, as it crosses and recrosses a field of coarse granite granules dotted with bedrock outcropping. Despite the sievelike drainage of this slope, flowers are frequently seen. High up on the slope two adjacent year-round streamlets nourish gardens of yellow mimulus and lavender shooting stars. At windy Franklin Pass, views are panoramic. Landmarks to the northwest include Castle Rocks and Paradise Peak; to the east the immediate unglaciated plateau about the headwaters of Rattlesnake Creek, and Forester Lake (on the wooded bench just north of Rattlesnake Creek). East of the Kern Trench and plateaus, one can make out Mt. Whitney on the Sierra Crest.

The initial descent from the pass, unlike the west-side ascent, is an ad-lib plunge down a slope mostly covered with a layer of disintegrated quartz sand and oddly dotted with small, wind-sculpted granite domes. After crossing this bench, the trail drops steeply down rocky, rough, blasted switchbacks that twine back and forth over some of the headwaters of Rattlesnake Creek. This steep descent levels out on the north side of the creek, and enters a friendly forest of young lodgepole pines broken by pleasant meadow patches. Several excellent campsites (10,300') line the creek here. Fishing for brook trout (to 8") is good to excellent, and the stream is ideal for fly fishermen. These streamside campsites are fine base camps for angling side trips to the several nearby lakes situated on the benches on each side of Rattlesnake Creek Canyon.

2nd Hiking Day: Retrace your steps, 10 miles.

97

Mineral King to Little Claire Lake

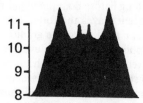

TRIP   From Mineral King to Little Claire Lake via
Franklin Pass, Rattlesnake Creek, Forester Lake
(round trip). Topo maps *Mineral King* (W.P.V.) 15′;
Mineral King 7½′. Best mid-to-late season; 26
miles.

Grade	Trail/layover days	Total recom-mended days
Leisurely	....	....
Moderate	4/0	4
Strenuous	2/1	3

HILITES For fine fishing, superlative scenery and a whole
range of side-trip possibilities, this trip is hard to
beat. As the opportunities for recreation are varied,
so are the watersheds that this trip visits. After
crossing Franklin Pass, this route hooks around to
visit the alpine headwaters of two tributaries of the
Kern River.

DESCRIPTION (Moderate trip)

1st Hiking Day (**Mineral King** to **Franklin Lakes**, 6 miles): Follow the
1st hiking day, trip 96, as far as Franklin Lakes.

2nd Hiking Day (**Franklin Lakes** to **Little Claire Lake**, 7 miles): Follow
the 1st hiking day, trip 96, to the campsites on **Upper Rattlesnake
Creek**. From the streamside campsites the trail descends
moderately through an increasingly dense forest cover of
lodgepole pine. In ¼ mile we pass the Shotgun Pass Trail, and in
another 0.2 mile reach the Soda Creek Trail (Forester Lake,
Little Claire Lake, Big Arroyo). Leaving Rattlesnake Creek, we
fork left here. A short distance beyond the junction, the trail

fords a little stream and then ascends gently over a rocky slope. Soon the trail arrives at the charmingly meadowed west side of Forester Lake, where fine campsites look across the azure blue waters to a dense forest fringe, and an occasional dimpling on the surface indicates the presence of brook trout. Turning northwestward, the trail ascends through a moderate forest cover to a meadowed bench, and then makes another ascent to the sandy crown of the ridge dividing the Rattlesnake and Soda Creek drainages. From this rounded summit the crests of Sawtooth Peak and Needham Mountain are easily visible to the north, and they continue to be seen as the trail descends moderately to the south end of Little Claire Lake. The effervescent, burbling call of the Brewer blackbird and the raucous call of the Clark nutcracker frequently are heard as the traveler skirts the east side of Little Claire Lake (10,450') to the good campsites at the north end of the lake, around the outlet. Fishing for brook trout is excellent (to 11").

3rd and 4th Hiking Days: Retrace your steps, 13 miles.

Main Franklin Lake

Mineral King to Little Five Lakes

TRIP   From Mineral King to Big Five Lakes via Franklin
              Pass, Little Claire Lake, Lost Canyon, return via
              Little Five Lakes, Black Rock Pass, Timber Gap
              (loop trip). Topo maps *Mineral King* (W.P.V.),
              Kern Peak 15'; *Mineral King, Chagoopa Falls*
              7½'. Best mid or late season, 40½ miles.

Grade	Trail/layover days	Total recom- mended days
Leisurely	....	....
Moderate	6/1	7
Strenuous	4/1	5

HILITES   This is perhaps the best knapsacker's route for
              looping the fine fishing country east of Mineral
              King. Challenging passes and remote lakes are the
              attractions for the hiker. For the angler, the chance
              to wet a line in excellent golden-trout waters should
              be sufficient inducement.

DESCRIPTION (Moderate trip)

1st 2 Hiking Days: Follow trip 97 to **Little Claire Lake**, 13 miles.

3rd Hiking day (**Little Claire Lake** to **Unnamed Lake at 10,000'**, 7
miles): The trail west of the outlet stream from Little Claire Lake
follows well-graded switchbacks down a steep, forested slope for
over a mile. At the foot of this precipitous duff-and-rock slope,
the route fords Soda Creek, descends gently over duff and sand
through a moderate forest cover, and then becomes steeper.
Marmots on the rocky slopes south of the creek whistle excitedly
as unexpected visitors to their domain pass by, but they do not
usually stir from their watching posts unless the traveler shows
more than passing interest.

During the next several miles of steady descent through lodgepole forest, somewhat away from Soda Creek, we hop across numerous refreshing tributaries and pass a half-dozen campsites of uneven quality. Among the evergreens one finds an occasional silver pine, and then red fir appears. Clumps of sagebrush space the stands of timber, and nestled next to their aromatic branches are much Douglas phlox and Indian paintbrush. The appearance of Jeffrey pines heralds the approach of the junction where a trail down into Big Arroyo branches right and our route starts a steep, rocky, exposed ascent to the foot of Lost Canyon. Nearing the creek in this canyon, we double back to the northwest and suddenly leave the dry south slope for a cool, moist, verdant bower at a ford of Lost Canyon Creek (difficult in early season). Beyond the ford we veer away from the creek on a steady ascent up a duff-and-sand-trail. More than a mile beyond the ford, just before a second ford of Lost Canyon Creek, the trail to Big Five Lakes branches right (north) and climbs the steep north wall.

This ascent makes a clear series of short, steep switchbacks which afford fine views west to the barren headwaters of Lost Canyon and the cirque holding Columbine Lake. Mostly lodgepole and foxtail pine, the timber cover thickens as the trail approaches a small, unnamed lake (due east of a granite spur, in the *Kern Peak* quadrangle). Fields of red heather highlight the luxuriant growth of the wildflowers around this lake's meadow fringes, and above the treetops in the north, the barren, massive, brown hulk of Mt. Kaweah rises just barely higher than the serrated Kaweah Peaks Ridge west of it. The excellent campsites at this little lake allow the dusty hiker to have a leisurely swim in water much warmer than can be found most places in the Sierra.

4th Hiking Day (**Unnamed Lake at 10,000′** to **Little Five Lakes**, 5 miles): From the north side of the little lake, our trail crosses a long ridge that is heavily overlaid with fallen snags. The ground trail is sometimes faint, but it is well-ducked. Above Big Five Lakes, the trail tops the ridge and we have views of Black Rock Pass to the west, and the lowest of the Big Five Lakes (9840′) immediately below. The descent to the good campsites near the outlet and along the north side of this lake is a rocky, steep downgrade.

Beyond the log-jammed outlet of the lake, the trail leads west

toward a reed-filled bay. At a junction we take the right fork and
embark upon a steep, rocky, switchbacking climb of ½ mile. Just
before the top of this climb, at a T junction where the left fork
leads to another of the Big Five Lakes, our right fork is the Little
Five Lakes Trail. Topping the ridge, we proceed to undulate for a
dry mile, with periodic great views of Mt. Kaweah, the Kaweah
Peaks Ridge and, at the ridge's west end, Red Kaweah and Black
Kaweah.

The dry stretch ends when the trail dips into a small, intimate
valley where a stream flows at least until late summer. From this
brook we ascend for several hundred vertical feet in a moderate
lodgepole forest, level off, and then gain sight of the main Little
Five Lake and its large bordering meadow. In a few minutes our
trail reaches the base of the lake's north-end peninsula, which
contains many good-to-excellent campsites. The one nearest the
peninsula's tip is surrounded by a wonderful carpet of grass,
sedge and dwarf bilberry which shimmers in the delicate light of
late afternoon, and an evening meal here may be raised to four-
star quality by the alpenglow on the Kaweah Peaks across Big
Arroyo. Across the bay is a summer ranger station where
emergency services are usually available.

5th and 6th Hiking Days: Reverse the 2nd and 1st hiking days of
Trip 91, 15½ miles.

Unnamed lake at 10,000 feet

Mineral King to Big Five Lakes

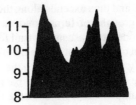

TRIP From Mineral King to Big Five Lakes via Sawtooth Pass, Lost Canyon, return via Little Five Lakes, Black Rock Pass, Spring Lake, Glacier Pass, part cross-country (semiloop trip). Topo maps *Mineral King* (W.P.V.), *Kern Peak* 15′; *Mineral King, Chagoopa Falls* 7½′. Best mid or late season, 22½ miles.

Grade	Trail/layover days	Total recommended days
Leisurely	....	....
Moderate	4/2	6
Strenuous	....	....

HILITES This fine, short, looping trip is an angler's delight. The route, part cross country, passes 15 lakes, providing a variety of both trout water and trout.

DESCRIPTION (Moderate trip)

1st Hiking Day: Follow trip 95 to **Upper Lost Canyon**, 7½ miles.

2nd Hiking Day (**Upper Lost Canyon** to **Lower Big Five Lake**, 4½ miles): From the alpine-meadowed bench below Columbine Lake, the trail enters forest cover (sparse lodgepole and foxtail), and then drops steeply over broken granite and meadowy sections. This stepladdering descent keeps to the north side of Lost Canyon Creek for about 1 mile, and then fords the creek twice in the space of the next mile. The second ford returns to the north side of the creek, where our route branches north, away from Lost Canyon, on the poorly signed Big Five Lakes Trail. From this junction, proceed as described in the second half of the 3rd hiking day and the first half of the 4th hiking day, trip 98.

4th Hiking Day (**Lower Big Five Lake** to **Spring Lake**, 5½ miles, part cross country): From the junction near the reed-filled bay on the north side of the lowest Big Five Lake, our trail goes west around the lake's north side and then ascends along the north side of the inlet through rank growths of ferns amid moderate stands of foxtail pine. This moderately ascending trail fords the stream ¼ mile below the outlet of the largest lake in the Big Five chain, and climbs over glacially smoothed granite to the lake's east shore. Our route fords the outlet and passes a packer campsite and several primitive campsites before crossing the swampy area around the north inlet of the lake. Just west of this inlet, our trail passes a trail to Little Five Lakes (or back to the lowest lake in the chain) branching right and continues west up the Big Five Lakes basin. Fishermen will find the angling for golden trout good to excellent in all the lakes of the upper basin except the highest.

The ascent to the third lake we pass is gentle over grass and swampy areas, and, near the outlet of this lake, the trail passes two primitive, exposed campsites. We follow the grassy trail about three-fourths of the way around this lake before turning sharply right (northwest) to begin a crosscountry ascent of the steep granite ridge separating the Big Five Lakes and Little Five Lakes drainages. After thrashing through a little brush, we head for the forested area and pick out an occasionally ducked route that ascends by grass-topped ledges to the saddle just south of the uppermost lake of the Little Five Lakes chain.

From this ridge one can see across Big Arroyo to the Kaweah Peaks and Red Spur. To the west, aptly named Black Rock Pass stands out in startling relief from the surrounding white granite. The steep, difficult, rocky descent on the north side of the ridge is clearly ducked, but some scrambling is required to bring one to the edge of the uppermost lake. (Fishing for golden in the two lower lakes of this chain is good.) Crossing the outlet stream from this lake, our ducked route meets and turns left onto the Black Rock Pass Trail. First ascending across alpine meadows, the trail veers north and then climbs a steep, very rocky series of switchbacks to the summit of Black Rock Pass (11,630'). This pass provides one of the finer viewpoints on this trip. Looking east one can see the Kaweah Peaks Ridge, the wooded flats of Chagoopa Plateau, a considerable length of Big Arroyo, and both the Little and the Big Five Lakes basins. On the south side of the pass, there are heart-stopping panoramas of the deep Cliff

Creek drainage and towering Empire Mountain, seeming to be almost at fingertip distance.

Descending on the west side of the pass, the rocky trail makes one long traverse and then drops by steady and steep zigzags toward the grass-bottomed basin just north of Spring Lake. Where we almost touch a year-round stream, at a hairpin bend in the trail, a route of use takes off for Spring Lake, visible in the distance, and we take this route. Following this unducked, rough route consists mainly of crossing talus fans. Do not try to stay high as the route drops, or you will find yourself confronting steep, water-slick slabs with much exposure. After crossing the last of the talus, we are below Spring Lake. Then, after fording the tributary northeast of the lake, we work our way upward through meadows and willows to Spring Lake, arriving at the good campsites (somewhat exposed) on the east side of the outlet and in the sparse timber cover of the northwest shore (10,050'). Views from these campsites of the massive cirque headwall and the ribboned waterfall inlets are satisfying, and fishing for brook trout (to 8") is good. (Less experienced backpackers should not go via Spring Lake but should stay on the trail from Black Rock Pass down Cliff Creek to the Timber Gap Trail and return via it; 1st hiking day, trip 90.)

5th Hiking Day (**Spring Lake** to **Mineral King**, 5 miles, part cross country): Reverse the 1st hiking day, trip 94. Note that Glacier Pass is the third saddle to the left of Empire Mountain.

Kaweah Peaks Ridge over middle Little 5 Lake

100   Mineral King to Crescent Meadow

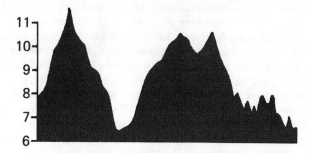

TRIP

From Mineral King to Crescent Meadow via Franklin Pass, Rattlesnake Creek, Kern River, Hamilton Lakes (shuttle trip). Topo maps *Mineral King* (W.P.V.), *Kern Peak, Mt. Whitney* (W.P.V.), *Triple Divide Peak* (W.P.V.) 15′; *Mineral King, Chagoopa Falls, Mt. Kaweah, Triple Divide Peak, Lodgepole* 7½′. Best mid or late season; 56 miles.

Grade	Trail/layover days	Total recommended days
Leisurely	....	....
Moderate	8/2	10
Strenuous	6/1	7

HILITES

This loop trip is one that should be taken by all who would say, "I know the Great Western Divide country" or "I know the Kern Trench and its wooded plateaus." This route surveys a 5000-foot range of Sierran biota, and the scope of the glaciated terrain one travels over reads like the synopsis of a geology textbook.

DESCRIPTION (Strenuous trip)

1st Hiking Day: Follow trip 96 to the campsites on **Upper Rattlesnake Creek**, 10½ miles.

2nd Hiking Day (**Upper Rattlesnake Creek** to **Rattlesnake Creek/Kern River**, 8 miles): Traveling down through the upper reaches of Rattlesnake Creek is a delightful study in intimate meadows, dense stands of lodgepole pine and a classic, murmuring mountain creek. About ¼ mile from the timberline campsites, our trail passes the Shotgun Pass Trail leading south across the creek, and in another 0.2 mile passes the Soda Creek Trail. Then it fords the winding meadow stream, only to return to the north side a few hundreds yards downstream. Soon we pass the Upper Rattlesnake Creek drift fence, the first of four seasonal stock fences in the canyon. As we descend, the creek picks up speed as its meandering course is constricted by narrowing canyon walls, and the trail climbs briefly on the north wall. In the narrow canyon the trail stays fairly close to the swiftly tumbling creek waters as it descends on a long, steady, rocky traverse of the canyon wall. After rounding the fractured granite nose of a ridge, the trail descends steeply to ford an unnamed tributary cascading down from the north wall, and then rejoins Rattlesnake Creek in the level stretches at Cow Camp Meadows.

This green grassland is frequented by the many mule deer in the vicinity and an occasional bear. Reflecting the lower altitude, the meadow's fringes show a forest cover of lodgepole, fir and some juniper, and as the trail continues to descend steadily, Jeffrey pine and aspen begin to make their predictable appearance.

Just above the final steep descent into the Kern Trench, our trail passes a trail to Big Arroyo, branching north, and then it switchbacks down abruptly to the good packer campsites just south of the junction with the Kern River Trail. Fishing for rainbow in the Kern is excellent (to 20″).

3rd Hiking Day (**Rattlesnake Creek/Kern River** to **Moraine Lake**, 7½ miles): Reverse the last part of the 4th hiking day, trip 70 to the junction of the Kern River Trail and the High Sierra Trail. Then proceed west on the High Sierra Trail, reversing the steps of the first part of the 4th hiking day, trip 81.

4th, 5th and 6th Hiking Days: Reverse the first 3 hiking days, trip 81, 30 miles.

Trip Cross-reference Table

Trip No.	No. Hiking Days	Season			Pace			Trip Type			
		Early	Mid	Late	Leis.	Mod.	Stren.	Round	Shuttle	Loop	Semiloop
1	2	X		X	X			X			
2	4	X		X	X			X			
3	3	X		X		X				X	
4	6		X	X		X		X			
5	7		X	X		X					X
6	4		X	X		X		X			
7	6		X	X			X			X	
8	4		X	X		X			X		
9	7		X	X		X					X
10	7		X	X		X					X
11	6		X	X	X			X			
12	2		X			X		X			
13	4		X		X			X			
14	5		X	X		X			X		
15	7		X	X		X				X	
16	2		X	X	X			X			
17	3		X	X		X		X			
18	2		X	X	X				X		
19	2		X	X	X			X			
20	2		X	X	X			X			
21	2		X	X	X					X	
22	2		X	X	X			X			
23	2	X	X		X			X			
24	2	X	X			X				X	
25	2	X	X		X			X			

Trip No.	No. Hiking Days	Season			Pace			Trip Type			
		Early	Mid	Late	Leis.	Mod.	Stren.	Round	Shuttle	Loop	Semiloop
26	4	x	x		x			x			
27	4		x	x	x			x			
28	6		x	x	x						x
29	6		x	x	x			x			
30	7		x	x		x					x
31	6		x	x	x			x			
32	5		x	x		x			x		
33	6		x	x			x		x		
34	4	x	x		x			x			
35	6		x		x			x			
36	4	x	x		x						x
37	2	x			x			x			
38	4	x	x		x			x			
39	7		x	x	x			x			
40	2		x	x	x			x			
41	2		x	x		x					x
42	2		x	x		x		x			
43	2		x		x			x			
44	6		x	x		x					x
45	8		x	x		x			x		
46	8		x	x		x			x		
47	4		x	x			x	x			
48	5		x	x			x	x			
49	2	x					x	x			
50	4		x	x			x	x			

Trip No.	No. Hiking Days	Season			Pace			Trip Type			
		Early	Mid	Late	Leis.	Mod.	Stren.	Round	Shuttle	Loop	Semiloop
51	4		x				x		x		
52	4		x	x			x	x			
53	4		x	x			x		x		
54	3	x		x		x		x			
55	5		x	x		x		x			
56	6		x	x			x		x		
57	3	x	x			x		x			
58	5		x	x	x			x			
59	7		x	x		x		x			
60	5			x		x		x			
61	6			x		x				x	
62	5			x		x			x		
63	4		x	x		x		x			
64	6			x			x				x
65	9		x	x		x					x
66	2	x	x		x			x			
67	6		x	x	x				x		
68	3		x	x			x	x			
69	4		x	x			x	x			
70	6		x	x			x		x		
71	8		x	x			x		x		
72	2		x	x	x			x			
73	4		x	x			x	x			
74	6			x			x	x			
75	8		x	x			x				x

Trip No.	No. Hiking Days	Season			Pace			Trip Type			
		Early	Mid	Late	Leis.	Mod.	Stren.	Round	Shuttle	Loop	Semiloop
76	8		x	x			x	x			
77	5		x	x			x		x		
78	2		x	x		x		x			
79	6		x	x		x		x			
80	6			x		x			x		
81	8		x	x		x			x		
82	13		x	x		x					x
83	2		x	x	x					x	
84	4		x	x	x			x			
85	4		x	x	x					x	
86	7		x	x		x			x		
87	4		x			x		x			
88	5		x	x		x			x		
89	5		x	x		x			x		
90	2		x			x		x			
91	4		x	x		x					
92	6		x	x		x		x			
93	6		x	x		x					x
94	2		x				x	x			
95	2		x				x	x			
96	2		x	x			x	x			
97	4		x	x		x		x			
98	6		x	x		x				x	
99	4		x	x		x					x
100	6		x	x			x		x		

Index